PRAISE FOR *IMPACT COACHING*
BY RAYMOND L. SMITH AND JULIE R. SMITH

The authors do a great job of sharing the benefits of coaching and elaborating on how the coaching partnership should and could look. The book is very relevant, clearly based on research, and has some great checklists to further clarify the recommended steps.

Kathy Rhodes, Principal
Hinton Elementary
Hinton, IA

This book is full of valuable information that is presented in a clear and concise way. Due to its organization and conversational writing style, the book readily lends itself to a book study with collaborative teams.

Jessica McMillan, Instructional Coach
Ferry Pass Middle School
Pensacola, FL

This book is well organized and cohesive. Examples and tables provide support throughout, and key takeaways at the end of each chapter help to reinforce the main points.

Angela M. Mosley, High School Principal
Essex High School
Tappahannock, VA

Impact Coaching

This book is dedicated to all of the inspired and passionate educational leaders that have influenced our life and who have given voice and authenticity to the pages within this book.

Impact Coaching
Scaling Instructional Leadership

Raymond L. Smith
Julie R. Smith

Foreword by Jim Knight

CORWIN
A SAGE Publishing Company

FOR INFORMATION:

Corwin
A SAGE Company
2455 Teller Road
Thousand Oaks, California 91320
(800) 233-9936
www.corwin.com

SAGE Publications Ltd.
1 Oliver's Yard
55 City Road
London EC1Y 1SP
United Kingdom

SAGE Publications India Pvt. Ltd.
B 1/I 1 Mohan Cooperative Industrial Area
Mathura Road, New Delhi 110 044
India

SAGE Publications Asia-Pacific Pte. Ltd.
3 Church Street
#10-04 Samsung Hub
Singapore 049483

Publisher: Arnis Burvikovs
Development Editor: Desirée A. Bartlett
Editorial Assistant: Eliza Riegert
Production Editor: Tori Mirsadjadi
Copy Editor: Jared Leighton
Typesetter: C&M Digitals (P) Ltd.
Proofreader: Ellen Brink
Indexer: Wendy Allex
Cover Designer: Anupama Krishnan
Marketing Manager: Nicole Franks

Printed in the United States of America

Library of Congress Cataloging-in-Publication Data

Names: Smith, Raymond L., author. | Smith, Julie R., author.

Title: Impact coaching : scaling instructional leadership / Raymond L. Smith, Julie R. Smith.

Description: Thousand Oaks, California : Corwin, a SAGE company, [2018] |

Includes bibliographical references and index.

Identifiers: LCCN 2017034821 | ISBN 9781506361826 (pbk. : alk. paper)

Subjects: LCSH: School principals—Training of. | Educational leadership. | Mentoring in education.

Classification: LCC LB2831.9 .S63 2018 | DDC 371.2/012—dc23

LC record available at https://lccn.loc.gov/2017034821

This book is printed on acid-free paper.

SFI label applies to text stock

18 19 20 21 22 10 9 8 7 6 5 4 3 2 1

Contents

Foreword by Jim Knight   ix

Preface   xi
    Retain Your Investment in Leadership   xii
    Promote Continuous Learning   xiii
    Where Do Impact Coaches Come From?   xiii
    Special Features   xiv
    Who Is This Book For?   xv
    Introducing Rachel Hazel, Featured Coachee   xvi

Acknowledgments   xvii

About the Authors   xxi

Chapter 1: Why Do School Leaders Need Coaching?   1
    The Dubious Quality of Traditional Professional Development   3
    Common Forms of Coaching   5
    Research on Leadership Coaching   13
    Key Takeaways   14
    Going Deeper   15

Chapter 2: Leveraging Your Five Big-Winner Leadership Practices   17
    The 80/20 Rule   18
    High-Impact Instructional Leadership Practices   19
    Key Takeaways   27
    Going Deeper   27

Chapter 3: What Does Impact Coaching Look Like?   29
    The Impact Coaching Cycle   30
    Key Takeaways   48
    Going Deeper   48

Chapter 4: Partnership Principles and Theories of Practice   49

    Knight's Partnership Principles   49

    Theories of Practice   51

    Key Takeaways   62

    Going Deeper   63

Chapter 5: Impact Partner Communication   65

    Why Conversations About Improvement Can Be Difficult   66

    Conducting Open-to-Learning Conversations   68

    Key Components of an Open-to-Learning Conversation   72

    Engaging in Behaviors That Mediate Thinking   72

    Key Takeaways   81

    Going Deeper   82

Chapter 6: Engaging School Leaders and Starting the Journey   83

    Getting School Leaders Amenable to Coaching   83

    Making Change Happen: Hall and Hord   84

    Key Functions of Change and Professional
       Learning in Schools   88

    The Components of Impact Coaching   88

    Key Takeaways   100

    Going Deeper   100

Chapter 7: Modeling, Observing, and Collaboratively Exploring Data   103

    Impact Coaching Process Tools   103

    Key Takeaways   136

    Going Deeper   136

Chapter 8: The End of Impact Coaching: Scaling
Instructional Leadership   137

    What Do We Now Know?   138

    Learning About Impact Coaching During Coaching   142

    Our Challenge to You   145

Appendices   147

    Section 1: Feedback Cue Card   148

    Section 2: Instructional Leadership Elements Rubrics   150

    Section 3: *Linking Walk* Evidence-Gathering Templates   172

    Section 4: Theories-of-Practice Self-Assessment Tool   176

Glossary   179

References   181

Index   185

Foreword

In *Impact Coaching: Scaling Instructional Leadership*, Ray and Julie Smith have done educators a great service by broadening the conversation on instructional leadership. No doubt you, like I, have heard again and again that principals must be instructional leaders. I have always agreed vigorously with such statements, but I've also wondered just who was going to help administrators develop that kind of leadership. In *Impact Coaching* Ray and Julie go a long way toward helping us better understand how to support school leaders so they can have a significant, positive impact on educators and children's lives.

Their phrase "impact coaching" is a powerful one. I might be a bit biased about that phrase since the concept of impact is at the heart of much of my work. I see an emphasis on impact as an emphasis on action over talk—and not just any kind of action; action that will have the greatest positive impact on children's lives. As the authors explain, referencing Vivian Robinson's research in a section of the book that I found extremely helpful, some leadership practices have much more positive impact on students' lives than others. They refer to these as High-Impact Instructional Leadership Practices.

Taken together, as I see them, Ray and Julie Smith's High-Impact Instructional Leadership Practices make a lot of sense. My understanding of the descriptions of those practices is that leaders need to

1. engage staff in the construction of a shared vision or goal for the school;

2. find and organize resources so that the goal can be pursued;

3. engage educators in dialogue around instructional practices;

4. create, shape, and participate in professional learning that helps educators (including themselves) learn what they need to learn in order to hit the goal for the school;

5. and use data to monitor progress toward the goal.

To help leaders implement these five High-Impact Instructional Leadership Practices, the impact coaches described by the authors use a coaching cycle based on the one I describe in *The Impact Cycle: What Instructional Coaches*

Should Do to Foster Powerful Improvements in Teaching (2018). That cycle involves some deceptively simple moves. Coaches help people get better by helping them surface a clear picture of reality, set a goal, and identify strategies that can be used to hit the goal. This is the Identify stage. Then coaches help people learn those strategies by describing and modeling them. This is the Learn stage. Finally, coaches help others make adaptations and modifications until the goals are hit. This is the Improve stage.

The Impact Cycle

I have long felt that the impact cycle could be used to help principals get better at the important, complex work they do, so I'm very grateful to Ray and Julie for writing this book so that I can see just how that can happen. But this book is much more than an application of the cycle in a new setting. The authors' theories of practice (TOPs), for example, flesh out the actions that coaches can take to support educational leaders, and their description of open-to-learning conversations (OLCs) should be helpful to any coach in any context. Most importantly, I think, the authors provide a great service by suggesting numerous moves and strategies coaches can use to apply the impact cycle to incredibly important work of helping leaders get better.

There are two basic ideas that make this book so important. For a long time we've known that principals play a vitally important role in the overall success of a school. Also, we've long known that coaches can help professionals get better at what they do. Now we have a book that puts these two ideas together, and by putting these ideas together, Ray and Julie Smith have described in detail how coaches can help principals learn how to be the educational leaders our children deserve.

Finally, we have a way to help school leaders become instructional leaders.

—Jim Knight

President, Instructional Coaching Group and the Impact Research Lab
Research Associate, University of Kansas Center for Research on Learning
Author, *The Impact Cycle, Better Conversations,* and *Focus on Teaching*

Preface

Our interest in leadership coaching began selfishly as we reflected on the support we received (or in many cases did not receive, but desperately needed) when we served as public school principals. This lack of support was aspirational for us. As time passed, our appetite for coaching school leaders grew, intensified, and consumed much of our professional thinking and actions as our respective roles shifted from serving as principals to serving principals—enhancing the leadership skills of the principals and assistant principals assigned to our care—as central office leaders. Then, as adjunct professors at two universities teaching within the respective aspiring leaders program, our passion for coaching deepened. And now, over the past decade, as educational consultants assisting state-, district-, and school-level leaders throughout the world with the improvement of leadership practices (i.e., John Hattie's Visible Learning research) it has become abundantly clear that coaching for instructional leadership is essential.

Therefore, the aim of this book is threefold. The first purpose is to offer an unadorned, straightforward delivery of the essence (or in Michael Fullan's words "the skinny") of impact coaching—that is, to inspire and show school leaders how they can and should be sharply focused on the stuff that matters most about instructional leadership in order to achieve their most ambitious change goals. The thing that distinguishes impact coaching from other coaching models is that impact coaching guides school leaders into placing a laser-sharp focus on developing the strategies that will have the most impact on improving student learning and achievement. Second—and perhaps most importantly—it is our hope that this book, in some way, stirs within our readers a desire to engage in more focused, critical, and nonjudgmental dialogue about—and therefore, inspire the implementation of—those leadership practices that research suggests lead to the biggest impact on teachers and students. Last, the purpose of this book is to encourage school leaders to follow the urging of Dr. Russ Quaglia (2016), founder of the Quaglia Institute for Student Aspirations, in his book *Principal Voice*, for principals to "utilize their voice to genuinely influence policy and practices" (p. 3) within their school. According to Dr. Quaglia (2016), when principals use their voice to guide policy and practice it creates an "opportunity to better understand [their] school, colleagues, students, and community, thus allowing [them] to lead, and support growth school-wide with the trust and support of those around [them]" (p.3). This book, then, is as much about coaching leaders to scale instructional leadership as it is about improving the culture of our schools and school districts.

RETAIN YOUR INVESTMENT IN LEADERSHIP

Strengthening and improving the practice of school leaders in your district by implementing the impact coaching model can go a long way toward protecting your investment in good leaders. A primary focus of school systems that are trying to improve their individual and collective efficacy is attracting and retaining talented, well-trained school leaders. Toward that end, numerous recent studies show how critical an effective school leader is to teacher effectiveness and, therefore, to improved learning and student achievement (Robinson, Lloyd, & Rowe, 2008). However, school systems face three major problems in their pursuit, selection, and retention of highly capable, skilled school leaders: (1) Principals require ongoing support, (2) the principal turnover rate is higher in more challenging schools, and (3) the principalship is a complex job that takes a long time to master.

The first problem is that school leaders are being hired but then simply being given the keys to the building without being given adequate, sustained support—a long-standing organizational practice that must be changed, as it negatively impacts schools, teachers, and students. A recent study by the School Leaders Network (2014) found that as many as one out of every two newly hired principals will leave those critical leadership positions in the first three years of their employment, largely due to a lack of support. Rapid principal turnover such as this deeply hampers the ability for our schools, particularly high-poverty schools, to initiate and sustain school improvement efforts necessary to achieve real gains for students.

Another problem—and perhaps the most urgent of the three—is that principal turnover in schools occurs at a higher rate in more challenging schools than in less challenging ones. Each year, approximately 20 percent of principals leave their schools (Beteille, Kalogrides, & Loeb, 2012), some driven by the decisions of district leaders but others initiated by principals themselves. When principals initiate a change of schools, the pathway they follow tends to lead them away from schools with lower-achieving students from less advantaged socioeconomic backgrounds to their more advantaged, higher-achieving counterparts. Moreover, schools with high turnover rates are inclined to employ less skilled principals who possess fewer years of school-specific experience.

This finding gives rise to yet a third problem, in that "jobs that involve the complexities of people or nature seem to take the longest to master" (Gawande, 2011, p.44). Suffice to say, the world of a school leader is rife with complexities—uncertain, ambiguous, constantly changing, intensely human, and relentless—punctuated by a series of ongoing challenges to be faced, assessed, and resolved effectively.

Therefore, school systems would be wise to protect their front-end school leadership investment (attracting and hiring skilled leaders) by supporting their back-end (retention) investment. District officials can provide school leaders with critically necessary back-end support by ensuring coaching beyond the first two years of their employment.

PROMOTE CONTINUOUS LEARNING

Highly skilled school leaders understand that the knowledge and skills needed to make a significant impact on learning for all and significantly impact student achievement are constantly evolving. Therefore, school leaders, as with other professionals, have to keep enhancing their capabilities to avoid falling behind. Leadership expertise is not a static condition but one that school leaders must continually build on and sustain throughout their careers.

Inasmuch as school leaders maintain a capacity for learning and growing throughout their tenure, experience alone is insufficient to promote continuous learning. Regardless of how well prepared school leaders are in their formative years, few can achieve and maintain their best performance on their own. Top-performing school leaders, like top-performing athletes, CEOs, and musicians, take advantage of coaching to make certain they are as good as they can be—experts in their field. Leadership expertise, then, is a by-product of "deliberate practice"—sustained, sharply focused efforts to develop the full range of abilities that success requires (J. Smith & R. Smith, 2015). You have to work at what you're not good at. As Atul Gawande (2011) reminds us in his *New Yorker* piece, "Personal Best," the coach provides "the outside ears and eyes" (p. 47) and makes you aware of where you're falling short. In other words, the coach helps a school leader reflect on her or his experience and use metacognitive strategies that allow her or him to exercise active control over the cognitive processes engaged in learning.

Moreover, applying the principles, processes, and tools associated with impact coaching is a way for district and school personnel (i.e., superintendents, associate superintendents, and central-office directors) who evaluate school leaders to build and sustain those high-impact instructional leadership practices through coaching that research has found to have the greatest impact on learning and student achievement.

WHERE DO IMPACT COACHES COME FROM?

Some school systems we have encountered have the luxury of staffing full-time coaches for school leaders. However, we also know that many more schools and school districts do not have the resources to hire coaches for school leaders. This book is concerned not with the hiring of coaches for school leaders but rather with coaching the leaders you hire. That is, if you hire and evaluate school leaders, then we believe you have an obligation to support them (i.e., provide coaching, mentoring, professional learning opportunities, etc.) in areas that will make the greatest difference to teachers and students within your schools.

School systems of all sizes and contextual variations (i.e., large, small, urban, suburban, and rural) can engage in impact coaching strategies with and for their school leaders. How is this possible? Impact coaching is made possible when those whose primary responsibility is to evaluate school leaders (i.e., superintendents, assistant superintendents, directors, and school principals) view their role through the lens of ten theories of practice. (We offer a full description of these theories in Chapter 4.) In support of this point, Meredith Honig (2012) suggests the principal supervisor be tasked with leading both one-to-one coaching and principal peer networks, in addition to previously held supervision responsibilities.

We believe that the most influential evaluators of school leaders are individuals who

- Continuously seek feedback from school leaders about their impact

- See themselves as agents of cognitive change in school leaders

- Talk more about learning with school leaders than about leadership and teaching practices

- See assessment as feedback about their impact

- Engage in dialogue with school leaders, not monologue

- Enjoy the challenge and never settle for simply "doing their best"

- Believe that it is their role to develop relational trust with school leaders and teachers in schools and classrooms

- Develop and use a shared language of learning with school leaders

- Reinforce with school leaders that learning is hard work

- Believe that working together with school leaders and teachers yields a greater impact than working alone

SPECIAL FEATURES

Here you will find a very practical approach to coaching school leaders. Each chapter contains features to help readers develop a clearer picture of what impact coaching is and the skills and processes coaches can use to support school leaders. If you're really in a pinch, the good news is that much of the coaching process we present can be implemented using a self-coaching process. To aid both coaches of school leaders and those school leaders engaged in self-coaching, we offer the following features:

- Insights from leaders who have personally experienced the impact coaching process

- Vignettes that provide real-world examples of how impact coaching has influenced day-to-day leadership practices

- Rachel Hazel's story—an extended narrative of one principal's experience with coaching, which we weave throughout the book

- Useful checklists that readers can use to facilitate their coaching process

- Evidence-gathering templates

- Tables summarizing the instructional practices that have the most impact on student achievement

- Rubrics for assessing teacher clarity

- Self-assessment for instructional leadership practices

- Several models, tips, examples, and strategies to facilitate effective coaching conversations

- A list of key takeaways at the end of each chapter

- Suggestions at the end of each chapter for delving deeper into the chapter topics

- Appendices containing additional scaffolds, forms, checklists, rubrics, and other impact coaching tools

WHO IS THIS BOOK FOR?

This book is for educators who hire and evaluate school leaders. Our aim is to motivate those of you who are so inclined to engage in impact coaching in order to take to scale instructional leadership. The tools offered here will help you focus on the leadership practices that have the greatest impact on learning and student achievement.

It is also our intent to help shape, within districts and schools, a coaching culture for school leaders. And absent the luxury of having an assistant principal or principals with whom the role of leader is shared, we want you to be able to utilize the various coaching tools and processes referenced throughout the book to coach yourself in order to achieve maximum impact on teaching and learning for all.

Potential readers of this book fall into two main categories: school leaders and central-office administrators. The school leader group consists of school principals, assistant principals, and perhaps teachers working on their administrative license. The central-office group consists of school district staff, including the superintendent, assistant superintendents, and their respective directors.

INTRODUCING RACHEL HAZEL, FEATURED COACHEE

 Rachel Hazel is a nineteen-year veteran educator. Throughout her career, she has served as a clerk, project assistant, special education teacher, program specialist, assistant principal, principal, and now executive director of K–12 curriculum and instruction in Volusia County, DeLand, Florida.

When we first started our coaching relationship with Rachel, she was principal at Spruce Creek Elementary School. Spruce Creek is one of eighty-four schools in Volusia County. It serves 770 preK–5 students who come from a largely middle-class community in east central Florida, 65 percent of whom qualify for free and reduced lunch.

At the time of Rachel's appointment in June of 2015, Spruce Creek had enjoyed historically high student achievement with strong parental support. However, past successes were not reflected in current student performance and parent perceptions of the school. Consequently, Rachel knew that the instructional and leadership practices pursued by the staff at Spruce Creek in the past would not provide a path forward for them in the future. In Rachel's words, "I knew that I needed guidance." So she reached out to us for coaching support.

Rachel's coaching story, as well as the coaching stories of other school leaders with whom we have had the great privilege to work, is featured within our book to illustrate the practical application of concepts we discuss and ground them in real-life settings. It is our hope that the coaching stories provide a picture for our readers as to what the implementation of impact coaching might look like.

This book is our attempt to provide an uncomplicated, straightforward map so that educators (school principals, assistant principals, instructional coaches, central office staff, and all other educators) can focus on those practices that matter the most in order to have a significant impact on learning and student achievement. A school leader should only be asked to attend a workshop, participate in a network of professional learning, partner with a coach, or be observed by a principal or central office staff member if those events will serve to scale those practices that result in all students experiencing a minimum of a year's worth of growth for a year's worth of input. Our goal here has been to create a map that is simple enough to be understood and yet sophisticated enough to guide central office staff and school leaders to their most impactful versions of their role.

Acknowledgments

It seems like this book has been in the making for over thirty-five years, as it was during these years serving in roles of principal and principal coaches that we were led and influenced by many great principal leaders. Now as educational consultants and authors we remain surrounded by individuals whose own research and life's work continues to directly and indirectly shape, clarify, and at many times challenge and redefine our thinking.

As you read through our book you will see the names and hear the voices of many of these influential thought leaders. Authors and leaders that have directly impacted our own voice throughout this book are John Hattie, Russ Quaglia, Viviane Robinson, Michael Fullan, Robert Garmston, Art Costa, Laura Lipman, Jim Knight, Carolee Hayes, and Jane Ellison. We particularly want to deeply thank Jim Knight and the work of the Kansas Coaching Project and Instructional Coaching Group researchers for the development of the instructional coaching cycle and for giving us permission to use their coaching model, which has guided our thinking in the development of our leadership impact coaching model. We are especially indebted to Rachel Hazel for her willingness to expose her thinking during the coaching process, thereby contributing her voice to this book by retelling her personal coaching story.

During the past eighteen months we have counted on, leaned on, whined to, and yes listened to and taken great advice from yet another influential leader and that is Arnis Burvikovs. We continually heard his voice saying, "Just write something every day, even if you delete every word. Keep focused, keep learning, and keep writing." Great advice from our esteemed friend and lead editor. We are forever grateful for your inspiring us to continue to write about our leadership passion and keeping us on track. We also thank his creative and talented editorial team of Desirée Bartlett, Tori Mirsadjadi, and Jared Leighton.

But most of all we want to thank our family and friends—they have endured this book, shaped the many versions of the message, and provided the feedback that only a loving family and a caring circle of significant others can give. Similar to most children who are asked about their day at school each night at the dinner table, we too have endured the same interrogation every night from our family and friends: How is the book progressing? What are you learning? When will the book be published? Thanks to Chenin and Sean Carlton for their unwavering friendship, for their support and continued interest in our writing, for their willingness to pass along their thoughts and ideas about coaching, and for sharing with us their fermented fruit! Winegrowers typically say it takes a lot of beer to make a good wine. In our case it takes a lot of wine to make a good writer. And lastly, thanks to our children—Lindsay and Lauren—to their spouses Mike and Jeff, and to our grandchildren—Marek, Silas, Ashlyn, and Kyler—you are our inspirations for living and the future benefactors of district leaders and school principals who wisely adopt the impact coaching principles espoused in this book.

PUBLISHER'S ACKNOWLEDGMENTS

Corwin gratefully acknowledges the contributions of the following reviewers:

David G. Daniels, High School Principal
Susquehanna Valley Senior High School
Conklin, NY

Clint Heitz, Instructional Coach
Bettendorf Community School District
Bettendorf, IA

Scott Hollinger, Principal/Professor
Teachers College Columbia University
McAllen, TX

Jessica Johnson, Elementary Principal/District Assessment Coordinator
Dodgeland School
Juneau, WI

Dr. Charles L. Lowery, Assistant Professor of Educational Administration
Ohio University
Athens, OH

Jacie Maslyk, Assistant Superintendent
Hopewell Area School District
Aliquippa, PA

Jadi Miller, Director of Curriculum
Lincoln Public Schools
Lincoln, NE

Roberto Pamas, Principal
Holmes Middle School
Alexandria, VA

Dr. Tricia Peña, Adjunct Professor
Northern Arizona University
Vail, AZ

Kathy Rhodes, Principal
Hinton Elementary
Hinton, IA

About the Authors

Dr. Raymond L. Smith is an author consultant with Corwin. Prior to joining Corwin, Dr. Smith served as adjunct professor at the University of Colorado, Denver Health Sciences Center, teaching within a principal preparation program. Dr. Smith's diverse experience includes over thirty-eight years of teaching and leadership at the building (high school principal), central-office (director of secondary education), and university levels.

Subsequent to completing his doctorate in educational leadership and innovation in 2007, Dr. Smith pursued his area of specialty and passion in leadership development by authoring several articles for the Ohio Department of Education, co-authoring four books, the first titled *School Improvement for the Net Generation* (2010), the second titled *The Reflective Leader: Implementing A Multidimensional Leadership Performance System* (2012), the third titled *Evaluating Instructional Leadership: Recognized Practices for Success* (2015), and the fourth titled *Impact Coaching: Scaling Instructional Leadership* (2018).

In addition to writing about leadership and leadership development, Dr. Smith is an activator of learning, leading others in workshops around Professor John Hattie's research in visible learning, as he is one of twenty-one Visible Learning^Plus Consultants with Corwin. He also conducts workshops in Dr. James Popham's research around designing and implementing defensible teacher evaluation programs.

Dr. Julie R. Smith is a thirty-eight-year veteran educator, international speaker, consultant, adjunct professor, and author. Her area of focus and expertise is building leadership capacity within people and systems; school improvement planning; and teacher-, principal-, and district- instructional evaluation models. Dr. Smith continues her learning by providing workshops in North America, Canada, and Australia around Professor John Hattie's research in visible learning as a Visible Learning Consultant with Corwin. She is also trained to provide workshops in Dr. James Popham's research around designing and implementing defensible teacher evaluation programs and in Dr. Russ Quaglia's *Student Voice* and *Aspiration Framework*. Dr. Smith is co-author of *The Reflective Leader: Implementing a Multidimensional Leadership Performance System* (2012), *Evaluating Instructional Leadership: Recognized Practices for Success* (2015), and *Impact Coaching: Scaling Instructional Leadership* (2018). She lives in Oregon on the Pacific Coast with her husband.

CHAPTER 1

WHY DO SCHOOL LEADERS NEED COACHING?

> *There was a moment in sports when employing a coach was unimaginable—and then came a time when not doing so was unimaginable. We care about results in sports, and if we care half as much about results in schools and in hospitals we may reach the same conclusion.*
>
> —Atul Gawande, *Personal Best* (2011)

This chapter addresses the question "Why do school leaders need coaching?" We could provide exhaustive testimonials from our own public education experiences about the power of coaching and the difference it has made in the leadership capacity of educators. However, as an introduction to coaching, we think it might be more illustrative to draw from our experiences outside of education. Along with our friends, coaches Sean and Chenin Charlton, we have a passion for wine and music. Coaching examples from these two fields can go far to illustrate the power and impact of coaching in the lives of all professionals and in all meaningful pursuits.

We recently watched an episode of the reality talent show *The Voice*. As many of you may already know, *The Voice* is an American reality television singing competition. The purpose of the series is to find new singing talent (solo or duets) in a contest of aspiring singers, age fifteen or over, drawn from public auditions. Television viewers voting by telephone, Internet, text message, and iTunes Store purchases of the audio-recorded artists' vocal performances determine the winner of any particular series. The series employs a panel of four coaches who critique the artists' performances and guide their respective teams of selected artists through the remainder of the season. They also compete to ensure that one of their acts wins the competition, thus making her or him the winning coach.

In conversation with Sean Carlton, he mused that

> there are two aspects of *The Voice* that I find compelling regarding coaching. First, the coaches are each masters in the art of music, and someone who is a master musician must also be a master of harmony. In each of the twelve scales of music, there are specific combinations of eight notes, all of which are in varying degrees of harmony with one another. Inclusion of any of the other four notes introduces dissonance, or disharmony. One of the qualities of a good coach then is someone who can help you orient your growth around harmony rather than dissonance. Second, all of the feedback the coaches give is positive. Sure, they point out flaws and errors, but the vast majority of the coaching is 100 percent "grade A" inspiration.
>
> This analogy perfectly parallels winemaking. As winemakers, we aim to be masters of grape harmony, or a balance of flavors. That is, all of the different elements to winemaking focus on this idea of harmony. For example, grape ripeness has to balance flavor ripeness. And we have make sure all the base elements are in harmony with the grape itself. A pinot noir is going to need a different balance between flavor, tannin, acid, and oak than cabernet sauvignon would need, but each has to be in harmony with itself. It is the relativity of these elements that is important. (Sean Carlton, winemaker, personal correspondence, March 19, 2017)

The takeaway here is that coaching, whether it's for wine or for music, involves parallel coaching processes. Each of the contestants on *The Voice* is assigned a coach because there is an understanding within the vocal music industry, as within the wine industry, that for artists to produce their best performances and help their coaches win the contest, each of the artists needs a personal guide observing their performances and activating the path to improvement. As accomplished as the musical artists are, few, if any, of them would be able to produce their best performance on their own. The coaches provided these vocalists critical outside ears and eyes to help them make needed refinements to their performances.

"Coaching done well may be the most effective intervention designed for human performance," observed Atul Gawande (2011) in his fascinating *New Yorker* article. Skillful coaching is the epicenter for high-performance teams and athletes worldwide. Similarly, skillful coaching is the heart of peak leadership performance, whether it is surgical, musical, relational, or instructional performance (Bickman, Goldring, De Andrade, Breda, & Goff, 2012). The next section of this chapter will address the question "If we know that there are specific practices, which, when learned and executed well, elevate human performance, why has traditional professional development failed our principals?" (Darling-Hammond, LaPointe, Meyerson, Orr, & Cohen, 2007).

THE DUBIOUS QUALITY OF TRADITIONAL PROFESSIONAL DEVELOPMENT

Regardless of which side the political aisle you find yourself on, the No Child Left Behind (NCLB) Act, followed by the Every Student Succeeds Act (ESSA) legislation, has riveted the nation's attention to the way teachers teach, leaders lead, and the impact teachers and leaders are having on student learning. The need for professional development to focus on instruction emanates from the critical research finding that the quality of instruction is a key determinant of the variation in student achievement (Hattie, 2015b). In order to support teacher effectiveness and reduce the variability among teachers and the effect that they have on student learning, school leaders need to acquire and develop capacity in understanding and improving instructional expertise. However, the professional development that many school leaders get is of dubious quality, long on seat time, and short on transfer of training (Darling-Hammond et al., 2007; Prothero, 2015; Rowland, 2017).

There are many reasons why traditional professional development for principals has failed to meet school leaders' leadership development needs. A few of the more frequent explanations for this failure include such things as traditional professional development offerings

1. Are inconsistent with our best understanding of how learning occurs

2. Are a one-size-fits-all experience that lacks customization

3. Are squeezed into the first few years of a principal's tenure but are not ongoing

4. Are not job embedded

5. Are not focused on principals applying new knowledge and skills to real-world leadership problems

6. Are reinforcing isolation and don't promote networking opportunities

7. Regardless of the quality of the professional development, sitting principals suggest that the demands of the job limit the time she could devote to her own professional development

These failures in professional development, however, can and must be overcome. School leaders require professional development (new learning) that employs four key principles for optimizing learning. These four professional development qualities align nicely with the professional development standards set forth by Learning Forward (2017). First, the professional development (PD) must be learner centered. Rather than simply expecting school leaders to attend prearranged, one-size-fit-all workshops, we need to be asking school leaders where they need help and then specifically structuring learning to meet those needs. Next, the PD should be knowledge centered. School leaders must be introduced to high-impact instructional leadership practices at the same time they are afforded the opportunity to understand why, when, where, and how the practice might be valuable to them. More important is the need for school leaders to integrate these high-impact practices with the district's school leader evaluation process. Then the PD should be assessment centered. In order for school leaders to change their practices, they need opportunities to try things out in their schools and then receive feedback. Lastly, school leaders' PD should be community centered. School leaders must be provided the opportunity for continued support, coaching, networking, and follow-up as they work to incorporate new ideas into their leadership practices. In Rachel Hazel's view,

Traditional [professional development] lacks the ongoing relationship and follow-up. Even with the best of intentions, it is impossible to present to a group of forty or more people ... [and] follow up with them to ensure that they have implemented what was taught. I love that coaching allows me the opportunity to discuss with my coach when something doesn't work and try it a different way. I view [professional development] as two-dimensional. You gain ideas and can ask questions while you are engaged in the lesson, but the opportunity to talk through success and failure is not there. Coaching is three-dimensional. You have the opportunity to try ideas, discuss the impact, and follow up. (personal communication, September 24, 2015)

Schools must have high-impact instructional leaders.

Characteristics of High-Impact Instructional Leaders

- Make frequent formal and informal classroom observations
- Provide effective feedback
- (Together with teachers) Interpret and use the results of test scores to inform next steps
- Stipulate that teachers are proficiently collaborating in planning and evaluating the instructional program both vertically and horizontally
- Insist that teachers expect a minimum of a year's worth of learning for a year's worth of teaching
- Establish that the staffroom and classroom atmosphere is conducive to learning for all

To achieve these rigorous expectations, school leaders need to learn continuously and effectively implement high-impact instructional leadership practices. As our friends and colleagues Jane Ellison and Carolee Hayes (2013) write in their book *Effective School Leadership: Developing Principals Through Cognitive Coaching*, "When principals are coached, the likelihood that new practices will be sustained and institutionalized is increased to statistically significant levels. Given the rate of change and learning in today's educational systems, we must provide structures for assisting principals in becoming more effective and efficient in learning the changing skills required by their profession" (p. 70). Impact coaching for instructional leadership represents one efficient method to help school leaders learn better, more impactful ways to lead teachers and students, thereby improving learning for all and increasing student achievement (Bickman et al., 2012).

COMMON FORMS OF COACHING

As long as humans have lived on this planet, coaching has been a fundamental element to the advancement of the human race. From our earliest days, the older or more skilled among us taught the young how to hunt, protect ourselves and our families, cook, paint pictures on cave walls, and be useful and effective members of our tribes and communities. The contemporary practice of coaching involves helping others to improve, develop, learn new skills, find personal success, achieve aims, and manage life change and personal and professional challenges. Coaching, in all manner of professional (and personal) endeavors, is a useful practice to enhance the performance of leaders and the productivity of organizations. What follows is a brief description of various coaching models so that we can make clear what characteristics we borrowed from previous coaching models and which characteristics are unique to impact coaching.

Executive Coaching

The most comprehensive literature on coaching comes from the business world, where executive coaching has become a booming industry. Workplace or executive coaching is essentially a one-to-one learning and development intervention that uses a collaborative, reflective, goal-focused relationship to achieve professional outcomes that are valued by the coachee. Robert Hargrove (2003), in his book *Masterful Coaching*, describes the process as "expanding people's capacity to create an extraordinary future" (p. 2) for themselves and their organizations.

The Core Features of Executive Coaching

- Formation and maintenance of a helping relationship between the coach and coachee
- A formally defined coaching agreement or contract, setting personal development objectives
- The fulfillment of this agreement (i.e., achievement of the objectives) through a development process focusing on interpersonal and intrapersonal issues
- Striving for growth of the coachee by providing the tools, skills, and opportunities he needs to develop himself and become more effective

---

Source: Smither (2011).

Leadership Performance Coaching

Our colleague Elle Allison (2011), like so many of us, was drawn to coaching because of the impact that coaching had on her personally. Elle described the process of being coached as "[providing] an essential support system [for] . . . leaders who want to accomplish great things . . . [because they] should not have to go it alone" (p. xi). Elle's leadership performance coaching (LPC) framework, similar to executive coaching, is grounded in the premise that coaching is a partnership in thinking, weaving together a relationship with others to help them accomplish their goals. This partnership comes to life through the professional conversations that routinely occur between the coach and the coachee. However, her LPC involves considerably more than a conversation.

Allison's Seven Steps for Each Coaching Conversation

1) **Greet and Hold Accountable**—Both coach and coachee welcome one another into the conversation, build rapport, and connect back to the leadership actions committed to during the prior coaching conversation.

2) **Focus the Conversation**—The coachee discusses with the coach the events that occurred since last they met and, in light of what took place, identify a goal for the current conversation.

3) **Listen**—The coach invites the coachee to talk about the goal they have established for the current coaching episode and then listens, without interruption, to the coachee.

4) **Deepen Understanding**—To gain a deeper understanding of the coachee's situation, the coach summarizes and paraphrases what she has heard the coachee say.

5) **Interact Through Questions**—Once the coach believes that she deeply understands the situation, and the coachee acknowledges that he has been understood, then, through the use of open-ended mediating questions, the coach helps the coachee to expand his perspective and how he might begin to shift the current reality.

6) **Reflect and Brainstorm**—The coach acknowledges the coachee's new perspective and then invites the coachee to think about possible next action steps to move his project forward.

7) **Commit to Action**—As a result of the present conversation, the coach asks the coachee to commit to action. The coaching conversation process is dynamic in that both the coach and the coachee are continually making adjustments as they attempt to navigate how to proceed.

Leadership Coaching for Educators

Much like Elle Allison's LPC framework, Karla Reiss (2007) views coaches as being "success partners" who together with the coachee work to develop a relationship in which the coachee feels heard and understood and provide inspiration and encouragement for the coachee as he attempts to navigate through change. Reiss created a five-part, structured framework for conducting coaching sessions, depicted in Figure 1.1.

These coaching sessions typically range between twenty and sixty minutes, and all follow the five-part structure. That is, they begin with clarifying what the coachee wants to accomplish within the organization and his goals, as well as what he needs by the end of the session. Then the conversation shifts to illuminating the issues at play, the obstacles that need to be overcome, and nurturing, within the coachee, the resourcefulness required to produce a successful outcome. Next, the coach helps the coachee think about the various actions available to him and which actions are the most plausible to which the coachee can commit. Afterwards, the coach functions as an emotional support, a champion of new ideas and behaviors. At the same time, she helps the coachee think about time management issues that will increase the likelihood of goal attainment. Lastly, the coach causes the coachee to reflect on the conversation, underscoring commitments, identified strategies to overcome obstacles, and next steps for the coachee to take.

Blended Coaching

Although the last two coaching frameworks both involved straightforward, conversational, step-by-step approaches, the blended coaching framework is considerably more elaborate. The blended coaching framework, created by

FIGURE 1.1 Reiss's POWERful Coaching Framework™

P — **Purpose:** What is the purpose of this session or of sessions in the future?

O — **Outlook and Obstacles:** What perceptions are at play? What obstacles are in the way?

W — **What:** What can the coachee do? What choices are there?

E — **Empathize, Empower, Encourage:** Offer emotional support, boost their spirits

R — **Recap and Record:** Review commitments, record assignments

Gary Bloom, Claire Castagna, Ellen Moir, and Betsy Warren (2005), takes on a more multifaceted approach. Convinced that there is "no single 'right' way to approach" (p. 53) the complex art of coaching, the authors begin by acknowledging a set of skills essential to successful leadership coaching (relationship building, listening, observing, questioning, paraphrasing, and giving feedback). Then, they set about the task of describing a series of five *blended coaching strategies* (facilitative coaching, instructional coaching, collaborative coaching, consultative coaching, and transformational coaching) that make up their coaching framework.

Blended Coaching Strategies

Facilitative Coaching. The *facilitative coaching* approach is used by a coach who wishes to enhance a coachee's existing knowledge, skills, interpretations, and beliefs by helping the coachee modify, deepen, or extend leadership capacity through reflective practice. In other words, the coach refrains from sharing her professional expertise and simply helps the coachee gather and interpret feedback so that the coachee can make his own analysis and determine next steps.

Instructional Coaching. Conversely, coaches who sense that their coachee lacks certain requisite knowledge and skills would employ the *instructional coaching* strategy, an approach in which the coach shares her own experience, expertise, and craft wisdom with the coachee by using traditional teaching strategies.

Collaborative Coaching. If, however, the coachee possesses a significant amount of knowledge of the school context, as well as positional authority to implement the actions, the coach might want to use a *collaborative coaching* approach, where the coach works alongside the coachee offering her expertise, resources, and perspective.

Consultative Coaching. In the *consultative coaching* approach, the coach shares her perspective, knowledge, and advice but does not own or participate in any action that results from the coaching process.

Transformational Coaching. Inasmuch as each of the preceding coaching approaches is designed to support the coachee's acquisition of new knowledge and skills, *transformational coaching* is focused on shifting individuals' views, values, and sense of purpose. This approach helps a coachee learn new ways of being (i.e., personality, disposition, and interpersonal skills). The goal here is for the coach to attempt to shift the coachee's perspective and help him construct new interpretations and new stories that open up possibilities for effective action.

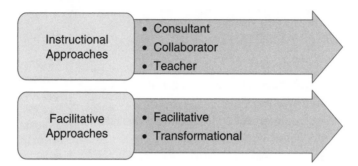

FIGURE 1.2 Blended Coaching Framework

In brief, it is the authors' claim that effective coaches move between instructional coaching approaches, in which the coach operates as expert consultant, collaborator, and teacher, and facilitative coaching approaches, in which the coach assumes a "meditational" role, with a primary focus upon building the coachee's capacity through metacognition and reflection (see Figure 1.2).

Cognitive Coaching for Principals

Perhaps one of the most widely used forms of coaching in American schools today is cognitive coaching (Costa & Garmston, 2002). Arthur Costa and Robert Garmston (2002), along with their colleagues Jane Ellison and Carolee Hayes (2013), have articulated a theory of coaching that has provided thinking tools that assist coaches in their work with teachers and school leaders. Specifically, the cognitive coaching literature and professional development outlines an efficient process for enhancing educators' professional learning, describes useful communication and relationship-building tools that coaches can utilize, and grounds those tools and procedures in a coherent theoretical foundation.

The cognitive coach utilizes three conversation maps that guide them through the cognitive territory of the principal's thinking. These maps, as depicted in Figure 1.3, serve to focus the conversation between the coach and the coachee, keeping it on course and supporting the productive use of time. A coach who wants to assist the principal in preparing for an upcoming event uses the "Planning Conversation Map." Conversely, a coach who endeavors to assist her coachee in a process of self-reflection would employ the "Reflecting Conversation Map." At times, coaches find themselves in a position to mediate a coachee's thinking, in which case they would use the "Problem-Resolving Conversation Map."

The cognitive coach's primary focus throughout all conversations and events is "on mediating [the principal's] thinking, perceptions, beliefs, and assumptions toward the goals of self-directed learning and increased complexity of cognitive processing" (Costa & Garmston, 2002, p. 5). Throughout the process, the unique focus of the cognitive coach is to develop the leader's ability

FIGURE 1.3 Cognitive Coaching Maps

CONVERSATION MAP	THINKING REGIONS (STEPS TO EXPLORE)	PURPOSE
Planning Conversation	• Clarify goals • Specify success indicators and a plan for collecting evidence • Anticipate approaches, strategies, decisions, and a plan to monitor them • Establish personal learning focus and processes for self-assessment • Reflect on the coaching process and explore refinements	Assists the principal in preparing for an upcoming event (i.e., planning professional development, engaging in focused classroom observations)
Reflecting Conversation	• Summarize impressions and recall supporting information • Analyze causal factors • Construct new learning • Commit to application • Reflect on the coaching process and explore refinements	Serves the principal in analyzing and learning from experiences
Problem-Resolving Conversation	• Honor existing state • Frame desired state • Locate and amplify resources • Check for congruence • Reflect on coaching process	Supports the principal when she feels stuck, helpless, unclear, or lacking resourcefulness; experiences a crisis; or requests external assistance from a coach

to engage in "relational and extended abstract thinking" (Biggs, 1995). That is, the coach helps the principal make important connections between action and purpose. Moreover, the coach assists the principal in ways that cause him to apply the concepts learned to familiar problems of leadership work that give rise to the coachee making connections not only within the current coaching focus but also beyond it.

Impact Coaching

Now that you have read a brief description of several common coaching models, it will be clear to you that we have strategically incorporated qualities of other coaching models into the impact coaching model because they have proven to be effective. To briefly summarize, successful impact coaches do the following:

- Build relationships with their coachees (several coaching models)
- Establish clear goals and expectations (several coaching models)
- Use coaching behaviors designed to mediate the thinking of the coachee, such as pausing, paraphrasing, and probing for specificity (several coaching models)
- Strive for coachees' growth by providing them with the tools, skills, and opportunities they need to develop themselves and become more effective (executive coaching)
- Foster a partnership characterized by a thinking relationship (leadership performance coaching)
- Endeavor to develop within coachees the ability to self-direct their own learning (cognitive coaching)
- Mediate the thinking of coachees (cognitive coaching)
- Utilize conversation maps as guides for planning, reflecting, and problem solving (cognitive coaching)

While the impact coaching model contains many characteristics of other coaching models, it differs in two fundamental ways: focus and quantification. We elaborate on these qualities in Figure 1.4.

FIGURE 1.4 Qualities Unique to Impact Coaching

UNIQUE QUALITY	BRIEF DESCRIPTION
Focus	This book and our coaching model is a call to action for coaches and school leaders to engage in sharply focused, critical, and nonjudgmental dialogue about and therefore effective implementation of those leadership practices that research suggests have the most significant impact on learning for all and student achievement.
Quantification	This book and our coaching model expect coaches and school leaders to evaluate the effect of their coaching and leadership practices on learning and achievement. Moreover, our coaching model requires the coach and school leader to understand the impact on students of all teachers and their own impact as school leaders and to act on that impact.

The remainder of this book is devoted to explaining the impact coaching model, the process tools coaches use, and what impact coaches do. In this sense, we use the term *coach* to refer to a variety of individuals who are normally operating within a school district or a school. District or school personnel that could serve as impact coaches to school leaders include the following:

- Central office staff who supervise school principals, and while coaching is certainly not supervision, highly effective supervisors provide a great deal of coaching

- School principals who supervise their respective assistant principals

- Individual school leaders who use our impact coaching skills and processes to guide themselves through a self-reflective process in order to leverage their high-impact instructional leadership practices

Essentially, impact coaches work with school leaders to help them focus on and effectively implement high-impact, research-based instructional leadership practices in their role as school leaders. When impact coaches work with school leaders, they do so with the primary goal of demonstrating how these research-based, high-impact instructional leadership practices look when implemented at a proficient or higher level. Similarly, impact coaches, much like executive coaches, must be skilled at unpacking their clients' (collaborating leaders) goals so that they can help them create a plan for realizing their professional goals. And impact coaches, like leadership performance and cognitive coaches, rely on a repertoire of well-honed communication skills, along with the ability to build rapport, empathize, and listen with the intent of understanding the coachee's perspective. Further, impact coaches, similar to leadership performance and cognitive coaches, must be highly skilled at facilitating school leaders' reflection about their instructional leadership practices and become the champions of new leadership ideas and behaviors. Most important to the impact coach is surfacing the school leader's constructed realities (based on surface and deep knowing), which is the major legacy of impact coaching.

Lastly, like the coaches who use a blended model, impact coaches have to possess the knowledge and skills in a wide variety of high-impact (i.e., practices that are ≥ 0.40 effect size) leadership practices. (An effect size of 0.40 roughly translates into a year of academic growth.) However, unlike those individuals operating under a blended coaching model, impact coaches orchestrate the coaching relationship and interaction on the understanding that a school leader's impact varies dramatically from one set of leadership practices to another. A few leadership practices, aimed at a limited number of goals—say two to three—end up making the major contributions to their total leadership impact. Moreover, impact coaches understand that school leaders can improve their leadership impact only by allocating their professional leadership time and resources more strategically. In other words, impact coaches help school leaders understand that they must spend more of their time, energy, and influence on the high-payoff, big-winner leadership practices that have a significant impact on student learning. (We discuss these big-winner leadership practices in detail in the next chapter.)

Only by sharply focusing on leadership practices that matter most can leaders achieve the critical mass of energy required for significant impact. The primary fuel source for school leaders' ability to impact learning for all and to increase student achievement comes when their leadership energy is *contained . . . compressed . . .* and *channeled*. It's simply a matter of leaders giving themselves more fully on a much more narrow front. Leadership power accumulates quickly when there are fewer ways for it to escape. Effective impact coaches help their coachees say "no" to the many urgent but nonimpactful leadership practices so they can say "yes" to the impactful practices.

RESEARCH ON LEADERSHIP COACHING

How do we know that coaching school leaders actually results in schools that make a positive difference for students? Or does coaching have a positive impact? Unfortunately, there is very little research evaluating the effectiveness of coaching practices related to outcomes (i.e., improved student achievement), specific techniques, or that identifies essential coaching practices that move a school leader toward maximum effectiveness. That said, the research on leadership coaching is largely descriptive, involving case studies, observations, and interviews. The anecdotal and descriptive evidence offered thus far has generated hypotheses and theories but no explicit findings about what works in coaching or why it works (Stober & Grant, 2006). So what can we learn from the paucity of research on leadership coaching?

We learned, for example, from the research conducted by the Center for Research on the Context of Teaching (Talbert, David, Chen, & Lin, 2007) that principal leadership, as perceived through the eyes of teachers, was strengthened as a result of the coaching support principals received. A similar learning can be derived from the qualitative research conducted by Gloria Talley (2011). Among other things, she concluded that new principals participating in a yearlong leadership academy in which leadership coaching was provided valued and were grateful for the support and guidance they received from an experienced principal as they relied upon these leadership coaches to "show them they way" (p. 97). Another theme that emerged from her research was the important role coaches played in helping their coachees to become more reflective in their practice.

Bridget Heston (2013) conducted a case study of Connecticut Association of School's Executive Coaching model in five different school locales and contexts to look for patterns and trends. In addition to other findings, Heston reported that "when coaching was approached as an endeavor of joint work" (p. 35), principals perceived the coaching as meaningful and valuable to them. Additionally, principals who were paired with coaches who utilized effective skills (i.e., listening and questioning strategies) reported "their leadership practices, particularly those deemed instructional leadership practices—had changed as a result of working with a coach" (pp. 36–37).

Lastly, we have learned that leadership coaching is indeed valuable to novice school principals, principals placed in turnaround schools, and principals working to develop the capacity of leadership teams within their schools from the work of the New York City Leadership Academy (2015). Of the four hundred principals who received coaching in that year, an overwhelming majority responded to their annual survey that coaching led to improvements in classroom instruction, in their ability to advance the capacity of staff members, and in school culture.

In brief, we've learned from this research that leadership coaching is a worthwhile investment. It is not surprising that school leaders who receive coaching "done well" (Gawande, 2011) say they appreciate the support and that it has made a positive difference for them. Moreover, supported principals not only report that they are more engaged in instructional leadership, they actually are spending more time on the instructional issues and are addressing them with more skill than their unsupported colleagues.

CHAPTER 1: KEY TAKEAWAYS

- Coaching is no longer a fad. Coaching is the epicenter for high-performance individuals, teams, and athletes worldwide.

- The professional development that many school leaders get is of dubious quality, long on seat time, perhaps inspirational at the time, and short on transfer of training. A few of the more frequent explanations for this failure were reviewed. Coaching offers an excellent remedy to the typical professional development.

- There are a number of coaching protocols being utilized within the education arena. We briefly reviewed five of the most popular versions.

- We learned from the scant research that leadership coaching is a worthwhile investment. And when it is done well, principals who have been coached say they appreciate the support and that it has made a positive difference for them.

Further Reading:
The Innovation Process in Organizations

Richard Elmore, professor at the Harvard Graduate School of Education and a critical friend to educators throughout this nation, laments that good ideas about teaching and learning have so little impact on U.S. educational practice because of a "deep, systemic incapacity of U.S. schools, and the practitioners who work in them, to develop, incorporate, and extend new ideas about teaching and learning in anything but a small fraction of schools and classrooms" (Elmore, 1996, p. 1). Coaches of all stripes will most likely be involved in a coaching relationship that involves working with a school leader who wants to implement an innovation (i.e., teacher clarity, teacher questioning, metacognitive strategies, etc.). As Elmore suggests, implementing the innovation proficiently in more than a handful of classrooms, like effective feedback or classroom discussion, for example, is problematic for most school leaders. Therefore, we would encourage you to read the chapter section titled "The Innovation Process in Organizations" in Everett Rogers's book *Diffusion of Innovations* (Rogers, 2003), as it will help you understand the stages in the innovation process that are critical to successful implementation of any innovation.

CHAPTER 2

LEVERAGING YOUR FIVE BIG-WINNER LEADERSHIP PRACTICES

> *We are recognizing that leaders' impact on student outcomes will depend on the particular leadership practices in which they engage. If empirical research indicates that some leadership practices have stronger impacts on student outcomes than others, then both researchers and practitioners can move beyond a general focus on the impact of leadership, to examining and increasing the frequency and distribution of those practices that make larger positive differences to student outcomes.*
>
> —Vivian Robinson, Claire Lloyd, and Kenneth Rowe (2008)

In the last chapter, we suggested that an important part of the impact coaching process is helping school leaders focus on and spend more of their time, energy, and influence on those high-impact, big-winner leadership practices that research has shown have a significant impact on student learning (Robinson, Hohepa, & Lloyd, 2009). That is, a critical feature of the impact coaching model (one that distinguishes it from other coaching models) is the notion that our coaching partnership is based on the idea that impact coaches must concentrate on high-impact instructional leadership practices—just as Knight's (2007) instructional coaching model zeros in on "the big four" instructional practices (p. 139). If impact coaches are unfocused in their work, they can waste school leaders' and their own time, and ultimately, they can miss an opportunity to improve students' learning experiences. Impact coaches can increase their chances of having a big impact by focusing on high-leverage practices that truly respond to leaders' most pressing concerns.

To help describe the concept of identifying and leveraging high-impact instructional leadership practices, we will draw on a principle taken from the field of total quality management. Let's apply the Pareto principle—what's known as the 80/20 rule—to your leadership practices.

THE 80/20 RULE

The 80/20 rule argument goes something like this: Roughly 80 percent of your leadership impact will come from 20 percent of your leadership practices. Another way of saying this is that a significant few leadership practices will account for most of your leadership impact. The biggest part of your leadership practices—say approximately 80 percent—will be so much less impactful that they will produce only 20 percent of your effect on learning and student achievement. As school principals, we experienced this phenomenon as it related to student discipline. Over the many years, as we dealt with student disciplinary problems, we came to realize that as much as (if not more than) 80 percent of our disciplinary problems came from a significant few of our students—20 percent or fewer of our student population. Critical to reducing the number of disciplinary problems in our school then became a matter of identifying the 20 percent of our students that were producing 80 percent of our disciplinary problems and developing intervention strategies to address that specific population of students.

Additionally, there are many economic conditions that clearly demonstrate the 80/20 rule—for example, the distribution of wealth and resources on planet Earth, where a small percentage of the population controls the biggest chunk. There are business examples in which 20 percent of employees are responsible for 80 percent of a company's output, or 20 percent of customers are responsible for 80 percent of the revenues (or usually even more disparate ratios). These are not hard rules; not every company, school, or school district will be like this, and the ratio won't be exactly 80/20. But chances are, if you look at many key metrics in a school district, there is definitely a minority creating a majority.

At a micro level, just by looking at your daily habits, you can find plenty of examples where the 80/20 rule applies. You probably make most of your phone calls to a very small number of the people for which you have contact information. You likely spend a large chunk of your money on few things (perhaps rent, mortgage payments, or food). There is a good chance that you spend most of your time with only a few people from the entire pool of people you know—minority-creating majority.

So the question is, "Have school leaders identified those significant few leadership practices that will account for their greatest impact on learning and student achievement?" Impact coaches need to help school leaders to "winnow" their practices. It's peculiar how things just seem to pan out this way if we let nature take its course. We spread our leadership time and energies around, investing in a variety of activities that seem worthwhile. But our impact varies dramatically from one set of leadership practices to another. A significant few leadership practices have a differential impact on student learning. A few leadership practices, aimed at a limited number of goals—say two to three—end up making the major contributions to your total leadership impact.

Just think how much you can improve your leadership impact by allocating your professional leadership time and resources more strategically. Spend your time, energy, and influence in the high-impact, big-winner leadership practices—*instructional leadership practices* (Robinson et al., 2009), and you could easily double or triple your impact.

Think about it this way: Leadership impact comes from disproportionate investment. That is, it happens when you focus on big-winner leadership practices . . . when you're unfair or stingy in the way you distribute your practices and professional resources.

School leaders won't get great results simply by staying busy or by being responsible or even by trying hard and turning out pretty solid work. It's not effort or activity that counts but the impact their leadership practices are having on learning and student achievement. Toward that end, impact coaches need to help school leaders examine their productive hours and identify what it is that seems to drive their leadership development the most. In particular, what do school leaders do and which practices do they engage in that contribute the most to learning and achievement? So which leadership strategies are considered high impact and should be the primary focus of coaching conversations?

HIGH-IMPACT INSTRUCTIONAL LEADERSHIP PRACTICES

To answer this question, we rely on the research of Viviane Robinson and her colleagues (2008, 2009). When Viviane Robinson, professor in the faculty of education at the University of Auckland, and her colleagues (2008) found in their study that "leaders' impact on student outcomes will depend on the particular leadership practices in which [leaders] engage" (p. 637) rather than on the type of leader one is, what did they mean? Simply put, leadership practice trumps the leadership label. The more leaders focus their relationships, their work, and their learning on the core business of teaching and learning, the greater their influence on student outcomes. Specifically, these researchers concluded that a combination of five interdependent leadership practices seemed to have greater impact on student results than other practices (see Figure 2.1).

These are the power leadership points, the big-winner leadership practices. They deserve the lion's share of school leaders' productive hours and energy because they'll bring them the most significant results. If school leaders want maximum impact, they shouldn't make the mistake of seeking "balance" in their workday or workweek routine. Rather, they should rely heavily on the

FIGURE 2.1 Big-Five High-Impact Instructional Leadership Practices

LEADERSHIP PRACTICE	EFFECT SIZE
Establishing a shared vision/mission, goals, and expectations	0.42
Strategic resourcing	0.31
Ensuring teacher and staff effectiveness	0.42
Leading and participating in teacher/leader learning and development	0.84
Providing an orderly, safe, and supportive environment	0.27

big-winner leadership practices to leverage their impact on learning and student achievement. Robinson et al. (2009) contend that "the more leaders focus their influence, their learning, and their relationships with teachers on the core business of teaching and learning, the greater their influence on student outcomes" (p. 40). Essentially, the authors determined that these five instructional leadership practices had the greatest impact on student achievement.

We settled on these five elements of leadership practices—practices that are associated with instructional leadership (Robinson et al., 2008)—because current research has concluded that the "mean effect size estimates for the impact of instructional leadership on student outcomes is three to four times greater than that of transformational leadership" (Robinson et al., 2008, p. 655). Specifically, the mean effect size (ES) for the impact of instructional leadership on student outcomes was 0.42, whereas the mean effect size for the impact of transformational leadership on student outcomes was 0.11 (Robinson, 2011). Effect size is a simple measure for quantifying the difference between two groups or the same group over time on a common scale. For example, an effect size of 0.40 indicates that the mean of the treated group is at the 66th percentile of the untreated group. That is, the average person in the treated group would score higher than 66 percent of the untreated group that was initially equivalent. As a general guide, an effect size of between 0.00 and 0.20 can be interpreted as showing no or weak effect; between 0.20 and 0.40, a small but possibly educationally significant effect; between 0.40 and 0.60, a moderate educationally significant effect; and greater than 0.60, a large and educationally significant effect.

Establish a Shared Vision, Goals, and Expectations

School leaders' impact student achievement through their emphasis on shared values and clear academic and learning expectations. Multiple conflicting demands that tend to make everything seem equally important characterize the work environment of most schools today; thus, impact coaches

FIGURE 2.2 Evidence of Impact in Goal Setting and Expectation Framing

- There is agreement in this school among teachers and administrators about the importance of the current learning and/or performance goals.
- Learning and/or performance goals in this school have been prioritized to reflect the two or three most important improvement needs.
- The alignment between overarching school goals and the goals set by content area or grade-level leaders is clear and well understood.
- Teachers are clear about the learning goals for which they are responsible.
- Teachers feel personally committed to achieving the goals for which they are responsible.
- Teachers possess or have confidence that they will acquire the knowledge and skills that are needed to achieve the goals for which they are responsible.
- Teachers have access to the resources (i.e., professional learning, time, support, and feedback) that are needed to achieve the goals for which they are responsible.

should guide school leaders to clearly articulate the school's learning intentions or SMART+ER goals (a complete discussion of SMART+ER occurs in Chapter 3) and **success criteria** (the markers faculty and school leaders use to describe what success in achieving the goal looks like) as the quality of leader clarity distinguishes for all within the school what is most important from what is least important and focuses staff and student attention and effort accordingly. More importantly, school leaders who place more emphasis on co-creating, with faculty, these learning intentions help the faculty to understand the academic language of learning.

Impact coaches work with school leaders to provide evidence of their evolving knowledge and skill in the area of setting goals and expectations by developing deliberate practice and school improvement plans and by applying new learning gained from participating in professional learning activities. Some examples of how leaders can demonstrate evidence of impact in this leadership element are identified in Figure 2.2.

Strategic Resourcing

The use of the word *strategic* indicates that this leadership element is about the deliberate practice of securing and allocating time, money, and people, precious resources that are aligned with and used to support the prioritized school goals, rather than the leadership skill in securing resources per se. In other words, the reader should not interpret this leadership practice as demonstrating skill in acquiring additional funds and/or materials through such means as business donations, fundraising, grant writing, and so forth, as these practices don't necessarily serve the planned purposes of the school.

Robinson (2011) suggested that leaders must possess three sets of skills to be successful in practicing this element of instructional leadership ability. To begin with, leaders and/or their designees have to be able to make thoughtful and informed staffing and instructional resource decisions that are more likely to result in goal attainment. Next, effective instructional leadership practice demands that leaders be able to determine the degree to which existing resource allocation practices are having the desired impact on the school's priority targets. Lastly, leaders and/or their designees must have strong human relations skills in order to successfully navigate the "human side" (p. 62) of the strategic resource allocation process as they work to reorganize the people, time, and money in their schools to match their priorities. Moreover, reorganizing how and where these precious resources are to be used requires school leaders and their leadership teams to be courageous, as well as persistent, in order to generate enough force to break away from the gravitational pull of prior patterns of resourcing that are not producing desired results.

Why must leaders be courageous and persistent? Leaders must be courageous because as they practice the first element of instructional leadership, setting goals and expectations, they establish, both with and through their staff, school-wide priorities. Consequently, they have to possess determined resolve to say that some things (i.e., instructional practices, curriculum scope and sequence, programs, staffing, etc.) are simply more important than others and then stay the course when champions of those lower-priority but favorite programs or practices wish to challenge the decision-making process.

FIGURE 2.3 Evidence of Impact in Strategic Resourcing

- School leaders routinely evaluate the degree to which the existing allocation of time, staffing, and money are having the desired impact on the school's priority targets.
- School leaders ensure sustained funding for instructional priorities.
- Staff recruitment is based on clear descriptions of teacher effectiveness found within the district's teacher evaluation framework and the students' areas of highest needs.
- School leaders subject the staff recruitment and selection process to an in-depth review and evaluation for the purpose of continuous improvement.
- School leaders can articulate the relationship between instructional programs being implemented and instructional resources being used and student achievement results.
- School leaders know how time is distributed within their schools and use this knowledge to make certain that instructional time is restructured to allocate high-quality instruction to students in the areas of highest need.
- School leaders routinely assess the degree to which relational trust exists among staff in order to successfully navigate the human element of the strategic resource allocation process as they work to reorganize the people, time, and money in their schools to match their priorities.

Leaders must be persistent because the process of reorganizing or reconstituting resources—including both human resources (i.e., the use of instructional aide positions, instructional specialists, reading coaches, etc.) and the resource of instructional time and how it is used—requires time: time to create a shared vision, time for the vision to take root, and time for the vision to bear fruit. For instance, anyone who has ever attempted to change instructional materials, decide on a new curricular sequence, alter the bell schedule, or implement new instructional practices understands that decisions regarding these resources take time to make and time to deeply implement.

Impact coaches assist school leaders in the demonstration of their knowledge and skills in the area of resourcing strategically by ensuring a tight alignment among key documents (i.e., the school's school improvement plan, the master schedule, and the annual budget) and processes (i.e., the school's selection and implementation of structured professional learning, hiring of staff, staffing assignments, etc.). Some examples of how leaders can demonstrate evidence of impact in this leadership element are identified in Figure 2.3 on the previous page.

Ensure Teacher and Leader Effectiveness

This leadership element makes a strong impact on student achievement (Robinson, 2011) and involves the orchestration of four leadership actions: (a) engaging faculty members in an ongoing dialogue about instructional practices and the effect that these practices are having on student learning; (b) collaborating with faculty members to coordinate and review the school's curriculum (i.e., develop clearly articulated learning progressions in the teaching of reading across all grade levels); (c) providing feedback to and securing feedback from teachers as a result of frequent classroom observations that help them answer the question "Where to next?" in relation to identified learning intentions; and (d) monitoring student progress numerous times throughout the year for the purpose of classroom, grade-level, and/or department improvement.

Information showing leaders' skill at enhancing the quality of teaching within their schools is primarily derived from four sources. First, the leaders' skill at improving the quality of teaching in classrooms happens based on the examination and use of information derived from face-to-face interviews and/or surveys that focus on both the frequency and quality of dialogue occurring among teachers, leaders, and leadership teams. Second, the leader's skill in the area of enhancing quality teaching results from the examination of key curriculum, instruction, and assessment documents (e.g., curriculum guides, pacing guides, teacher-made assessments, summaries of program evaluation). Third, leaders and teachers both routinely calculate and use effect size data to determine the growth in student learning that is or is not occurring. Fourth, leaders and teachers learn about the quality of teaching by tapping into student perspectives as to what learning looks and feels like. Impact coaches can

FIGURE 2.4 Evidence of Impact for Ensuring Teacher and Leader Effectiveness

- A clear understanding among teachers as to which high-priority academic standards are orchestrated horizontally within and vertically across all grade levels
- Agreement among teachers that the teaching of high-priority academic standards is driven by the use of a common instructional framework
- The level of agreement that exists between teachers and the leadership team about what constitutes effective teaching and learning
- The degree to which student evaluations of teachers are used as an index of teaching quality
- The percentage of teachers whose yearly effect size measures are ≥ 0.40
- The degree of understanding among the staff as to which instructional and leadership strategies and curricular programs are having the greatest impact versus the least impact on student achievement and use the results to inform next steps
- The frequency and quality of *LinkingTalks* (i.e., connecting teaching to student learning) that occur among teachers and leaders within the school
- The frequency with which leaders are present within classrooms in order to observe the impact of teachers' work on student learning and provide them with feedback
- The degree to which student achievement data are regularly monitored and used to determine program effectiveness

help school leaders demonstrate evidence of impact in this element of instructional leadership ability by achieving the examples described in Figure 2.4.

Lead and Participate in Teacher/Leader Learning and Development

This instructional leadership element requires school leaders to devote time and energy in two synchronized roles—both promoting as well as participating in teacher and leader development. The professional development in which teachers and leaders engage includes both formal (i.e., scheduled staff development throughout the year) and informal (i.e., planning period dialogue) learning opportunities. The research suggests that this leadership element had a strong impact on school performance (Robinson, 2011). In high-achieving schools, teachers report that their school principals are actively engaged in teachers' learning. That is, leaders of high-achieving schools have an acute awareness of teaching and learning in their schools, so they know firsthand what direct instructional support their teachers require (Seashore-Louis, Leithwood, Wahlstrom, & Anderson, 2010), and they act on that awareness. These leaders serve as the connective tissue of their organization by creating a powerful web of informed coordinated effort. In this sense, the principal facilitates collaborative effort, encourages knowledge sharing and information exchange, and is a critical source of instructional advice, which implies that she is both accessible and knowledgeable about instructional matters.

- The characteristics of effective professional learning, as described within the research, drive the design, selection, and implementation of teacher and leader professional learning opportunities.
- Teachers agree that leaders in their schools routinely participate with them as leaders or learners (or, at times, both) during professional learning opportunities.
- Teachers agree that as a group and as subgroups, they examine together how well students are doing, relate this information to how they are teaching, and then make the necessary adjustments in pedagogy.
- There are clear connections between the planned professional development and students' learning needs.
- Both teachers' and leaders' improvement plans reflect student learning needs.
- The leader can articulate the system that he uses to identify teachers with the expertise that is needed to help colleagues address targeted teaching problems.
- Teachers and leaders agree that they routinely measure the degree to which student learning has been impacted as a result of changes in pedagogy resulting from professional learning.

Impact coaches can help school leaders demonstrate their evolving knowledge and skill in the area of leading high-quality, collaborative teacher and leader learning and development by providing evidence that they are applying the research on professional learning that shifts teachers' practices and enhances student learning. Some examples of how school leaders can demonstrate evidence of impact in this instructional leadership ability element are identified in Figure 2.5.

Provide an Orderly, Safe, and Supportive Environment

This leadership element describes those leadership practices that ensure both teachers and students can focus their energy and time on teaching and learning. Leadership of high-achieving schools is characterized by its emphasis on and success in establishing an orderly and safe school environment through clear and consistently enforced behavioral expectations and discipline codes. Teachers in high-performing schools report that the principal is effective in buffering them from undue pressure from education officials and from parents (Bryk, 2010). Moreover, an orderly and safe environment is also one in which the leader addresses staff conflict quickly and effectively.

Academic achievement and social behavior are highly related (Durlak, Weissburg, Taylor, & Schellinger, 2011). More specifically, researchers have underscored how various interpersonal, instructional, and environmental provisions generate better student and adult performance through the following means: (a) well-established norms of conduct for both students and

FIGURE 2.6 Evidence of Impact in Providing an Orderly, Safe, and Supportive Environment

- The leader creates multiple opportunities for students to provide feedback about the quality of their classroom and school experience.
- The leader regularly uses surveys to assess students' sense of safety in a variety of in-school and out-of-school arenas, as well as their perceptions of bullying and intimidation.
- The leader regularly uses the results from student surveys to improve the quality of school life.
- The leader provides illustrative examples of leaders and/or leadership teams who have moved to redefine procedures and responsibilities designed to continuously reduce the potential risk to students throughout the school.
- Teachers agree that school leaders work to protect teaching time and buffer teaching faculty from distractions from their work.
- Parent involvement efforts are focused on increasing parental engagement with the educational work of the school.
- The leaders and/or the leadership team evaluate the effectiveness of parent involvement and use the results of the evaluation to improve those efforts.
- Teachers agree that school leaders address staff conflict quickly and effectively.
- The leader establishes clear and consistently enforced social expectations and discipline codes.

staff that communicate high expectations and support for academic success, (b) strong teacher–student relationships that cultivate personal commitment to learning and a connectedness to the school, (c) the use of engaging, high-impact teaching practices, such as class discussion, reciprocal teaching, and feedback (Hattie, 2012), in conjunction with proactive classroom management approaches, and (d) safe and orderly environments that promote and reinforce positive classroom behavior. Therefore, effective leaders distinguish themselves from their less effective counterparts through their work on three specific tasks within this instructional leadership ability element: (a) setting and enforcing clear expectations, (b) protecting teachers from outside pressures, and (c) addressing staff conflict quickly and effectively. Several recent studies highlight these key leadership practices.

Impact coaches help school leaders provide evidence of their evolving knowledge and skill in the area of ensuring an orderly and safe environment by providing evidence that they are applying the research on setting and enforcing clear expectations; protecting teachers' instructional time, using bridging strategies and buffering teachers from outside pressures; and addressing staff conflict quickly and effectively. Some examples of how leaders can be shown to demonstrate evidence of impact in this leadership element are outlined in Figure 2.6.

CHAPTER 2: KEY TAKEAWAYS

- Roughly 80 percent of your leadership impact will come from 20 percent of your leadership practices.

- Spend your time, energy, and influence in the high-payoff, big-winner leadership areas—*instructional leadership practices*.

- The more leaders focus their relationships, their work, and their learning on the core business of teaching and learning, the greater their influence on student outcomes.

- We presented the five high-impact instructional leadership practices that research suggests have the greatest impact on student achievement. They include establishing a shared vision, strategic resourcing, ensuring teacher and leader effectiveness, leading and participating in teacher/leader learning and development, and providing a safe and orderly environment.

GOING DEEPER

Suggested Activity: Time Audit

What percentage of your day or week is spent directly engaged in these big-five, high-impact instructional leadership practices? If you don't know, do a time audit. Maintain a log of time for one week. Examples of categories you might include are e-mails, planning, voice mail responses, reports, professional reading, observing classes, counseling direct reports, parent meetings, staff meetings, community meetings, leadership team meetings, personal time, family time, travel, and community service. After collecting at least one full week of daily records, construct a pie chart that reflects your actual time allocation for each category. Compare this with these five leadership practices. Evaluate what changes you need to make to more effectively allocate your time to your big-winner leadership practices.

CHAPTER 3

WHAT DOES IMPACT COACHING LOOK LIKE?

> *Instructional coaches who use a proven coaching cycle can partner with [leaders] to set and reach improvement goals that have an unmistakable, positive impact on students' lives. And that should be the measure of the effectiveness of any coaching program.*
>
> —Jim Knight et al. (2015)

In the Chapter 1 epigraph, you will recall that we cited a statement that Dr. Atul Gawande (2011), an acclaimed surgeon and research scientist, made in an article for the *New Yorker* titled "Top Athletes and Singers Have Coaches. Should You?" Specifically, he wrote, "Coaching done well may be the most effective intervention designed for human performance" (p. 53). In reflecting on his own professional development, Gawande researched instructional coaches—providers of job-embedded support—and found compelling proof of the positive impact that coaching can have on growth, both personally and organizationally. However, what is most important—and often missed—about Dr. Gawande's frequently cited words—and what stuck with us in our roles as teachers, school principals, district office leaders, and adjunct professors—is that it is specifically coaching "done well" that adheres to a "simple but powerful coaching cycle" (Knight et al., 2015, p. 12) gives you the biggest bang for your buck.

Wander back with us for a moment to our opening thoughts in the first chapter and how effective coaching works in many industries—specifically, the wine industry. Our friend Sean Carlton, who has been coaching people on wine appreciation for the past twenty-three years, helps us understand that a hallmark of wine "coaching done well" is the ability to make the complex simple. Sean believes that

> there are a lot of winemakers that have far greater technical ability than I do. I am reminded of the adage that says "I can explain something for you but I can't learn it for you." For sure, there is a lot

of truth to this, but what it fails to capture is that good coaches explain the content exceedingly better than bad coaches. I believe I am a better wine coach because I have found ways to provide relatively simple, real-life explanations for complex scientific processes. (Sean Carlton, winemaker, personal communication, March 20, 2017)

The notion that coaching must be high quality, infused with the knack for making the complex simple, in order to be effective at improving leadership practice may seem obvious. But delivering effective coaching in practice is not always so simple. Many instructional leadership coaching efforts fail to yield real improvement in leadership practice, teaching, and learning because they fail to take the time to develop a relationship with the coachee, and they are not grounded in a strong, shared understanding of what effective coaching is. Too often, coaching initiatives are implemented haphazardly, without a clear plan and, more consequentially, without an appreciation for the science behind coaching and what it takes to be successful. What, then, is impact coaching done well?

Our friend and colleague Dr. Jim Knight has been attempting to answer this question, along with his research team at the University of Kansas Center for Research Kansas Coaching Project and at the Instructional Coaching Group in Lawrence, Kansas, for the past five years (Knight et al., 2015). That is, they have been studying what good coaches do. The result of that research is an "instructional coaching cycle" (p. 12) good coaches employ that fosters the kind of improvement in performance Gawande describes.

Therefore, we have adopted and then modified the Knight et al. (2015) instructional leadership coaching cycle to align with our impact coaching process in order to scale instructional leadership ability. Additionally, our leadership coaching cycle is influenced by our leadership work with Dr. John Hattie, as well as by the research of Dr. Viviane Robinson and her colleagues (2009) around the concept of instructional leadership. As a result, we label the revised process as *the impact coaching cycle*. The remainder of this chapter will explain this process.

THE IMPACT COACHING CYCLE

The impact coaching cycle we use with school leaders is deceptively simple yet very powerful and is based on the research and work by Jim Knight (2007). Although the three components that Jim describes within his teacher coaching cycle (Identify, Learn, and Improve) are the same components we use within our leadership coaching cycle, we have added several additional substeps within each of these three components to fit with our focus on the work of school leaders. In order to provide our readers with a clear description of the impact coaching cycle ahead of a discussion about each of the substeps within the coaching process, we have identified the three components along with each of their related steps in Figure 3.1.

FIGURE 3.1 Impact Coaching Cycle Checklist

COMPONENT 1 – IDENTIFY: The impact coach, the school leader, and the faculty collaborate to identify a school-wide problem of practice related to prioritized student needs, set a SMART+ER goal, select a high-impact leadership strategy to try to meet the goal, and establish a monitoring and evaluation plan.		
	1	Identify a prioritized student-learning problem.
	2	Identify a school-wide problem of adult practice related to the prioritized student needs.
	3	The school leader creates a clear picture of reality by collecting, reviewing, and analyzing observation and/or perception data to determine next steps.
	4	Establish a SMART+ER goal.
	5	Select a high-impact leadership strategy to meet the goal.
	6	The school leader determines what he will do to know whether they are on track or not and how they will know they have achieved the goal at the end of the specified time period.
COMPONENT 2 – LEARN: The impact coach helps the school leader learn about the selected high-impact strategy and how to implement it at the proficient or higher level (using established success criteria).		
	1	Learn what research says about the selected high-impact leadership strategy.
	2	Describe what successful implementation of the selected high-impact leadership strategy looks like when implemented at the proficient or higher level (i.e., co-create the success criteria).
	3	Model successful implementation of the selected high-impact leadership strategy.
	4	Practice implementing the selected high-impact leadership strategy with feedback to determine next steps.
COMPONENT 3 – IMPROVE: The school leader and the impact coach monitor how the school leader implements the selected high-impact leadership strategy and the relation to goal attainment.		
	1	The impact coach along with the school leader assesses the **fidelity of implementation** (using the established success criteria).
	2	The impact coach, along with the school leader, assesses the impact on student achievement.
	3	The school leader creates "public displays of effection" that reflect the relationship between the implementation data and the student achievement data.
	4	The school leader uses the assessment information to determine next steps.

Thus, Figure 3.1 represents a straightforward sequence of steps, which constitute the impact coaching cycle and result in the development, implementation, and monitoring of a personal improvement plan. To begin with, the impact cycle is grounded in a targeted area of student performance and a school-wide instructional problem of practice, which directly relates to the prioritized student achievement need, followed by the school leader crafting a SMART+ER goal (this acronym will be explained in detail momentarily). Next, goal attainment is made possible by successfully implementing a research-based, high-impact leadership practice. The frequent monitoring of this practice results in data that leaders use to inform their next steps. Then the school leader's learning during implementation is shared with the faculty, as well as other school leaders, in "public displays of effection" (graphing, charting, and displaying the data) that depict the relationship between the practice being implemented (the percentage of faculty implementing the initiative or the percentage of faculty who agree or strongly agree that the school leader is implementing a particular leadership practice proficiently) and the impact it has had on student achievement (percentage of students scoring at the proficient or higher level of a school- or classroom-based assessment). Figure 3.2 offers a sample "public display of effection." Lastly, the school leader's learning journey forms the basis of the dialogue with his impact coach.

FIGURE 3.2 Sample Public Display of Effection

Leadership Strategy vs Student Achievement

	September	October	November	January	February	March	April	May
Leadership Strategy #1	5%	20%	40%	45%	52%	70%	73%	85%
Student Assessment #1	30%	40%	48%	54%	65%	69%	72%	82%

Frequency of Monitoring Progress Points

☐ Leadership Strategy #1   ■ Student Assessment #1

The following subsections of this chapter discuss in detail the component steps of the impact cycle and punctuates each with quotes from Rachel Hazel and other coachees with whom we have worked to help the reader understand how each coachee experienced the process.

Component 1: IDENTIFY—Set a SMART+ER Goal and Select a Strategy to Meet the Goal

Effective coaches put Michael Fullan's (2010) concept of "simplexity" to use as they begin the impact coaching cycle. What does that mean? It means that coaches and their coachees strive to focus the identified change efforts on the "fewest number of high-leverage, easy-to-understand actions that unleash stunningly powerful consequences" (p. 16). In other words, the idea is to attack the narrowest front, penetrating confusion, complexity, and change with a precise sense of what's most important for personal and organizational success. Therefore, the first component of the impact coaching cycle involves several steps.

Identify a prioritized student-learning problem. First, the coach and coachee gather and analyze evidence to identify a prioritized student-learning problem and a related problem of instructional and leadership practice (City, Elmore, Fiarman, & Teitel, 2009). In other words, the coach and coachee attempt to create a clear picture of the prioritized learning strengths and challenges of student learning, as well as the related instructional and leadership strengths and challenges, that may be contributing to the student-learning problem. Rachel and her coach identified student nonfiction writing as Spruce Creek's 2014–15 prioritized student-learning problem based, in part, on the Florida Comprehensive Assessment Test (FCAT) trend data reflected in Figure 3.3.

Identify a school-wide problem of adult practice related to prioritized student needs. The question that spurred considerable conversation between Rachel and her staff was, "What might be some of the adult practices, which they were either doing or not doing, that could be contributing to the dramatic loss in student writing performance?" Based on the collective teacher survey and dialogue with her faculty around this topic and on the classroom walkthrough data obtained during the first two months of the 2014–15 school year, Rachel and her staff concluded that "few if any teachers routinely posted learning targets (writing), targets were not aligned with instruction, and teachers were struggling with instruction that matched the [writing] standards" (Rachel Hazel, personal communication, March 9, 2017). That is, the faculty came to the conclusion that poor teacher clarity (i.e., communicating clear learning intentions and success criteria at beginning of the instructional cycle) and related practices were contributing to poor student writing performance. Studies have shown the importance of leaders identifying issues and fostering a collective, constructive approach to problem solving as an effective school improvement strategy, which entails in particular a willingness

FIGURE 3.3 Spruce Creek Elementary School Three-Year FCAT Trend Data

SCHOOL YEAR/ PERCENTAGE	READING	MATH	WRITING	SCIENCE	READING GAINS	MATH GAINS	READING LOW 25%	MATH LOW 25%	SCHOOL GRADE
Percentage Proficient 2012–13	70	65	76	69	68	80	74	69	A
Percentage Proficient 2013–14	66	59	65	63	65	62	54	49	B
Percentage Change From 2012–13	–4	–6	–11	–6	–3	–18	–20	–20	
Percentage Proficient 2014–15	65	60	38	60	62	60	69	46	C
Percentage Change From 2013–14	–1	+1	–27	–3	–3	–2	+15	–3	

among leaders like Rachel to consider how they are contributing to a problem (Robinson, Hohepa, & Lloyd, 2009).

Work with the school leader to creates a clear picture of reality. The next step in the impact cycle requires Rachel and her coach to develop a clear picture of Rachel's instructional leadership reality. In other words, how is Rachel's leadership supporting or not supporting her teachers' efforts to improve their collective writing instruction? Why? School leaders, in assessing their impact on student achievement, often have a myopic understanding of what their leadership looks like through the eyes of others until they receive feedback either in the form of video, audio, or perception data from staff and students. (A number of tools are described in detail in Chapter 7.) In Rachel's case, she developed a clear picture of her instructional leadership reality through the use of quarterly teacher perception surveys relating to the writing feedback she was providing during her classroom walkthroughs. The dark bars in Figures 3.4 through 3.7 reflect Rachel's baseline data.

Establish a SMART+ER goal. Based on the results of the analyzed data gathered, the coachee identifies a SMART+ER goal. What is a SMART+ER goal? We are assuming that most of our readers have by now been exposed to this familiar acronym. However, we have made a few significant alterations to this well-known phrase that merit some discussion.

In brief, the "S" suggests that the goal must be *specific* (that is, its meaning and implications are clear, so it leaves no one guessing as to the target). The

"M" indicates that the goal needs to be *measurable* (that is, it has both a baseline and a projected percentage gain measure). The "A" stands for *ambitious*, indicating that the goal should reflect a stretch from the existing to the desired level of performance. The "R" refers to *realistic* (indicating that

FIGURE 3.4 Helpfulness of Writing Feedback?

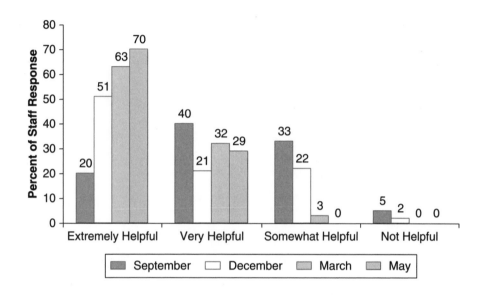

FIGURE 3.5 Meaningful Writing Feedback?

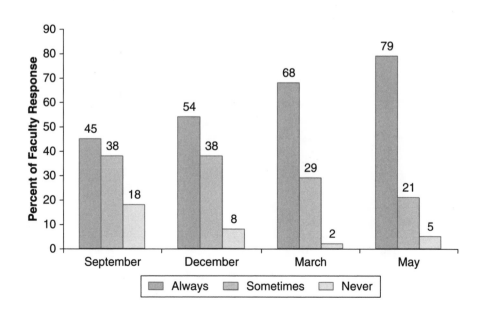

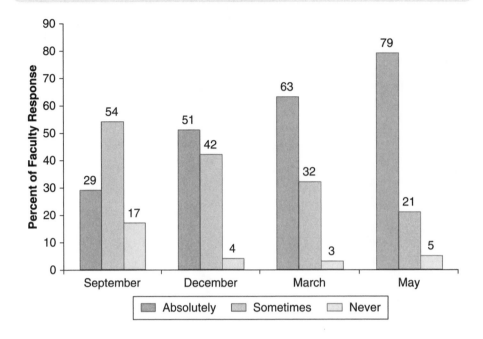

FIGURE 3.6 Writing Feedback Used?

FIGURE 3.7 Created Structures/Process for Meaningful Feedback?

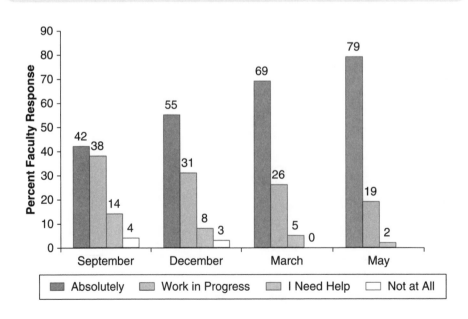

IMPACT COACHING: SCALING INSTRUCTIONAL LEADERSHIP

the goal needs to be grounded in factors over which the school has control and influence). The "T" stands for *time limited* (indicating that the goal has a defined deadline both to ensure accountability and to establish a sense of urgency). The "E" in the acronym refers to *evaluation*, as goals cannot simply be set without evaluating whether or not progress is being made toward goal attainment. Finally, the "R" refers to *reevaluation*, as goals must be continuously reevaluated over the course of the year (we suggest at minimum four times a year). Rachel's SMART+ER goal was this: "The percentage of students demonstrating [writing] proficiency will increase from 38 percent to 55 percent by spring 2015 as measured by the FCAT Assessment and reevaluated quarterly using WriteScore" (Rachel Hazel, personal communication, March 8, 2017).

Identify a high-impact leadership strategy to meet the goal. One thing is clear: In high-performing schools, leaders were more likely to do frequent, spontaneous classroom observations—"20–60 observations a week [that] enabled them to make formative observations that were clearly about learning and professional growth, coupled with direct and immediate feedback" (Louis, Leithwood, Wahlstrom, & Anderson, 2010, p. 86). Teachers in such schools reported that their leaders set and adhered to clear performance standards for teaching as well as feedback from regular classroom observations that helped them improve their teaching (Robinson et al., 2009). Therefore, targeted classroom observations with feedback focusing on writing instruction (e.g., whether writing learning targets were posted prominently in classrooms, the frequency with which teachers referred to the posted learning targets during instruction, and the degree to which learning activities directly supported teachers' posted learning targets) was the high-impact leadership practice identified by Rachel in order to achieve the stated SMART+ER goal.

Identify a strategy to know whether school leaders are on track or not, and how school leaders will know they have achieved their goals. The final substep within this first component of the impact coaching cycle involves the coach and coachee identifying the data the coachee intends to monitor that will help her know if she is on track as she goes along, as well as the evidence the coachee would accept that informs her of the degree to which she has achieved the goal at the end of the specified time period. Figure 3.7 identifies two strategies Rachel determined would help her know if she and her teachers were on track (progress monitor), as well as two strategies that will help the school evaluate their improvement efforts.

Component 2: LEARN—Learn About the Strategy and How to Implement It Proficiently

Once the coach and the school leader have identified a high-impact instructional leadership strategy to be implemented, the coach must explain the leadership strategy to her coachee—a step in the process that is easy to say

FIGURE 3.8 SMART+ER Goals and Monitoring Plan

GOAL	WHAT WILL WE DO TO KNOW WHETHER WE ARE ON TRACK AS WE GO (REEVALUATION)?	HOW WILL WE KNOW WE HAVE ACHIEVED OUR GOAL AT THE END OF THE SPECIFIED TIME PERIOD (EVALUATION)?
The percentage of students demonstrating [writing] proficiency will increase from 38 percent to 55 percent by the spring of 2015 as measured by the FCAT Assessment and reevaluated quarterly using WriteScore.	Quarterly teacher survey results indicate a growing percentage of teachers believe that • Feedback on writing instruction is helpful, meaningful, and implemented WriteScore results indicate a growing percentage of intermediate students are performing at the proficient or higher level in writing.	End-of-year teacher survey results indicate that • Feedback on writing instruction was helpful, meaningful, and implemented FCAT results indicate a significant percentage of intermediate students performing at the proficient or higher level in writing.

but considerably more difficult to do! What makes the translation process so difficult? Two factors complicate the task: (a) Research does not come in leader-friendly formats, and (b) the research is typically not deconstructed into rich narrative descriptions (checklist or **rubric**) of the instructional leadership strategy, along with clear "word picture descriptions" (Hall & Hord, 2011, p. 48) of the strategy, to deepen and enrich the leader's understanding of what each is expecting the school leader to be able to do in practice.

Learn what research says about the selected high-impact leadership strategy. For illustration purposes, let's use Rachel's selected leadership strategy, effective feedback, which Dylan Wiliam (2011), an emeritus professor of educational assessment at the University College London Institute of Education, suggests can double the rate of learning as its effect size is 0.75 (i.e., when implemented well results in almost two years worth of student achievement growth). In other words, the leader is interested in providing teachers with effective feedback as a result of her routine classroom observations.

To be clear, effective feedback is a difficult strategy to comprehend. Some mistakenly think that the advice, praise, suggestion, or evaluation one might offer another about their performance is feedback. Guidance such as this is, at best, viewed as irrelevant by the recipient and at worst seen as useless information (Wiggins, 2012). What is effective feedback—and how might a coach clearly explain this to her coachee? In brief, the aim of feedback is to bridge the gap between where the coachee is (existing state) and where he should be (desired state). In our work with clients who have elected to focus on effective feedback for their leadership strategy, we rely upon the often-cited research of John Hattie and Helen Timperley (2007) to develop "good checklists" (Gawande, 2009, p. 120) for and with our coachees—these instructional tools are clear-cut, efficient, to the point, and easy to use, even in the most difficult situations. In an effort to interpret what the research says about effective feedback, whether it's between leaders and teachers or between teachers and students, we have created a four-part "Effective Feedback Checklist" tool to be used with school leaders (see Figure 3.9).

Given the complexity of this instructional leadership practice, Figure 3.9 serves to identify for the coachee what she would be doing if she were providing teachers effective feedback (the way it's described in the research) as a result of classroom walkthroughs. The feedback checklist is synthesized from the Hattie and Timperley (2007) research. Figure 3.9 is categorized into four parts, with each part containing clear, open-ended descriptive statements of leadership practice. The aim is to help the coachee attain a deep understanding of what she would be doing (i.e., the success criteria of effective feedback) in order to enjoy the impact research suggests the instructional influence has on student achievement.

The first part of the feedback checklist consists of open-ended statements about the instructional leader's skill at *gathering feedback from teachers* about his application of new learning in one or more instructional strategies (i.e., the teacher's use of learning intentions and success criteria, teacher questioning, student engagement, etc.). While Part 1 is relatively short considering the number of open-ended statements embedded within each of the remaining three parts, it is perhaps the most important part, as it gives the school leader much-needed information, which allows him to make adjustments to his leadership strategies to better support the teacher's needs.

Part 2 of the checklist describes the expected practices in which the school leader would be engaged when he is *giving feedback to the teacher* about his use of a selected instructional practice. And Part 3 of the checklist provides the coachee guidance as to the practices she needs to consider when *planning teacher professional learning and assessment.*

The last set of expected practices, Part 4, communicate the required practices in which the school leader must be mindful of that help the teacher *develop the ability to monitor her own learning*—to encourage teachers to be drivers of their own learning. Prompts such as these open-ended statements help the coachee to organize, plan, and monitor her feedback practices. Moreover, such prompts help the impact coach provide feedback to his coachee in an effort to bridge the gap between prior or current achievement and the success criteria. The more transparent impact coaches can make this status for their coaches, the more those coaches can help to get themselves from the points at which they are to the success points and thus enjoy the fruits of feedback from their practices.

FIGURE 3.9 Effective Feedback Checklist

Success Criteria for Feedback (Leaders/Teachers)—Consider each of the following statements, and indicate U (Usually), S (Sometimes), or R (Rarely) by checking the appropriate box immediately to the right of each statement.			
Part 1: Gathering feedback FROM teachers about learning	**U**	**S**	**R**
I use a variety of assessment strategies (i.e., self-assessment, feedback logs, etc.) to gather feedback about teachers' learning.			
I note where teachers need further instruction and support, and adjust my leadership practices accordingly.			
Part 2: Providing feedback TO teachers about their learning	**U**	**S**	**R**
Feedback includes three components: what was done well, what needs improvement, and specific suggestions for how to improve.			
Feedback relates to the learning goal(s), which I shared and clarified with teachers at the outset of the learning cycle.			
Feedback is based on only the success criteria, which I shared and clarified with teachers at the outset of the learning cycle.			
Feedback is prioritized to focus on the aspects of teacher learning that need the greatest attention.			
Feedback is focused on the task, the processes used, or on teachers' self-regulation, not on the teacher as a person.			
Next steps are incremental and specific enough so that teachers know what to do but without doing the improvements for them.			
The amount of feedback I provide teachers at any one time is manageable (e.g., limited to two or three specific items).			
Feedback is expressed in a respectful, positive tone and in language meaningful to the teacher.			
The timing of my feedback (oral or written) provides teachers opportunities to use the information while they are still learning and practicing the requisite knowledge and skills.			
I use strategies to monitor teachers' responses to feedback (e.g., feedback log).			
Part 3: Considering feedback when planning professional learning and assessment	**U**	**S**	**R**
I identify and share incremental learning goals, based on the overall and specific expectations, which describe what teachers are to know and be able to do.			
I identify the criteria for successful achievement of the learning goals and plan how to develop and/or share those criteria with the teachers at or near the outset of the professional learning.			

IMPACT COACHING: SCALING INSTRUCTIONAL LEADERSHIP

Part 3: Considering feedback when planning professional learning and assessment (continued)	U	S	R
I identify critical points in the learning where the teachers and I engage in assessment and feedback to determine who is learning and who needs further professional development and support.			
I plan activities that provide teachers with the opportunity to practice and demonstrate their learning so that feedback can be given and received.			
I plan opportunities for teachers to act on feedback with my support.			
I look for ways to maximize feedback to teachers while helping them take on greater responsibility for providing peer feedback and for self-assessing:			
• Provide group feedback to teachers who share similar strengths and needs.			
• Provide oral feedback during conversations and observations.			
• Schedule routine interactions (e.g., face to face, electronic) to provide feedback on their learning.			
Part 4: Developing teachers' ability to monitor their own learning	U	S	R
I explicitly make connections between the purpose of a task and the learning goal(s).			
I encourage teachers' to think continuously about the criteria for success and to look for the criteria in their demonstrations of learning.			
I involve teachers in defining and applying success criteria.			
I use a variety of strategies (e.g., a think-aloud) to explicitly model providing feedback.			
I have teachers use criteria to provide feedback to peers and to self-assess.			
I provide teachers feedback on the quality of the peer assessments and self-assessments.			

Helpful feedback then is key to coaching effectiveness. Karen Beattie, principal at Chisholm Elementary School in Volusia County Schools, DeLand, Florida, a veteran educator but a new elementary principal participating in a coaching relationship, says,

> I thought I knew what I was doing in my new role. However, it wasn't until I was the recipient of relevant learning, effective feedback, and ongoing support that I hit my stride as a principal. Being a principal should not come with the "you have arrived stamp of approval," but with a challenge to continue to learn. Coaching brings challenges to the thinking of those leading resulting in improved professional practice. (Karen Beattie, principal, Chisholm Elementary School, personal communication, March 20, 2017)

As mentioned previously, coaches need to have a deep knowledge of a small number of high-yield leadership strategies. District- and school-level leaders with whom we work are taught the five key instructional leadership practices (see Figure 3.10) we describe in *Evaluating Instructional Leadership: Recognized Practices for Success* (J. Smith & R. Smith, 2015), along with the strategies that are embedded within them.

However, inasmuch as possessing a deep knowledge of these practices is important, it is not, by itself, sufficient. In addition to a deep knowledge of high-impact instructional leadership practices, coaches must apply such tactics as

- Clarifying the research for their coachees through their own personal reading, writing, and synthesizing of what they plan to tell leaders

- Breaking down the research into manageable pieces related to the specific leadership strategies to be implemented

FIGURE 3.10 Five Elements of Instructional Leadership Ability

ELEMENT	DESCRIPTION
Establishing a shared vision/ mission, goals, and expectations	Involves the establishment, communication, and monitoring of performance as well as learning goals and expectations. Internal and external stakeholders should be engaged in the process to achieve clarity and ownership in the vision/mission and goals.
Strategic resourcing	Involves linking the selection and allocation of resources (i.e., money, people, materials, and time) to the school's priority goals. Includes the recruitment, selection, and retention of staff with suitable expertise.
Ensuring teacher and staff effectiveness	Includes the leader's direct involvement in supporting and evaluating teaching through frequent classroom observations, with feedback provided to and collected from teachers to determine next steps. Involves establishing a coherent instructional program, ongoing dialogue with teachers about the relationship between instructional practice and student achievement, and monitoring of student performance data to drive continuous program improvement.
Leading and participating in teacher/leader learning and development	Involves leaders who both lead and participate with teachers in targeted professional development that is either formal or informal in nature.
Providing an orderly, safe, and supportive environment	Involves creating an environment that provides assurances that teachers and students can focus on learning by setting and enforcing clear expectations. This involves protecting teachers from outside pressures and addressing staff conflict quickly and effectively, and creating an environment where it is okay to make and learn from mistakes.

- Seeing the research through the eyes of school leaders, so they can address the practical concerns leaders might have as they attempt to implement a strategy

- Simplifying the research in ways that make the complex clear through the use of stories, metaphors, rubrics, and the like without reducing the complexity of the concept

These tactics are presented in more detail in Chapter 6. Coaches who explain strategies in precise and provisional ways lay the groundwork for high-quality implementation yet give school leaders the freedom to use their learning about implementation during implementation (Hattie, 2012) to modify leadership strategies that more accurately align with the success criteria and better meet teachers' needs.

Model the successful implementation of the selected high-impact leadership strategy. The next step within the second component of the impact coaching cycle is modeling. To understand how to proficiently implement the selected leadership strategy, school leaders need to see it being implemented by someone else. As we have engaged in the coaching process with clients, we have found that modeling can occur in at least three ways—in the school, in a colleague's school, and engaged in simulations during a seminar.

- *In the school.* While impact coaches conduct classroom walkthroughs and provide teachers feedback according to the established success criteria checklist, the school leader completes the same checklist as she watches the demonstration. Immediately after the classroom observations, the impact coach debriefs with the school leader to answer questions she may have as a result of the process. Later, the roles can be reversed, with the impact coach and school leader conducting the classroom observations with teacher feedback using the established success criteria checklist. During the debriefing session immediately following the classroom observations, the school leader would compare the feedback she would provide teachers with the feedback the coach would provide.

- *Visiting other principals' schools.* When school leaders are learning new leadership strategies, they may elect to visit other principals' schools to see how they implement them. Another variation of this strategy is that visiting principals could participate in their colleagues' "in the school" modeling process, as described previously. That is, they, along with the school's principal, would participate in the classroom walkthroughs and craft their own feedback. At the end of the process, all walkthrough participants compare notes and the identified feedback.

- *During a seminar simulation.* In some cases, we have conducted modeling sessions, which are simulated to small groups of coachees during a seminar setting. While modeling of this nature is not ideal, it does provide school leaders safe "practice fields" on which to try out their newly acquired skills.

Practice implementing the selected high-impact leadership strategy with feedback to determine next steps. The final sub-step within the second component of the impact cycle involves the impact coach providing the school leader feedback and/or the school leader's teachers providing the school leader feedback regarding the degree to which they are effectively implementing the identified high-impact leadership practice. Rachel's feedback came directly from her teachers in the form of a survey (see Figures 3.4 through 3.6, which we presented earlier in this chapter). Rachel and her coach would review each quarter's survey results from teachers and, together with her coach, would determine the needed adjustments to leadership practice. These adjustments in leadership practice were then implemented during the next quarter's classroom walkthroughs, which is explained in greater detail within the final component of the impact cycle.

Component 3: IMPROVE—Monitor Implementation and Measure the Effects

Instructional coaches, together with their coachees, perform four critical maneuvers in this last component of the impact coaching cycle: (a) They monitor and access how well the coachee is implementing the chosen high-impact strategy; (b) they use the results of the monitoring to inform next steps—next coaching steps, as well as adjustments to leadership practice; (c) they assess the impact on student achievement (a formative assessment in the same academic area as the SMART+ER goal); and (d) they create graphic displays of the data (measures of the leadership practice, along with measures of student achievement), which we call "public displays of effection," or impact data. Let's take each one of these four actions and discuss them in greater depth.

Assess the fidelity of implementation. Impact coaches, along with the coachee, monitor and assess to what degree the coachee proficiently implements the chosen high-impact leadership strategy. Impact coaches can accomplish this by surveying teachers. In other words, the coachee asks teachers to respond to the established success criteria checklist (see Figure 3.9 parts 1, 2, and 4) so they can see, through teachers' eyes, how well they are implementing the instructional leadership strategy—effective feedback. Armed with summary data of teacher perceptions, coaches and coachees better understand which aspects of the high-impact instructional leadership strategy are being implemented well and those aspects that require further work (i.e., additional clarification, modeling, etc.).

The general storyline created by the data presented in Figures 3.4 through 3.7 scream *Feedback is powerful!* In other words, school leaders who use the feedback they secure from teachers learn about their implementation efforts during implementation (Fullan, 2010). In this case, Rachel learned how helpful and how meaningful her writing feedback was to teachers and their writing instruction and the degree to which her teachers were using her feedback to improve their writing instruction. Rachel recalled that the feedback she gave teachers "evolved as [their] learning evolved. For example, in the beginning, I gave feedback that was more general" (Rachel Hazel, personal communication, June 5, 2017) and then, over time, the feedback became more specific. Samples of feedback that Rachel gave her teachers as a result of her classroom observations are depicted in Figure 3.11.

Each quarter, Rachel used the results from that quarter's implementation efforts to make adjustments to her feedback practices, which she applied during the next quarter. And in all cases, Rachel saw an increase in both the helpfulness and meaningfulness of her feedback, as well as in teachers' use of her feedback. In this manner, Rachel demonstrated the power of feedback, as the information she secured from teachers was used to change her practice.

The data depicted in Figures 3.4 through 3.7 tell another important but rarely told story. While most school leaders collect mountains of student achievement (effect) data, few leaders that we have encountered collect adult (cause) data. Collecting one without collecting the other tells only half the achievement story and perpetuates "factless debates" as to what adult practices caused learning to happen or not. That is, collecting student effect data (see Figures 3.11 and 3.12) without attempting to understand the degree to

FIGURE 3.11 Samples of Rachel's Feedback to Teachers

Feedback in the beginning included . . .

- *Four out of five of the students were unclear about the success criteria for the lesson. What might you do to make this clearer?*

- *Seven students reported that they were learning about a particular subject (like birds, when the question was why would birds make great pets). However, the actual learning intention was to be able to write a persuasive paragraph.*

- *Three out of five students asked were unable to use the academic language in the learning intention correctly. Could you use a different color to highlight the academic language and specifically teach it?*

As these practices became second nature, the feedback then became more focused on individual students. Such as . . .

- *[Kyler] was able to tell me exactly where his writing is on the rubric but was unclear about how to move to the next level. Is there an example that can be shown to him to illustrate what is being asked of him?*

- *[Ashlyn's] writing has moved two levels from our last walkthrough. What strategy has helped her the most? Why?*

which the adult practices were contributing or not contributing to student learning deprives school leaders and teachers of the opportunity to make needed adjustments to leadership and instructional practices in a timely way. The goal here is to determine which teachers are having the greatest impact, find out what they are doing or how they are doing it, and then move to replicate those instructional practices in the practices of other teachers—to scale instructional expertise.

The hypothesis that Rachel and her faculty devised went something like this: If we increase the percentage of faculty that are using the writing feedback to make adjustments to writing instruction, then student writing performance would increase. The essence then of Rachel's Deliberate Practice Plan (the growth plan she developed with her coach) was to test this hypothesis. As you can see from what is depicted in Figures 3.4 through 3.7 and 3.10 through 3.11, her plan was successful.

Assess the impact on student achievement. Assessing progress in the identified area of student achievement can be realized by administering a formative assessment in that area. For example, Rachel's identified student-learning problem was prioritized to the area of writing (specifically fourth- and fifth-grade writing performance)—the percentage of students writing proficiently on the Florida Standards Assessment. Given the state assessment occurs only one time each year, Rachel and her faculty decided to have their students take a quarterly writing assessment developed and scored by WriteScore (a third-party vendor) to provide them the benchmark data they needed to judge progress and make just-in-time adjustments to instruction and leadership strategies (see Figures 3.12 and 3.13).

FIGURE 3.12 Fourth-Grade WriteScore Performance

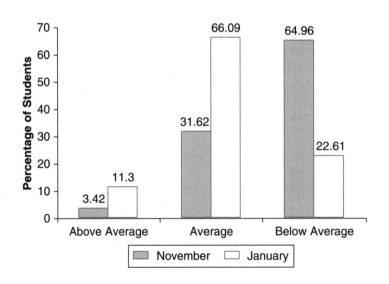

IMPACT COACHING: SCALING INSTRUCTIONAL LEADERSHIP

FIGURE 3.13   Fifth-Grade WriteScore Performance

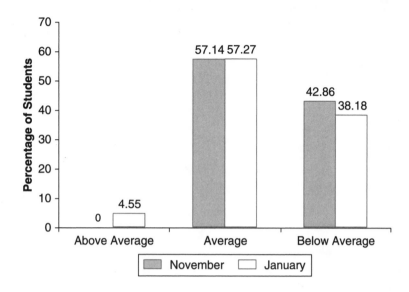

Create "public displays of effection," and determine next steps. The "public display of effection," or impact, is created by showing the relationship between two measures—the degree to which the instructional leadership strategy is implemented proficiently (writing feedback) and the percentage of students scoring at the proficient or higher level on the formative school-wide assessment (writing). Figures 3.4 through 3.7 depict the data Rachel monitored and used to measure her leadership strategy. That is, as quarterly adjustments were made to the feedback Rachel was providing to her teachers, the number of teachers reporting that the feedback was meaningful and helpful increased, and more teachers were making use of the feedback to change their writing instruction. The result was that student writing performance in the targeted areas was positively impacted.

"Public displays of effection" such as these (Figures 3.4 to 3.7 and 3.11 and 3.12) form the basis for the coaching conversations between Rachel and her coach. In Rachel's view,

Coaching has given me confidence that I would have never had without it. I feel confident that what I am doing makes a difference. The evidence is clear. Difficult conversations with teachers about the direction of our school, conversations with my supervisors, and even with parents have become easier because there is indisputable evidence that what we are doing is the right thing. In this regard, coaching has made the really hard decisions easy. (Rachel Hazel, personal communication, September 24, 2015)

- Specifically, it is coaching "done well" that gives you the bang for your buck!

- Coaching is about building relationships with school leaders as much as it is about instructional leadership. The heart of relationships is emotional connection.

- The simple but powerful instructional leadership coaching cycle we use with clients involves a number of steps that are embedded within three components—Identify, Learn, and Improve.

- Instructional leadership coaching begins by developing a clear picture of instructional leadership reality.

- Focus the identified change efforts on the fewest number of high-leverage, easy-to-understand actions.

- Coaches support leaders by having a deep knowledge of a small number of high-yield leadership strategies.

- SMART+ER goals are developed based on the results of the analyzed data gathered.

- Coaches model in the school, in other schools, or in seminars so that school leaders can see what correct implementation of a high-impact leadership practice looks like.

- Examining both adult practices and the impact of those practices on student achievement is essential.

- "Public displays of effection" drive the coaching dialogue.

GOING DEEPER

Further Reading: *Research on Implementation*

Want to learn more about what the research says about implementation? Dean Fixsen, Sandra Naoom, Karen Blase, Robert Friedman, and Frances Wallace (2005), in *Implementation Research: A Synthesis of the Literature*, reveal the science related to implementing "evidence-based practices and programs" (p. vi) with fidelity and good outcomes for consumers. This research synthesis supports many of the concepts presented within the instructional leadership coaching cycle.

CHAPTER 4

PARTNERSHIP PRINCIPLES AND THEORIES OF PRACTICE

> *Our human yearning for caring connections, for peace rather than war, for equality rather than inequality, for freedom rather than oppression, can be seen as part of our genetic equipment. The degree to which this yearning can be realized is not a matter of changing our genes, but of building partnership social structures and beliefs.*
>
> —Riane Eisler (2017)

When Riane Eisler, a social scientist, attorney, and award-winning author who has perhaps written more about the concept of partnership than anyone suggested that the natural human desire for a caring relationship can be realized best by creating partnership social structures and belief systems (Eisler, 2017), what did she mean? She meant that relationships, which are mutually respectful and caring, where individuals feel both valued and valuable and help each other grow mentally, emotionally, and spiritually, are productive partnerships. Effective coaching can only grow and flourish in such a partnership. In our coaching model, as in Jim Knight's (2007) coaching model, it is the *partnership philosophy* that forms the basis for how impact coaches interact with their coachees. But what exactly are the principles—or as we shall call them, the theories of practice (TOP)—behind that approach? And how does our thinking about this approach compare to Jim Knight's thinking about the same?

KNIGHT'S PARTNERSHIP PRINCIPLES

In Jim Knight's (2007) book *Instructional Coaching: A Partnership Approach to Improving Instruction*, Jim identified seven principles that were intended to provide coaches with a "conceptual language" (p. 40), a set of values, if you will, that underpin their work with teachers thus creating a partnership relationship. These seven principles represent the glue that holds together Jim's systematic approach to instructional coaching. The seven partnership principles are briefly identified and described in Figure 4.1.

FIGURE 4.1 Knight's Seven Partnership Principles

PARTNERSHIP PRINCIPLE	DESCRIPTION
Equality: Instructional coaches and teachers are equal partners	Is about believing the people we collaborate with are no less important than we or anyone else and that, consequently, their ideas, thoughts, and opinions are no less important than our own
Choice: Teachers should have choice regarding what and how they learn	Is about believing that choices lie at the heart of professional practice and that when we take away others' choices, we treat them as if they are not professionals. We have found that when we offer others choices, we actually increase the likelihood that they will embrace what we have to offer. Taking away choice is a bona fide recipe for resistance.
Voice: Professional learning should empower and respect the voices of teachers	Is about valuing the opinions of everyone with whom they collaborate. When a coach empathetically listens to another person's ideas, thoughts, and concerns, the coach communicates that the other person's life is important and meaningful. This may be the most important service that a coach can provide.
Dialogue: Professional learning should enable authentic dialogue	Is about believing in the importance of conversations that enable people to think together. During dialogue, people inquire into each other's point of view to surface assumptions of their own and others' assumptions in order to make meaning.
Reflection: Reflection is an integral part of professional learning	Is about believing that learning can be enhanced when we have numerous opportunities to consider how what we're learning might impact what we have done in the past, what we are doing now, and what we will be doing in the future.
Praxis: Teachers should apply their learning to their real-life practice as they are learning	Is about believing that learning is most meaningful when we reflect and re-create knowledge so that we can use it in our personal or professional lives. When teachers learn, reflect, and act, they are engaged in praxis.
Reciprocity: Instructional coaches should expect to get as much as they give	Is about believing that every learning experience we create provides as much of a chance for us (coaches) to learn as it does for our learning partners. All members of the partnership are rewarded by what each individual contributes.

THEORIES OF PRACTICE

Our impact coaching model incorporates Jim Knight's (2007) "Partnership Principles," which, like in Jim's coaching model, underpin our coaching process. These partnership principles, together with our ten theories of practice (TOPs) form the basis for our leadership partnership relationship. The "Partnership Theories of Practice," similar to the Costa and Garmston (2002) "Five States of Mind" (p. 125) and John Hattie's (2012) ten "Mindframes" (p. 169) offer a theoretical construct that binds together the practices of coaches and school leaders, which are played out within the leadership impact coaching cycle. That is, like these other authors, we rely upon these theories of practice—ways of thinking that serve as a guide to the coaching process with and between school leaders. We wrote about nine TOPs in our book *Evaluating Instructional Leadership: Recognized Practices for Success* (J. Smith & R. Smith, 2015). Subsequent to its publication, we have added a tenth theory of practice to the original nine. Our ten TOPs represent individual beliefs, which require changes in how impact coaches view their roles within the coaching process. These ten TOPs describe how coaches go about working with school leaders. Figure 4.2 provides brief descriptions of our ten partnership theories of practice.

This chapter describes the TOP that is foundational to the leadership partnership relationship work. Additionally, we breathe life into these TOPs by adding Rachel Hazel's perceptions of how these ten TOPs have impacted her coaching experiences. Descriptions of these ten theories of practice, as well as examples of critical questions that impact coaches and school leaders might be attempting to answer when operating within each theory of practice, follow.

Evaluate Your Impact

Impact coaches believe that their most essential undertaking is to continuously evaluate their impact on school leaders and, based on the results, alter, enhance, or continue their coaching strategies. In a formative sense (i.e., development at a particular time), enacting this theory requires coaches to alter their coaching "on the fly" (Hattie, 2012, p. 160) on the basis of the leader's feedback about the effect of coaching practices used. That is, formatively, effective impact coaches acting on this belief would, for example, be routinely collecting evidence on such things as leaders' perspectives (responses to clarifying and/or probing questions, paraphrases, etc.) on the effectiveness of the coaching strategies being employed.

From a **summative** point of view (i.e., the outcome of coaching), operationalizing this theory of practice would mean, among other things, that impact coaches are systematically evaluating the impact that they are having on the school leader by assessing and analyzing leaders' responses to the "Success Criteria Checklist for the Instructional Leadership Impact Cycle" (more about this assessment tool in Chapter 8). Critical questions that impact coaches and school leaders might be attempting to answer when operating within this particular theory of practice are reflected in Figure 4.3.

FIGURE 4.2 Brief Descriptions of the Ten Partnership Theories of Practice

TOP	TOP DESCRIPTION
#1: Evaluate impact	Is about coaches believing that their most essential undertaking is to continuously seek feedback about their influences on leaders and, based on the results, alter, enhance, or continue their coaching strategies
#2: Activate change	Is about coaches seeing themselves as agents of cognitive change, which requires a belief that leaders' success is not a fixed trait but rather a dynamic, constantly changing characteristic as a result of coach and leader dedication and hard work
#3: Focus on learning	Is about believing that learning is most meaningful when we reflect and re-create knowledge so that we can use it in our professional lives. Professional discussions are about learning and not leadership practices. We debate learning and discuss the impacts school leaders are having on teachers' learning.
#4: View assessment as feedback	Is about coaches and leaders debating and agreeing about where they are going, how they are going, and where they are going next. We need to move from the prepositional divide of assessment as "assessment of" and "assessment for" to assessment as feedback for the leader.
#5: Engage in dialogue	Is about believing in the importance of conversations that enable people to think together. During dialogue, people inquire into each other's points of view to surface assumptions of their own and others' assumptions in order to make meaning.
#6: Embrace the challenge	Is about believing that the art of coaching is about understanding that what is challenging to one leader may not be to another. We need to pay constant attention to individual differences. Challenge will be through mutually developed clear learning intentions and success criteria that require us to ask three questions: (a) Where am I going? (b) How am I going? and (c) Where to next?
#7: Develop relational trust	Is about believing that relational trust is built by practicing and expecting others to practice four essential qualities to a successful coaching partnership: (a) demonstrating respect by valuing the ideas of others, (b) employing deep listening skills designed to understand others' assumptions and points of view, (c) believing in others' capability, and (d) ensuring words match deeds.
#8: Perpetuate the language of learning	Is about the development and use of a shared language of learning within the coaching partnership. For example, both coach and leader use clearly established learning dispositions (paraphrasing, open versus closed questions, perseverance, checking assumptions, etc.) within the coaching cycle.
#9: Reinforce that learning is hard work	Is about reinforcing with leaders the value of concentration, perseverance, and deliberate practice in order to bring about the desired changes
#10: Collaborate with others	Is about believing that by working together we can make a greater difference and have a more positive impact on learning and student outcomes than we ever could by working alone. Effective collaboration happens when the criteria for successful collaboration are mutually established and implemented with fidelity to the success criteria, structures for collaboration are created, and relationships are mutually beneficial and enable information and ideas to flow in all directions.

FIGURE 4.3 Critical Questions for Evaluating Your Impact

✓ What evidence might I gather that would convince me this coaching or leadership strategy is working?

✓ In what ways might I compare this strategy with that strategy?

✓ What is the degree of significance of the effect on the coachee or teacher?

✓ What evidence would I accept that I mistakenly used these strategies?

✓ How are my coaching or leadership practices reinforcing with school leaders or teachers the value of reflecting on what they have done in the past, what they are doing now, and what they will be doing in the future?

Activate Change

Impact coaches for instructional leadership believe that success and failure in the coaching process is a byproduct of their action or inaction. That is, they see themselves as agents of cognitive change, which requires a belief that the school leader's capacity for improvement is not fixed but rather a dynamic, constantly changing quality as a result of his dedication and hard work (Dweck, 2006). It is about impact coaches having confidence in their ability to cause learning to happen. It is also about impact coaches being willing to challenge the status quo and understand the benefits to all of working with the school leader to create clear learning intentions and success criteria. Impact coaches who are activating change and helping school leaders see that their individual achievement is "enhanceable" and is never immutable or fixed, for instance, would make certain that school leaders are monitoring, measuring, and analyzing the relationship between their practices and the impact on student results. Thus, impact coaches understand that the degree to which school leaders learn or not is based primarily on what they do or do not do.

[My coach] was not there to be a crystal ball full of answers and quick fixes, but she was there to be a resource, a sounding board, and, most importantly, someone who kept me on track. . . . In this manner, I saw real change. I learned that as I reflect on my practice, I add depth to my experiences while creating new knowledge to guide my decisions and monitor my impact. (Rachel Hazel, personal communication, September 24, 2015)

Critical questions that impact coaches and school leaders might be attempting to answer when operationalizing this particular theory of practice are reflected in Figure 4.4.

Focus on Learning

Skilled impact coaches thrive on dialogue about learning rather than on conversation about leadership practices—not because the conversation is

FIGURE 4.4 Critical Questions for Activating Change

- ✓ In what ways am I encouraging help-seeking behaviors within my coachee or teachers?
- ✓ How am I helping my coachee or teachers acquire and use multiple learning strategies?
- ✓ How effective have I been at developing assessment-capable school leaders or teachers?
- ✓ How am I encouraging peer interactions in order to improve learning?
- ✓ How am I reinforcing with my coachee or teachers that critique, error, and feedback are powerful opportunities for improving learning?
- ✓ In what ways am I demonstrating that the coaching/leadership process provides as much of a chance for the coach or leader to learn as it does for the coachee or teacher?

not important but because it often blocks important dialogue about learning. That is, coaches see themselves as "Michelangelos" of learning, where the ongoing dialogue attempts to paint a picture as to how both the coach, as well as the coachee, learn, secure evidence of learning, and understand how to reflect and re-create knowledge so that each can use it to enhance her personal and professional life. Too many professional learning sessions are about best leadership practice, new strategies for leading others, or examination of student assessment results, which is far too late to make a difference in the practices of teachers or of leaders. Moreover, we seem to like these safe, nonthreatening topics within these professional learning sessions. Our intent here is to amplify the importance for impact coaches and coachees to converse about how they each are learning, evidence of teachers' learning in their multiple ways, and how to learn differently.

Consequently, to engage in dialogue about learning and about our impact on learning requires impact coaches that are supportive of school leaders being learners and evaluators. School leaders need to be adaptive learning experts, to know multiple ways of leading and learning, to be able to model different ways of learning, and to become the best error detectors in the teaching and learning business.

Through our coaching relationship, I have increasingly gained the ability to accurately articulate where I am on my continuum of learning and the subsequent impact on my school. (Rachel Hazel, personal communication, September 24, 2015)

Critical questions that impact coaches and school leaders might be attempting to answer when operating from this particular theory of practice are reflected in Figure 4.5.

FIGURE 4.5 Critical Questions for Focusing on Learning

> ✓ Are the school leader's and the teachers' learning goals clearly articulated, few in number, and measurable?
>
> ✓ Have I co-created with the school leader and teachers the success criteria that result from their professional learning?
>
> ✓ Where and when during our coaching or teaching interactions do we engage in dialogue about learning and about our impact on this learning?
>
> ✓ Am I helping the school leader or teacher to learn, reflect, and act on that learning?
>
> ✓ Am I coaching and modeling different ways of learning and to be the best error detectors in the business?

View Assessment as Feedback

Of the 400-plus influences on student learning that Hattie (2009, 2012; Hattie & Donoghue, 2016) has researched, feedback is among the top ranked—and this is also the case for school leader learning. School leaders need feedback about their effects on each teacher—hence, the notions of assessment as leader feedback, leaders as evaluators, and school leader colleagues and teachers as peers in the feedback equation. School leaders, like teachers, need to debate and agree about where they are going, how they are doing, and where they are going next.

Likewise, impact coaches should operate from the standpoint that assessment is feedback to them regarding their impact. Consequently, both the impact coach and the school leader need to identify and use "rapid formative assessment" (Yeh, 2006)—that is, short-cycle formative assessment opportunities that provide invaluable information about his effects on the school leader and students and teachers.

School leaders, much like students, need to have a clear understanding of the goal they are pursuing, where their performance is in relation to that goal, and what next steps might look like that move them toward goal attainment. In other words, the concept of assessment as feedback for school leaders works on the same level as "assessment as feedback for teachers" (Hattie, 2012, p. 163), where leaders also need feedback about their effects on each teacher.

> *I realize now that coaching really isn't about my individual actions but about my ability to assess my own learning and change course accordingly. Coaching has given me confidence that I would have never had without it. I feel confident that what I am doing makes a difference.* (Rachel Hazel, personal communication, September 24, 2015)

FIGURE 4.6 Critical Questions for Viewing Assessment as Feedback

✓ Which school leaders or teachers did we teach well and not so well?

✓ What did we teach well and not so well as a result of the professional learning experience?

✓ Where specifically are the gaps in school leader or teacher learning, where are the strengths, what was learned, and what has still to be learned?

✓ How do we develop a collective understanding of progress among coachees or teachers in the district or school?

Critical questions that impact coaches and school leaders might be attempting to answer in this particular theory of practice are reflected in Figure 4.6.

Engage in Dialogue

Dialogue is a reflective learning process in which partners in the coaching process seek to understand each other's viewpoints and deeply held assumptions. The word dialogue comes from the Greek word *dialogos*. *Dia* meaning "through" and *logos* meaning "the word." In this "making meaning through words," both coaches and coachees inquire into their own and the others' beliefs, values, and mental models to better understand how things work in their world.

The dialogue between [my coach and me] really drove the coaching process. Our conversations allowed me to verbalize my concerns and fears, as well as allow us to share feedback with each other. (Rachel Hazel, personal communication, September 24, 2015)

Each learning partner does much of the deepest work internally. Dialogue creates an emotional and cognitive safety zone in which ideas flow for examination without judgment. In dialogue, there is free and creative exploration of complex and subtle issues—a deep "listening" to one another and exposing one's own views, beliefs, and assumptions—because the purpose of dialogue is to make meaning rather than to make decisions. Critical questions that impact coaches and school leaders might be attempting to answer in this particular theory of practice are reflected in Figure 4.7.

Embrace the Challenge

Impact coaches recognize the many challenges school leaders face as they endeavor to address the needs of those they serve. Further, the art of coaching is about understanding that what is challenging to one school leader may not be to another. Consequently, the impact coach must pay thoughtful attention to the particularized differences inherent in the school and community and help the school leader choose and pursue collective opportunities

FIGURE 4.7 Critical Questions for Engaging in Dialogue

✓ What evidence will I accept that I am engaging in effective use of active listening skills with my coachees or teachers to better understand how and whether they are learning to improve their instructional leadership or instructional performance?

✓ In what ways do I reinforce with my coachees or teachers that their ideas, thoughts, and opinions are no less important than my own?

✓ What are the skills of effective dialogue that we would be using when we come together to collectively reflect on our impact?

✓ How do I participate in my coachees' or teachers' collective reflection so that I support them engaging in effective dialogue?

---

for teachers to work together with the principal to make the greatest difference. Toward that end, the impact coach and school leader's role is to determine where and how best to enlist teachers in the challenge of the learning.

For me, this journey was challenging while simultaneously confirming what I knew instinctually to be true about learning. Our dialogue led to reflection, which often resulted in a change of practice and even greater accomplishment. (Rachel Hazel, personal communication, September 24, 2015)

Essential to engaging teachers in the challenge of learning is the development of clear learning intentions and success criteria. Use of learning intentions and success criteria are a critically necessary part of the learning journey because when teachers understand these, they can see the purposes of the challenge that are so essential to success in learning. Likewise, when impact coaches make clear the learning intentions and success criteria for school leaders, they too can see the reasons of the challenge essential to their success in learning. Critical questions that impact coaches and school leaders might be attempting to answer in this particular theory of practice are reflected in Figure 4.8.

FIGURE 4.8 Critical Questions for Embracing the Challenge

✓ What are the key processes I use to ensure that school leaders or teachers are provided choice in determining what and how they learn?

✓ Have I worked with my coachee or teachers to co-construct school-wide learning goals and success criteria?

✓ What key strategies am I using that provide me access to the particularized differences that exist within the school and school community?

✓ What are key strategies I am using to make clear the learning intentions and success criteria for the coachee or teachers so they can see the reasons of the challenge essential to their success in learning?

Develop Relational Trust

Impact coaches highly regard their role in developing relational trust with school leaders and within the school community. Why? Because there is persuasive evidence that links the level of trust among members of a school community and the way they work together and the level of social and academic progress of students (Bryk & Schneider, 2002). In short, as the level of trust between the impact coach and coachee grows, the social and academic progress of the school leader increases.

An impact coach builds relational trust by displaying and expecting from others the four qualities on which it is based (Bryk & Schneider, 2002). The first and perhaps the most fundamental of these qualities is respect. Coaches demonstrate respect by valuing the ideas of other people, which means that they practice active listening and are open to influence. Next in developing relational trust is demonstrating a personal regard for others. Coaches gain trust by employing deep listening skills designed to understand others' assumptions and points of view. Third is the quality of competence. Impact coaches who are deemed to be competent by others work to achieve the common good. The last quality needed to build relational trust is personal integrity. The first question we ask is, "Can we trust the coach to keep his word?" Simply put, when individuals perceive that a coach's words are incongruent with his actions or when the coach doesn't settle disagreements that arise out of competing individual interests within a coaching session in a compassionate and impartial manner, the school leader comes to distrust that coach.

> *It is this reciprocal relationship [with my coach] that has proven to be an invaluable resource to help me find my voice as my school's instructional leader. Having a voice and feeling valued is motivating.* (Rachel Hazel, personal communication, September 24, 2015)

There are a number of important benefits to coaches as they scale relational trust. To begin with, strong relational trust between a coach and school leader makes it more likely that reform initiatives will be implemented deeply because trust reduces the sense of risk associated with the change in practice. When the coach and the school leader trust one another and sense mutual support, they feel safe to experiment with new practices. Likewise, relational trust promotes the necessary social exchanges between the impact coach and school leader as they learn from one another, engaging in "open to learning conversations" (Robinson, 2011, p. 40) about what's working and what's not, which means exposing their own ignorance and making themselves vulnerable. Without trust, genuine dialogue of this sort remains highly unlikely. Moreover, relational trust supports a moral imperative to take on the difficult work of school improvement (Fullan, 2003). Critical questions that impact coaches and school leaders might be attempting to answer in this particular theory of practice are reflected in Figure 4.9.

FIGURE 4.9   Critical Questions for Developing Relational Trust

- ✓ What evidence would convince me that my coachee or teachers trust me?
- ✓ What evidence would convince me that it is okay in this coaching or staff relationship to discuss feelings, worries, and frustrations with one another?
- ✓ What evidence would I accept that the school leader or teachers at this school respect those colleagues who are expert at their craft?

Perpetuate the Language of Learning

Excellent impact coaches are clear about the development and use of a shared language of learning within the coaching partnership. For example, both coach and school leader use clearly established and well-defined learning dispositions (i.e., paraphrasing, open versus closed questions, perseverance, checking assumptions, etc.) to help them navigate within and through the coaching cycle. Impact coaches who co-understand the importance of paraphrasing, posing open versus closed questions, perseverance, and checking assumptions are more able to have dialogue with their respective coachees.

The dialogue between [my coach and me] makes me feel supported, valued, and in control of my own learning. (Rachel Hazel, personal communication, September 24, 2015)

Critical questions that impact coaches and school leaders might be attempting to answer in this particular theory of practice are reflected in Figure 4.10.

Reinforce That Learning Is Hard Work

Skilled impact coaches know all too well and appreciate the fact that learning is not always enjoyable and easy. Often learning is a messy, frustrating, nonlinear, recursive process that, at times, causes the learner to operate at a

FIGURE 4.10   Critical Questions for Perpetuating the Language of Learning

- ✓ What strategies am I using within the coaching or improvement cycle to teach my coachee or teachers the importance of paraphrasing, posing open versus closed questions, perseverance, and checking assumptions?
- ✓ What opportunities am I providing for the coachee or teachers to choose from a range of activities that accommodate different schedules, preferences, and capabilities and communicate to others that their involvement and support has a positive impact on school leaders' or teachers' performance in the district or school?

variety of levels of the knowledge continuum, co-constructing and recon-structing knowledge and ideas with others as they wrestle with challenging problems.

> *As I reflected on our conversations, I always walked away with a feeling of accomplishment. That was huge for me! I often talk to my students about "brain sweat"—the exhaustive process of challenging work. For me, this journey was challenging while simultaneously confirming what I knew instinctually to be true about learning. Our dialogue led to reflection, which often resulted in a change of practice and even greater accomplishment.* (Rachel Hazel, personal communication, September 24, 2015)

Grappling with educational problems is not a new phenomenon to American educators. For example, with the passage in 1920 of the Nineteenth Amendment to the Constitution, which established voting rights for women, public educators realized that curriculum modifications were needed to ensure that all students, not just male students, obtained the reading, writing, and computational skills they would need to participate in American society. Now fast forward to our present challenges, spurred on by College and Career Ready Standards that require a number of fundamental shifts in instructional practice (i.e., cross-content literacy expectations).

Consequently, impact coaches must create and nurture a coaching environment in which error is not only tolerated but, more importantly, welcomed and celebrated, thereby communicating to the school leaders that they can be secure in their role as practicing learners, similar to a practicing physician or a practicing attorney, to "learn, re-learn, and explore knowledge and under-standing" (Hattie, 2012, p. 19). In short, learning is hard work and requires a great deal of concentration, persistence, and commitment to seek out the next additional challenging task. Critical questions that impact coaches and school leaders might be attempting to answer in this particular theory of practice are reflected in Figure 4.11.

FIGURE 4.11 Critical for Reinforcing That Learning Is Hard Work

- ✓ In what ways do I model for my coachee or teachers the qualities of concentration, persistence, and a personal commitment to seek out the next additional challenging task?
- ✓ To what degree are the qualities of concentration, persistence, and commitment to seek out the next challenging task reflected in coaching or teaching wide descriptions of what it means to be a good learner in this school?
- ✓ How am I developing my and school leaders' or teachers' capacity to cope with overload (e.g., paying attention, working slowly, increasing the level of practice, rereading materials, finding a peer support)?

Collaborate With Others

In the traditional hierarchical organization, administered according to the scientific management principles first presented by Fredrick Taylor (1911), the school leader's role was clear. It was to plan, monitor, and control—in general, to get people to behave in a way that furthers the organization's aims. However, the global economic playing field is leveling off, and the world works at a faster and faster rate with each passing day. A shift is underway from the traditional organizational structure dominated by command-and-control leadership to a new paradigm of business character-ized by collaboration and connection or agency and on a scale never before imagined. As impact coaches and school leaders transition into this new world, the skills they'll utilize and the mindset required to activate the part-nership approach and successfully negotiate the myriad changes confronting school leaders and organizations must also change.

Certainly, the school leader's role retains the functions of integrating, orga-nizing, coordinating, and representing the group but changes from super-vising to activating. In this sense, instructional leadership within today's educational organizations is a social process—something that happens between and among people. As such, it depends not on what one person decrees but on how people collaborate to make sense of the situations that they face.

In the beginning of our work together, I was unsure of the coaching process and found that our dialogue consisted of me answering questions, reflecting, and then following up with questions that I had in an e-mail or during our next meeting. Over time, I began to gain confidence and become more aware of my impact. Our dialogue shifted. I found myself reflecting on my practice before the conversation and formulating questions of my own. I now feel that we have more of a mutual exchange of information. . . . The dialogue between [my coach and me] makes me feel supported, valued, and in control of my own learning. (Rachel Hazel, personal communication, September 24, 2015)

In this sense, the coaching partnerships we are advocating are like string quartets: members are reciprocally interdependent, using one another's out-puts as their own inputs and vice versa. Their interdependence is also com-plete and immediate. Their work is done only as a unit; they cannot perform a string quartet composition without all of the members of the quartet work-ing together simultaneously. Thus, impact coaches and school leaders are artists who collaborate; they must simultaneously devote their concentration to their own and to each other's playing in order to produce the harmonic discourse or the desired result of the coaching process. Critical questions that impact coaches and school leaders might be attempting to answer in this particular theory of practice are reflected in Figure 4.12.

FIGURE 4.12 Critical Questions for Collaborating With Others

✓ How am I reinforcing the belief that the people with whom we collaborate are no less important than we or anyone else and that their ideas, thoughts, and opinions are no less important than my own?

✓ What strategies do I employ that underscore the importance that choices lie at the heart of professional practice?

✓ How am I demonstrating that I value the opinions of everyone with whom I collaborate?

✓ How am I, through my words and actions, modeling the importance of dialogue that enable people to think together—inquire into each other's point of view and surface assumptions to make meaning?

At the core of the coach–school leader relationship, as we define it, there is a deep respect for the professionalism of school leaders. We base our work with school leaders on these ten theories of practice: evaluate impact, activate change, focus on learning, view assessment as feedback, engage in dialogue, embrace the challenge, develop relational trust, perpetuate the language of learning, reinforce that learning is hard work, and collaborate with others. It is our sincere hope that the impact coach will be considered to be just like another school leader within the organization. If the impact coach is viewed in such a way, and school leaders come to see her as a colleague they can trust, there is a good chance that the impact coach can make a difference in the way school leaders provide quality instructional leadership and that learning for all (school leader, coach, teachers, and students) predominates.

CHAPTER 4: KEY TAKEAWAYS

We have proposed that human beings, in their interactions with one another, design their behavior and hold theories for doing so. These theories of action, as we have called them, include the values, strategies, and underlying assumptions that inform individuals' patterns of interpersonal behavior.

In this book, we propose ten theories of practice, which combined with Knight's (2007) partnership principles, are the essence of creating a partnership relationship between the impact coach and the school leader. They are the core notions on which this partnership is based if there is to be success at having major impacts on the school leader, teachers, and students in their learning and achievement.

- *Evaluate impact*—Is about impact coaches and school leaders evaluating their effect on others.

- *Activate change*—Is about impact coaches and school leaders seeing themselves as change agents.

- *Focus on learning*—Is about impact coaches and school leaders talking more about the learning than the leadership.

- *View assessment as feedback*—Is about impact coaches and leaders seeing assessment as feedback about their impact.

- *Engage in dialogue*—Is about impact coaches and school leaders engaging in dialogue versus monologue.

- *Embrace the challenge*—Is about impact coaches and school leaders enjoying the challenge and never retreating to "doing their best."

- *Develop relational trust*—Is about impact coaches and school leaders believing their primary role is to develop positive relationships.

- *Perpetuate the language of learning*—Is about impact coaches and school leaders informing all about the language of learning.

- *Reinforce that learning is hard work*—Is about impact coaches and school leaders reinforcing the value of concentration, perseverance, and deliberate practice in order to bring about the desired changes.

- *Collaborate with others*—Is about impact coaches and school leaders believing that working together is more effective than working alone.

GOING DEEPER

Further Reading: *Dialogue Skills*

Readers interested in learning more about the skills of dialogue should consider reading Donald Schön's (1987) *Educating the Reflective Practitioner*. Specifically, Chapter 5, "The Dialogue Between Coach and Student," provides a challenging but highly rewarding description of coaching, dialogue, and the mutual benefits of collaboration between the coach and the coachee.

James Nottingham's (2016) *Challenging Learning: Theory, Effective Practice and Lesson Ideas to Create Optimal Learning in the Classroom* offers advice and techniques for helping children of all ages (adults as well) develop into confident, thoughtful, and independent learners. Nottingham's description of the "Learning Pit" (p. 109) supports the TOP that learning is hard work and that "life skills [are] developed at the bottom of the pit" (p. 117).

CHAPTER 5

IMPACT PARTNER COMMUNICATION

> *Leaders need to be able to disclose their views and the reasons for them, listen to other's views and be open to reciprocal influence, give and receive tough messages, and detect and challenge their own and others' problematic assumptions.*
>
> —Robinson, Hohepa, and Lloyd (2009)

Communication breathes the first spark of life into the work of coaches and school leaders, and effective communication keeps collaborative effort alive. Nothing else is so crucial to coordination of collective effort. No other factor plays such a precious role in building and preserving trust between the coach and the coachee. Communication is the make-or-break issue.

It's not enough for the right hand to know what the left hand is doing. The right hand needs to know what the left hand intends to do. Both partners need a keen sense of what's planned if they are to execute with precision. There's no hope of orchestrating a coordinated coaching effort unless good communication precedes action.

Each individual within the coaching partnership needs to know what's going on. The information network should connect all of the players, wiring everyone into the nerve center of the coaching partnership. Impact coaches and school leaders need to meet . . . talk . . . engage in very open give-and-take discourses. Encourage all to air their differences, to go public with their opinions. That's the only way the coaching process can achieve understanding, hammer out the best approach, and end up with the school leader endorsing the outcome.

Impact coaches need to serve as relay persons, helping transmit information to others. Anyone who is left out of the loop—who gets information too late or doesn't get it at all—can foul up coordination or cause disaster. Also consider the coach as a quality control point in the communication process. The impact coach must do her share, along with the school leader, to make the data accurate, up to date, and meaningful. Any colleague who makes a move based on misinformation can wreck the results streaming from the coaching process.

Jammed-up information pipelines and warped messages cause conflict and cripple the performance of both the impact coach and coachee. In schools, school leaders are often confronted with and caught off guard by interpersonal dilemmas when on a journey of educational improvement and organizational change. That is, they are torn between the desire to maintain relationships and deal with a performance issue. The same is also true of impact coaches attempting to support school leaders within a coaching partnership. When faced with such challenges, impact coaches are often compromised by their need to advance improvement while also needing to maintain and protect the relationship within the coaching partnership. Challenging conversations with the school leader about improvement can be uncomfortable and can often lead to clogged information pipelines and "warped messages," which result in minimal or no positive change in practice or process.

What often leads to these confrontational and challenging conversations are the assumptions and inferences that individuals make about a situation and the conclusions they draw as a result. This puts impact coaches and school leaders in a bind as to how they approach difficult conversations about improvement. The concept of "open-to-learning conversations" (Robinson, 2011, p. 38), researched and written about by Professor Viviane Robinson at the University of Auckland, is a model that has its roots in the work of Chris Argyris, a social and organizational psychologist who has done extensive empirical and intervention research on the interpersonal effectiveness of leaders in real on-the-job situations. We have elected to use the "open-to-learning conversations" model of communication for our impact coaching framework and work in helping coaches to prepare for and have difficult conversations with their coachees because, in its various forms, it has a sound theoretical and research base.

WHY CONVERSATIONS ABOUT IMPROVEMENT CAN BE DIFFICULT

Engaging in dialogue about the quality of performance between impact coach and coachee are, at times, difficult because they have the potential to threaten relationships by eliciting discomfort and unintended defensiveness. In the face of such threats, impact coaches, as well as school leaders, often experience a dilemma between pursuit of their change agenda and protection of their relationship with the coachee. Inasmuch as impact coaches and school leaders may want to address what they see as a performance issue, they believe they cannot do so without potentially compromising the relationship. In other words, they feel that they cannot simultaneously address the performance issue and maintain a relationship with others. They feel stuck between a rock and a hard place.

Prior to providing some research-based guidance about how to effectively address these dilemmas, we need to explain how they arise in the first place. Why is it so common for people to experience a dilemma between addressing the task issues and maintaining relationships? Is the dilemma inevitable or is it a consequence of the values and skills that are often brought to such conversations? Figure 5.1 provides some insights.

It is important to note that with both the "soft-sell" and the "hard-sell" strategies, the impact coach has drawn the same conclusion: the feedback is of poor quality. In the soft-sell version, the impact coach does not reveal her evaluation, expects the school leader to disclose his own, and offers "gratuitous congratulations" about teacher receptiveness. This strategy addresses the person–task dilemma by giving the threat of damaged relationships greater importance than the possible threat to the learning of the coachee and teachers.

FIGURE 5.1 Two Unproductive Approaches to Address a Performance Problem

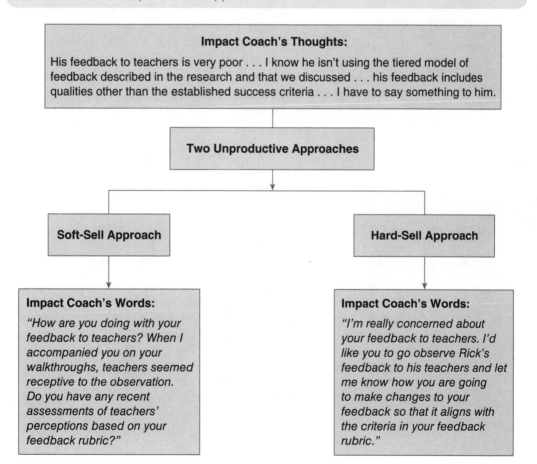

Impact Coach's Thoughts:

His feedback to teachers is very poor . . . I know he isn't using the tiered model of feedback described in the research and that we discussed . . . his feedback includes qualities other than the established success criteria . . . I have to say something to him.

Two Unproductive Approaches

Soft-Sell Approach

Hard-Sell Approach

Impact Coach's Words:

"How are you doing with your feedback to teachers? When I accompanied you on your walkthroughs, teachers seemed receptive to the observation. Do you have any recent assessments of teachers' perceptions based on your feedback rubric?"

Impact Coach's Words:

"I'm really concerned about your feedback to teachers. I'd like you to go observe Rick's feedback to his teachers and let me know how you are going to make changes to your feedback so that it aligns with the criteria in your feedback rubric."

In the hard-sell version, the impact coach assumes that her evaluation of the feedback the school leader is providing his teachers is correct and then instructs the school leader to make some changes. The relationship has been risked in the interest of addressing what the impact coach sees as the problem. In reality, however, while this hard-sell strategy is likely to result in the school leader's understanding the feedback, defensiveness and resentment may mean that the task issue is not advanced.

The dilemma between concern for the person and concern for the task is irresolvable in both of these examples because the impact coach leaves no opportunity for a shared or co-constructed evaluation of the leader's feedback. In the soft-sell strategy, the coach discourages debate by her unwillingness to disclose evaluation of the feedback. In the hard-sell strategy, the coach discourages dialogue by assuming the truth of her views. Neither strategy will produce the type of dialogue that is necessary to reach an equitable agreement about the quality of the feedback the school leader is providing teachers and about whether change is needed.

When impact coaches seek to impose their views rather than invite dialogue and co-construction, they face the dilemma of how to do so without creating negative emotional reactions. The key to resolving this dilemma is not, as we have seen, to hide one's own views in the hope that the school leader will express what the impact coach herself is reluctant to reveal. This strategy is just as "closed to learning" (Robinson, 2011, p. 38) as the more hard-sell strategy because the goal is still to achieve acceptance of one's views without being open to learning about the validity of those views. The fundamental issue here is to change the impact coach's thinking that leads her to assume rather than check the validity of her point of view. Resolving this dilemma requires the impact coach to use an open-to-learning rather than a closed-to-learning approach.

CONDUCTING OPEN-TO-LEARNING CONVERSATIONS

Acquiring and effectively using the skills of open-to-learning conversations can help impact coaches, as well as school leaders, become more attuned to their perceptions of situations. They can tell them how their perceptions influence their assessment of a situation and the way they approach difficult conversations about improvement. Most importantly, practicing open-to-learning conversations can help build a culture and environment of professional and relational trust foundational to partnership communication, and as a result, it can lead to the improvement of teaching and learning and to students' social and academic progress—our core business.

At the heart of this model of communication is the value of openness to learning from one another. Another way of saying this is, it is about maintaining openness to learning about the quality of the thinking and information that both partners within the coaching relationship can use when making judgments about what is happening, why it is happening, and what to do about it. Moreover, it is about impact coaches and school leaders developing trusting relationships while facing up to difficulties that are almost certainly to arise within the coaching process and helping the school leader to do the same. Some of the skills involved include the ability to describe problematic situations, listen to others' views, detect and challenge one's own and others' assumptions, invite consideration of alternative views, give and receive negative feedback, and deal constructively with conflict. These skills, however, are much easier to talk about than they are to put into practice. So let's take a look at the model that will help change the thinking that produces the types of dilemmas involved in discussion of many performance problems.

Open-to-Learning Conversations: The Model

The governing values and key strategies of an open-to-learning conversation are in direct alignment with the leadership partnership approach, which we described in detail in the previous chapter. The three governing values and their corresponding key strategies are depicted in Figure 5.2.

FIGURE 5.2 The Guiding Values and Key Strategies of an Open-to-Learning Conversation

GUIDING VALUE	KEY STRATEGIES
1. **Increasing the Validity of Information** Valid information includes thoughts, opinions, reasoning, inferences, and feelings	• Disclosing the reasoning that leads to your views • Providing examples and illustrations of your views • Treating own views as hypotheses rather than taken-for-granted truths • Seeking feedback and disconfirmation
2. **Increasing Respect** Involves treating others as well intentioned, as interested in learning, and as capable of contributing to your own thoughts, ideas, and perceptions	• Listening deeply to understand others' viewpoints, especially when others' views differ from your own • Expecting high standards and constantly checking how you are helping others to reach them • Sharing control of the dialogue and discussion, including the management of emotions
3. **Increasing Commitment** Involves fostering ownership of decisions through transparent and mutually shared processes	• Sharing the problem and the problem-solving process • Requiring accountability for collective decisions • Fostering public monitoring and review of decisions

The three guiding values in Figure 5.2 on the previous page are supported by a number of organization development experts, such as Warren Bennis, Edgar Schein, and Chris Argyris, in their writings on effective conversation and more recently by Robert Garmston and Bruce Wellman (1999), authors of *The Adaptive School: A Sourcebook for Developing Collaborative Groups*, who promote the notion that those "skilled in discussion employ many rigorous cognitive operations" (p. 57) such as

- Distinguishing between verifiable facts and value claims
- Determining the factual accuracy of a statement
- Identifying ambiguous claims and unstated assumptions
- Detecting bias

More importantly, these values are easy to talk about but considerably harder to put into practice in difficult conversations, which involve giving and receiving corrective feedback. Viviane Robinson (2011) calls conversations in which these values are actually put into practice "open-to-learning" conversations because each point of view is expressed openly rather than defensively, and such openness increases the chance of detecting and correcting faulty assumptions about the other person's thinking, about the problem or task, and about what to do.

The validity value is especially critical for impact coaches because of the potential impact on the quality of improvement effort for the school leader. Thus, impact coaches have an ethical obligation to make decisions "employing rigorous cognitive operations" (Garmston & Wellman, 1999, p. 57). Absent the value of respect, they will not be able to build the relational trust needed to give and get good feedback about their thinking and to build the collective responsibility and commitment required to improve instructional leadership practices. The interdependent values of valid information and respectful processes, which cause both impact coach and coachee to feel heard and have authentic opportunities to exercise influence, work together to cause leadership partners to feel more committed to decisions made within the coaching process.

Given this, let's return to the original task–person dilemma presented in Figure 5.1 and see how the values of an "open-to-learning conversation" can reduce the obvious conflict between the impact coach's desire to avoid negative emotion and to address the performance issue. The dilemma represented in Figure 5.1 is extreme because the impact coach thought about the school leader's performance in ways that were highly judgmental. ("His feedback to teachers is very poor.") The coach's own thinking put her in the bind of either having to be diplomatic (soft sell) or brutally forthright (hard sell), neither of which is a satisfactory outcome. Figure 5.3 presents a third, more desirable alternative in which the coach expresses her point of view in a way that invites the school leader to consider whether her concern is justified.

FIGURE 5.3 An Effective Approach for Communicating Performance Concerns

IMPACT COACH'S THOUGHTS . . .	IMPACT COACH'S WORDS . . .	ANALYSIS . . .
When I accompanied him on his classroom observations, I was surprised to see that his feedback to teachers was about instructional strategies that were not identified in his success criteria. I suspect that his feedback confused teachers and wasn't particularly helpful in guiding them to their next steps. I must talk to Mike about how to check the quality of feedback given to teachers . . .	*"When I accompanied you on your classroom observations, I got the impression that teachers were somewhat confused by your feedback. So I thought I should tell you that and work out with you just what teachers' current views of your feedback are . . .*	• The impact coach's concerns are revealed. • The grounds for the concerns are disclosed. • The impact coach indicates that his concern needs to be checked rather than simply assuming it to be a valid point of view. • The impact coach invites the school leader to influence how the checking is to be accomplished.

The alternative approach depicted in Figure 5.3 substantially reduces the dilemma because the coach's concern is communicated in a manner that neither prejudges the situation nor protects the school leader from the possibility that a change in practice might be needed. Consequently, if the impact coach continues to disclose his assumptions, check them against the leader's point of view, listen to the leader's thinking, and co-construct the assessment of the quality of feedback with the school leader and use the results to make modifications to the leader's practice, then the outcome should be a school leader who feels challenged yet respected. That is, the impact coach's thinking does not create an impossible choice between either tackling the leadership practice or damaging the relationship.

Stacey Honda, principal at Schurr High School in Montebello Unified School District, Montebello, California, described the impact of "open-to-learning conversations" on her personal leadership practice, as well as on her administrative team's practice, this way:

> [By] creating an atmosphere of mutual respect developed by [my coach], we (my administrative team) felt safe in sharing our ideas and thoughts even though we may not have agreed . . . I also believe that as a principal we are often viewed as having to have the "right" answer all the time, and working with a coach gave me "navigational" perspective . . . In other words, [my coach] made me see things that I didn't see before. (Stacey Honda, personal communication, December 9, 2016)

THE KEY COMPONENTS OF AN
OPEN-TO-LEARNING CONVERSATION

Open-to-learning conversations (OLC) are not guided by a structured set of rules because the shifts from less open to more open-to-learning are subtle, reflecting the changes in values, context, and ways of thinking as much as they are about changes in communication skills. Thus, hard-and-fast rules also do not work because good dialogue is like "collective verbal improvisation" (Schön, 1987, p. 30), with leadership partners continually improvising words in conversations and improvising solutions to problems on the spot. Nevertheless, it is possible to identify some of the recurring components of open-to-learning conversations. Figure 5.4 identifies some of the key components, along with an explanation, and shows how an impact coach might use them in conversations with school leaders about high-impact instructional leadership practices.

The examples in Figure 5.4 are our own compilation, but there are certainly other versions that are also worth exploring (Conzemius & O'Neill, 2002; Costa & Garmston, 2002; Garmston & Wellman, 1999; Scholtes, Joiner, & Streibel, 2001). In our experience of coaching school leaders at all levels, facilitating workshops for school leaders around effective coaching practices, or working with school leaders to scale up their instructional leadership practices, leaders can begin to identify and suspend their closed-to-learning communication patterns after a day or so of theoretical explanation, modeling, and coaching with feedback using their own on-the-job performance issues. We believe the skills involved in developing and honing your open-to-learning communication are worth the investment in order for coaches and coachees to address the tough issues related to improved instructional leadership performance. Moreover, we believe that open-to-learning moves beyond simply a series of strategies to be used in a coaching conversation. The values of valid information, respecting others, and commitment through ownership form the ethical and moral foundation for all leadership practice and for building a culture within schools of collaborative inquiry.

ENGAGING IN BEHAVIORS THAT MEDIATE THINKING

In addition to using open-to-learning communications, impact coaches, as well as school leaders, enhance their interaction with a number of other effective communication skills that support the enhanced partnership principles. Those skills include pausing, paraphrasing, probing for specificity, and inquiry. It's clear our world has a new tempo. People talk about "living on Internet time"—about "doing business at Web speed." This implies not only a much faster beat in the business of education but also a far more persistent rhythm. The new cadence calls for a constant sense of urgency. Sustained speed. The pressure to perform at a more intense pace just doesn't ebb and flow like it used to. So it might seem strange for us to say to you that the first tool that impact coaches and school leaders must use well is to

FIGURE 5.4 Key Components of an OLC About a Performance Concern

KEY COMPONENT	WHAT YOU MIGHT SAY	EXPLANATION
1. **Describe your concern as your point of view**	• *I need to tell you about a possible concern I have about . . .* • *I believe we may have different views . . .* • *I realize this may not be how you see it; however . . .* • *I'm really disappointed in the professional development because . . .* • *I am not certain I am right on this, but I was worried when I saw . . .*	State your concern without presuming that your point of view is "the reality" or is shared by the other person. You cannot be open to learning or expect others to be if you do not disclose your thinking. Avoid expressing your point of view via a series of manipulative questions that are designed to get the other person to say what you don't want to (e.g., "How did you think it went?" when you think it went badly but haven't said so).
2. **Describe the basis for your concern**	• *The reason for my concern is . . .* • *Yesterday, when we were conducting classroom observations, I heard . . .* • *If I am right, it's the third time our coaching session has been interrupted by . . .* • *I don't want teachers coming to me demanding that I address their student discipline concerns. I want to work with you to address their concerns . . .*	Disclose your views, along with the evidence, examples, or reasons on which they are based. This enables the other person to understand "where you are coming from" and to help you learn about the quality of your thinking. If you don't give the grounds on which you hold your views, then it is hard for you or others to check their validity. You then appear to be treating them as obvious and taken for granted—and this is a closed- rather than open-to-learning stance.
3. **Invite your coachee to share his or her point of view [Pause and look at the other person]**	• *What are your views on the matter?* • *You've been very quiet, what do you think?* • *In what ways do you see it differently?* • *I am certain there is another side to the story. What are your thoughts?* • *It's important to me to understand your point of view . . .* • *You are shaking your head; what have I missed?*	If you want to gain commitment to a problem-solving or change process, you need to learn your coachee's view of the current situation and of any proposed change. Respect for others implies openness to their views. Validity is increased if differences are treated as opportunities to learn about the relative merits of each view, rather than as opportunities for persuasion.
4. **Paraphrase his or her point of view, and check for understanding**	• *So, you are feeling . . .* • *You're noticing that . . .* • *In other words . . .* • *Hmm, you are suggesting that . . .*	In conversations where issues are complex and uncertain, the ability to paraphrase, summarize, and check for understanding keeps others emotionally connected and

(Continued)

FIGURE 5.4 (Continued)

KEY COMPONENT	WHAT YOU MIGHT SAY	EXPLANATION
4. **Paraphrase his or her point of view, and check for understanding (continued)**	• *You've recommended three approaches . . .*	provides some structure to the conversation. The proof of whether or not you have listened deeply to others is whether they confirm that your paraphrase or summary is an accurate reflection of their views and emotions.
5. **Detect and check important assumptions**	• *What leads you to believe that your teachers wouldn't do . . .?* • *What might be examples of that?* • *What might be other possibilities?* • *How might you know if your assumptions are wrong?* • *What evidence do you have about the effectiveness of this leadership practice?* • *What are some things you would expect to see or hear that would convince you your assumptions were wrong?*	A key value of open-to-learning conversations is valid information. This value is seen in efforts to detect and correct important assumptions that are being made in the conversation. The goal is to improve the quality of the information and reasoning being used by making important assumptions explicit and checking their accuracy by doing such things as saying "What leads you to your point of view?" or seeking counter examples and inviting others to critique your views, as well as express their own.
6. **Establish common ground**	• *We both agree that _____ is unacceptable as it is . . .* • *It sounds like we see the problem the same way.* • *We both want [summarize], but we have different ideas as to how to get there.* • *We see the cause of the disruption differently, but we both want to do something about it.*	When people disagree or are threatened, it is important to establish some common ground. The common ground might be based on an agreed process for resolving differences, a shared expressed dissatisfaction with the status quo, expressions of satisfaction with the conversation or relationship, or a shared purpose or goal. The common ground provides the motivation to keep the partners working together.
7. **Make a plan to get what you both want**	• *How would you like to learn more about _____?* • *Okay, you will talk with your colleagues and let me know next week how they explain the results.* • *What might be a goal on which you would like to work? What are some key strategies that would lead to goal attainment? What are some of the progress measures will you consider?*	It is not important who comes up with the plan as long as both partners have an opportunity to contribute and are committed to it.

slow down the cadence of communication—pausing the rhythm of dialogue in order to actively listen to, understand, and learn from the thoughts and ideas of those around you (Quaglia, 2016).

Pausing

The communication skill of pausing is grounded in the "wait time" research of Mary Budd Rowe (1972) and, more recently, the "think time" research conducted by Robert Stahl (1994). Wait time is the period of silence that follows the questions impact coaches ask and school leaders' completed responses. What Rowe discovered in her research was that teacher "wait time" rarely lasted more than 1.5 seconds in typical classrooms. More importantly, she discovered that when these periods of teacher silence lasted at least three seconds, many positive things happened to students' and teachers' behaviors and attitudes. For instance, when students are provided with three or more seconds of undisturbed "wait time" after a question is asked and before they are asked to respond to it, there are certain positive outcomes:

- The length and correctness of student responses increase.

- The number of "I don't know" and "no answer" responses decreases.

- The number of volunteered, appropriate answers by larger numbers of students greatly increases.

- The scores of students on academic achievement tests tend to increase.

Similarly, when teachers wait patiently in silence for three or more seconds after students have responded to a question before asking another question, positive changes in their own teacher behaviors also occur:

- Their questioning strategies tend to be more varied and flexible.

- They decrease the quantity and increase the quality and variety of their questions.

- They ask additional questions that require more complex information processing and higher-level thinking on the part of students.

Simply put, thinking takes time. Moreover, high-level thinking takes even more time. The point is that learning cannot be rushed. Thinking, like good coffee, requires percolation time. In other words, wait time provides both coach and school leader with time to percolate a question down through their brain cells and create an appropriate response. Furthermore, if impact coaches let the school leader's responses percolate before asking another question, they will end up with a better brew of thinking from the school leader.

You might be asking yourself "How does this research about teachers' practice apply to the interactions between an impact coach and her coachee?" The Commission on Behavioral and Social Sciences and Education (2000) found in its study of human learning that its research design framework assumed "that the learners are children, but the principles apply to adult learning as well" (p. 26). Thus, Rowe's (1972) "wait time" and Stahl's (1994) "think time" research findings dealing with adolescent learners can easily be generalized to adult learners—impact coaches and school leaders.

In her research, Rowe identified four "species of wait-time" (Rowe, 1972, p. 6)—structuring, soliciting, responding, and reacting:

- Structuring occurs after the teacher gives directions.

- Soliciting happens after someone asks a question.

- Responding takes place when an individual answers a solicitation or responds to a structuring suggestion or builds on the responses of others or reports on data.

- Reacting occurs when an individual evaluates statements made by others.

The first two types of wait time require both the impact coach and the school leader to monitor and control his own behavior. These are intentional pauses that provide the other partner with time to think. The person being asked the question controls the third type of wait time: responding. This is personal reflection time in which that person waits before answering. Often, a person will signal the need for this time by saying "Let me think about that for a minute." The last type of wait time, reacting, takes place throughout a dialogue between impact coach and school leader, who use shared pauses to allow ideas and questions to "percolate" and for personal reflection and/or note taking.

Pausing begins a conversational configuration in which paraphrasing, inquiry, and probing can be practiced. Impact coaches and school leaders greatly enhance the dialogue when they routinely practice this configuration: pausing, or extending to self and others the time to think; paraphrasing, or listening with the intent to support others' thinking; and inquiry and probing, or broadening the thinking of others or asking for details and precision in thinking.

Paraphrasing

Paraphrasing is perhaps one of the most valuable communication skills in an impact coach's conversational toolbox. By definition, paraphrasing simply is the restatement of a text, passage, conversation, or work giving the meaning in another form. This communication skill, when used by either the impact coach and/or the school leader requires two things: listening to understand and attempting to see the other person's point of view.

The architecture of a well-designed paraphrase includes three structural components. First, a good paraphrase reflects the speaker's content back to the speaker for further consideration. Next, it replicates the speaker's emotion about the content. Lastly, it constructs retainers that hold the speaker's thought processes (see Figure 5.5).

FIGURE 5.5 Architecture of a Well-Designed Paraphrase

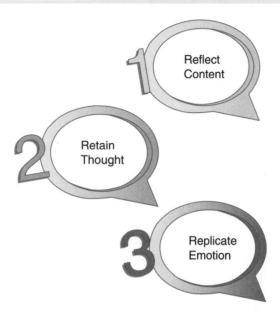

When both members of the impact coaching cycle consciously use well-designed paraphrases, they communicate a desire to listen, they establish rapport between themselves and the speaker, and they gain permission to probe or inquire for additional details, examples, and greater precision of thinking.

Here are several examples of sentence stems that can be used to begin a paraphrase (notice that the use of the personal pronouns "I" and "me," as in "I hear you saying . . . ," or "Let me see if this is what you mean . . . ," is avoided because the use of these first-person pronouns directs the attention from the speaker to the one paraphrasing. In addition, the use of personal pronouns communicates intent on the part of the listener to interpret, not reflect, the speaker's thoughts:

- You are concerned about . . .
- On the one hand, you think we should start now, but on the other hand . . .
- You value . . .
- So your short-term goal is . . .
- So far, you have identified three qualities . . .
- In other words, . . .
- You are noticing that . . .
- An assumption you are making is . . .
- You are feeling . . .
- So you believe that our objective is to . . .
- You are suggesting that we . . .

FIGURE 5.6   Three Types of Paraphrases

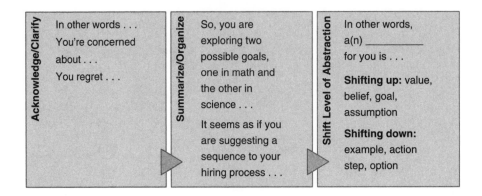

There are three basic types of paraphrases, which are described in Figure 5.6. Impact coaches and school leaders who become skillful in their use of the three types of paraphrases will increase the range of possible responses from others and, at the same time, will support understanding, relationships, and learning. The three types of paraphrases are acknowledge and clarify thinking, summarize and organize thinking, and shift another's level of abstraction.

Inquiry and probing by asking questions, as a communication skill, joins pausing and paraphrasing within the impact coach's and school leader's toolboxes to enable them to serve as activators of growth as a result of their coaching session and to aid in the successful completion of tasks as both members explore ideas, analyze cause-and-effect data, develop goals and strategies for improvement, monitor their collective efforts, and make adjustments to practice based on the results. Essentially, there are two types of questions impact coaches and school leaders may ask: those that open up the other person's thinking (inquiry) and those that focus another's thought processes (probing).

Another way of thinking about these two forms of questions is to liken them to the effects of a floodlight and a spotlight. For example, inquiry questions that open thinking, much like floodlights, shed light on a wide range of thinking, thereby inviting a diverse number of potential responses. Conversely, probing questions, similar to a spotlight that focuses a precise beam of light on a small area, serve to support precision in thinking by identifying and clarifying details.

Inquiry

Margaret Wheatley and Debbie Frieze (2010), in their article "Leadership in the Age of Complexity: From Hero to Host," said that we must abandon our reliance on the antiquated notion that some all-knowing leader-hero will sweep in and make all of our problems go away. Rather, these two authors believe we must replace our leader-as-a-hero notion with the idea of a leader as a host that reengages people in the problem-solving process. As a result, these leaders as hosts must consequently extend sincere invitations, ask good questions, and have courage to support risk taking and experimentation.

So how would impact coaches and/or school leaders operating as "leaders as hosts" ask good questions? What does a good question look like or sound like, if both members within the coaching partnership truly want to invite the other member into a conversation? What kind of question encourages open thinking and builds a culture of collaborative inquiry? Bruce Wellman and Laura Lipton (2004) contend that expert communicators invite thinking by paying attention to four invitational elements: sincere invitations, approachable voice, plural forms, and exploratory phrasing.

The process begins with *sincere invitations* and with the impact coach and school leader attending fully to one another, which signals that they are committing their undivided attention to the dialogue. Next, invitational questions are asked using an "approachable voice" . . . a voice that is "well-modulated and tends to rise at the end of the statement, paraphrase or question" (p. 18). Then, invitational questions should use plural forms (e.g., ideas instead of idea, choices instead of choice, thoughts instead of thought) so that those responding to the question need not be concerned about having to sort through or rank order ideas. Lastly, invitational questions ought to contain "exploratory phrasing" (p. 18)—words like might, some, possible, may, and promising, which serve to expand others' range of thinking, as depicted in Figure 5.7.

Probing

The second type of question, probing, introduces specificity to the conversation. These questions cause others to make their reasoning explicit, to explore more deeply their point of view, to clarify their assumptions, and to provide greater details in order to clear up vague thinking and language patterns.

One important way that coaching group members make a difference to one another is by supporting precision in thinking. Robert Garmston and

FIGURE 5.7 Sample Invitational Questions

- "In light of these results, what are some criteria you might use to help you determine which is most important?"
- "What are some of your hunches as to what might need to happen next?"
- "What might be some of the key instructional trends or patterns you observed during your *LinkingWalk*?"
- "If you take this course of action, what are some things you anticipate you will see or hear from staff that might influence your actions or outcomes?"

Bruce Wellman (2009), in their book *The Adaptive School: A Sourcebook for Developing Collaborative Groups*, identify five major categories of vague thinking and language patterns that are prominent within human speech— vague nouns and pronouns, vague verbs, comparator words and phrases, rule words, and universal qualifiers. These are briefly described in Figure 5.8.

As you read through the example phrases within each of the five categories of vague thinking and language in Figure 5.8, the speaker's intent is unclear and requires the person listening to these comments to follow up with a clarifying question. For example, within the vague nouns and pronouns category, the statement "Our students aren't capable of monitoring their own learning" is unclear and requires greater specification. You might, for instance, want to ask "So none of your students are able to monitor their own learning?" Or "Which students exactly do you think are unable to monitor their own learning?" Also, in the vague verb category, the comment "We will implement Marzano's nine classroom strategies that work" is equally ambiguous. In this

FIGURE 5.8 Vague Thinking and Language

CATEGORY OF VAGUE THINKING AND LANGUAGE	DESCRIPTION	EXAMPLE PHRASES
Vague nouns and pronouns	A part of one's speech that refers to people, places, or things as if each is clearly identified	"Our students aren't capable of . . ." or "The central office won't allow . . ." or "The union is uncooperative . . ." or "The parents are angry . . ." or "Our school administration is concerned . . ."
Vague verbs	A part of one's speech that refers to an action that is taking place as though it is plainly understood	"Implement . . ." or "understand . . ." or "improve . . ." or "be on time and prepared . . ." or "plan . . ."
Comparators	A part of one's speech that references an undefined qualitative or quantitative measure	"This meeting was better than the last one . . ." or "It's important that our students show growth in their achievement . . ."
Rule words	A part of one's speech that conveys to others the speaker's undefined beliefs as to how the world works and how people are to operate within it	"We have to . . ." or "We must . . ." or "We shouldn't . . ." or "I can't . . ."
Universal qualifiers	A part of one's speech that infers a universal truth understood by all	"All teachers in the school are upset with the new policy . . ." or "Everyone knows that this program is great . . ." or "Our students always do poorly on short, constructed response items . . ."

case, you might want to follow up with a question: "Implement how well?" Words are simply an externalization of the internal thinking process. Often, when words lack specificity, it is a reflection of a lack of clarity in thinking. The goal with these follow-up questions is for the impact coach to assist the school leader in moving toward greater clarity.

CHAPTER 5: KEY TAKEAWAYS

- Impact coaches and school leaders need to meet . . . talk . . . engage in very open give-and-take discourses.

- When faced with such challenges, impact coaches are often compromised by their need to advance improvement while also needing to maintain and protect the relationship within the coaching relationship.

- When impact coaches seek to impose their views rather than invite dialogue and co-construction, they face the dilemma of how to do so without creating negative emotional reactions.

- The "open-to-learning conversations" model of communication was selected for our impact coaching framework and works in helping impact coaches to prepare for and have difficult conversations with their coachees because, in its various forms, it has a sound theoretical and research base.

- Engaging in dialogue about the quality of performance between impact coach and coachee is, at times, difficult because it has the potential to threaten relationships by eliciting discomfort and unintended defensiveness.

- Acquiring and effectively using the skills of open-to-learning conversations can help impact coaches and school leaders become more attuned to their perceptions of situations.

- The governing values (valid information, respect, and commitment) and key strategies (disclose reasoning, provide examples, treat own views as hypotheses, seeking feedback, listen deeply, expect high standards and check how you are helping others reach them, share control of the conversation, share problems and problem solving, require accountability, and foster public monitoring and review) of an open-to-learning conversation are in direct alignment with the partnership approach.

- Open-to-learning conversations are not guided by a structured set of rules because the shifts from less open to learning to more open to learning are subtle, reflecting the changes in values, context, and ways of thinking as much as they are about changes in communication skills.

- In addition to using open-to-learning communications, impact coaches, as well as school leaders, enhance their practice by employing four effective communication tools that support the partnership principles: pausing, paraphrasing, probing for specificity, and inquiry.

GOING DEEPER

Further Reading: *On Dialogue and Discussion*

Jane Ellison and Carolee Hayes (2013), in their book *Effective School Leadership: Developing Principals Through Cognitive Coaching*, argue that at a time when principals are being asked to do more and more with less and less, the value of supporting principals with coaching builds their professional efficacy, consciousness, interdependence, flexibility, and craftsmanship. These five states of mind are nurtured through the effective use of cognitive coaching principles—concepts that are well aligned with the open-to-learning model of conversation.

Robert Garmston and Bruce Wellman (2009), in *The Adaptive School: A Sourcebook for Developing Collaborative Groups*, take the reader into a deeper understanding of two forms of conversation—dialogue and discussion—in Chapter 4 and in developing groups in Chapter 8. Both chapters underscore the key concepts presented in open-to-learning conversations.

Communicating effectively is a critical skill of impact coaches, as well as of school leaders. If you want to take your personal learning to a deeper level on the subject of communication, the topic of communication is described in the book *Better Conversations: Coach Yourself and Each Other to Be More Credible, Caring, and Connected* (Knight, 2016). Improving the way we communicate might be the most important "improvement initiative" anyone can bring to a school. The book contains a number of very helpful self-coaching strategies to improve your communication skills.

CHAPTER 6

ENGAGING SCHOOL LEADERS AND STARTING THE JOURNEY

> *Life is like an essay. Each day is a new draft—identify the strengths and build on them; identify the weaknesses and make them strengths. Then your life will get better and better.*
>
> —Arthur Costa (2009)

In this chapter, we'll explore the impact coaching partnership approach strategies we have successfully used with a variety of school leaders that helped them to increase support for their staff and build teacher leaders within their schools (the engage, identify, and teach components of instructional leadership coaching). We will explore in Chapter 7 the coaching components impact coaches can use to guide, teach, and support school leaders' deep implementation of research-based, high-impact practices (model, observe, explore, support, and reflect).

GETTING SCHOOL LEADERS AMENABLE TO COACHING

The way impact coaches interact with school leaders makes or breaks most coaching relationships. Even if impact coaches know a lot about content and pedagogy and have impressive professional pedigrees, experience, or postgraduate diplomas, school leaders will not embrace learning with an impact coach unless they're comfortable in that coaching relationship. Stacey Honda, principal at Schurr High School in Montebello Unified School District, Montebello, California, describes the importance of having a comfortable coaching relationship this way: "Effective coaches bring out the best in others, and that is through creating an environment of trust where it [is] is safe to explore unchartered ideas and thoughts" (Stacey Honda, personal communication, August 23, 2016).

Additionally, while emotional intelligence and communication skills contribute to a coach's impact, there is yet another factor that is crucial to successful coaching. How impact coaches think about coaching significantly enhances or interferes with their success as coaches. As we have suggested previously, we believe that impact coaches must engage in an *enhanced partnership approach* (Knight, 2007; J. Smith & R. Smith, 2015) to collaboration with school leaders. (This was discussed in detail in Chapter 4.)

The impact coaching partnership approach that we used with Rachel Hazel to promote her professional learning is dramatically different from the more traditional professional development sessions, which are grounded in the faulty assumption that change happens in single events (Fullan, 2009; Hall & Hord, 2011; Prochaska, Norcross, & DiClemente, 1994). What change scholars have concluded from their research is that deep implementation of change takes time, three to five years, practice in work settings, with feedback, coaching, and "is a process, not an event" (Hall & Hord, 2011, p. 8). Indeed, one of the main reasons why traditional, professional staff development has such a poor rate of success (Joyce & Showers, 2002) is that it is based on a flawed understanding of what happens when people and organizations are engaged in change. For that reason, before turning our attention to our discussion of the four specific components of impact coaching—enroll, engage, identify, and explain—we will review one well-researched change model that impact coaches, as well as school leaders, should consider utilizing during the impact coaching process.

MAKING CHANGE HAPPEN: HALL AND HORD

In our work with leaders across the country, we are often asked "What has changed about change leadership?" Our response to this question is, simply, "Nothing!" We know as much now about what happens when people and organizations are engaged in change as we did two decades ago. Thus, the problem educators face is not a "knowing" problem rather it is a "doing" problem (Pfeffer & Sutton, 2000). While knowing "what" to do is important, it is insufficient by itself. One must act on what she or he knows by translating the knowing into doing. One of the main reasons why the act of turning knowledge into action is so problematic is the tendency to liken talking about a needed change with actually doing something about it. In far too many organizations and with far too many individuals, there is an unspoken belief that once a decision is made to change a practice or procedure, no additional work is needed to make certain it is implemented with fidelity!

Gene Hall and Shirley Hord (2011) have spent much of their professional careers developing clarity about the change process in educational environments, identifying the key change facilitation strategies that school leaders and

FIGURE 6.1 Six Shared Functions for Facilitating Change

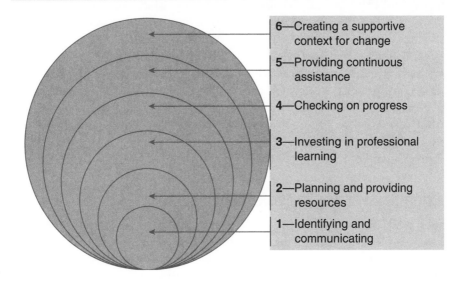

coaches must keep in mind and are most important to make change happen (see Figure 6.1).

Figure 6.1, much like a set of Russian matryoshka dolls, illustrates a design paradigm, known as the "matryoshka principle," or "nested-doll principle." In this instance, the figure depicts a relationship of six "support and assistance" functions (Functions 1–5) that are required for change to happen. These key functions reside within a supportive outer layer (Function 6) or the creation of a school and/or district context that undergirds the desired change. Moreover, you will notice that these six functions align nicely with the impact coaching cycle (see Figure 3.1) we presented earlier and each of its substeps. The six mutually interdependent functions for facilitating change are briefly described below.

Function 1: Identifying and Communicating a Shared Vision of Change

Impact coaches understand that the pathway toward any envisioned future of leadership practice and improved performance is paved with two important coaching and leadership strategies: creating a shared vision of the desired change and establishing clearly stated SMART+ER goals (Identify substep 4 in Chapter 3). Both of these coaching strategies serve the same end but address different purposes. For instance, the purpose of creating a shared vision is to clearly establish the *why* for impact coaches and school leaders. A shared vision gives both the impact coach and the school leader direction and purpose—a desired future. A shared vision inspires both individuals to move from an existing state to some desired state of leadership practice.

Function 2: Planning and Providing Resources

With the establishment of a vision and SMART+ER goal, planning for their realization and providing resources is both a logical and necessary next step. Some might argue that this is an obvious procedural step within any improvement process; however, as the researchers point out, many change efforts stall because over time, the necessary resources (i.e., time, money, schedules, equipment, materials, etc.) required to make the change happen are not procured. Moreover, one of the most important resources—and the one that is most often missing from the change journey—is time: time for practice, time for professional learning, and time for the impact coach and the school leader to do their work.

Function 3: Investing in Professional Learning

Change well done is learning—it's as simple and as complex as that! However, not all change is of the same magnitude. Some changes carry greater implications for school leaders and the organizations they lead. Therefore, changes of this nature are more difficult to implement proficiently than are other changes and require more time and support to deeply implement. For instance, a change in leadership practice, such as increasing the number of weekly classroom observations, is a change that is consistent with existing values and norms and one that can be implemented with existing knowledge and resources. Thus, a change of this degree is of a lower magnitude, or a "first-order" change (Marzano, Waters, & McNulty, 2005, p. 112). Conversely, a change that is not obvious as to how it will make things better for school leaders in their role; that requires school leaders to learn and implement new practices, such as providing teachers with effective feedback (Hattie & Timperley, 2007); or that conflicts with the prevailing values and norms of the organization is a more complex, or a "second-order," change (Marzano et al., 2005, p. 112), which requires perseverance and flexibility in thinking on the part of the school leader in order to implement it well.

Consequently, impact coaches (along with school leaders) who are contemplating a change in the school leader's leadership practice that involves a complex change—a "second-order" change—must weave professional learning with feedback into the change process. In other words, in order for school leaders to achieve improvement in their leadership practices, they must modify their unsuccessful practices, which requires learning.

Function 4: Checking on Progress

Because complex change, "second-order" change of the type we previously discussed, happens over time, the change process must be continuously monitored and reevaluated so that school leaders and their staff can learn from the results they are gathering and apply their learning to their practice (Improve substeps 1–4 in Chapter 3). Thus, frequent monitoring, measuring, and use of the data are critical to deep implementation (Hall & Hord, 2011). What this means for impact coaches and the school leaders is that they need to heed Michael Fullan's (2010) advice and "learn about implementation during the implementation" (p. 27). Frequently monitoring leadership practices, just like scheduling regular health check-ups, can help school leaders find problems before they start and identify problems early, when school leaders' chances for treatment (intervention) and assistance are better.

Function 5: Providing Continuous Assistance

The functions of providing assistance and checking on progress are interdependent. In other words, when needs or problems surface as a result of the implementation process, a response to those needs and problems is required to support those individuals directly involved with the implementation process. While there are a number of strategies impact coaches and school leaders should pursue (i.e., supplying implementers with more information, problem solving, providing follow-up professional learning, celebrating successes, etc.), Gene Hall and Shirley Hord (2011) are quick to emphasize the important impact that expert coaching can have on implementers, which, in large part, is why this book is being written.

Function 6: Creating a Context Supportive of Change

Jon Saphier and Matthew King (1985) have it right when they observe that "good seeds will not grow in weak cultures" (p. 67). What do they mean by this and what does this have to do with impact coaching? Metaphorically speaking, think about it this way: The seeds we plant that fall on stone and have no topsoil to accept the roots will not germinate. The seeds that fall in the weeds are choked out before they can reach the sun. However, the seeds that fall on fertile ground grow tall and strong. Likewise, the seeds of change (i.e., applying the findings from research on highly impactful leadership practices) that school leaders wish to sow into their leadership practice and school culture must also be planted in healthy soil. When we are talking about organizational change, healthy soil means a healthy school culture—a culture where people have some level of autonomy, where dialogue is open and respectful, where people make and learn from their errors, and where people work toward a clearly understood common purpose.

In this respect, impact coaches and school leaders understand that creating a context supportive of change means that they must address two critical cultural aspects: the physical aspect and the people aspect of the organization. The physical aspect of an organization's culture refers to its building facilities, master schedules, and policies; whereas the people aspect of the organization refers to such things as the beliefs, values, and norms that guide the actions of the members of the organization, the relational trust between these members, their attitudes, and so on.

KEY FUNCTIONS OF CHANGE AND PROFESSIONAL LEARNING IN SCHOOLS

Let's return to our recent coaching work with Rachel Hazel, as she provides an excellent illustration of how these key functions of change, as well as the leadership impact coaching cycle, work in a practical sense to support and assist her with the successful identification and implementation of a professional growth plan—a deliberate practice plan (DPP). Volusia County School District, as part of its school administrator evaluation process, requires each of its principals and assistant principals to "identify [one] to [four] specific and measurable priority learning goals related to teaching, learning, or school leadership practices that impact student learning growth" (Volusia County School District, 2012, p. 44). In brief, Rachel, through her actions, was required to demonstrate discernible progress on her priority goals, monitor progress toward them, use the monitoring data to make adjustments to her leadership practice, and provide measurable evidence of growth in personal mastery of the targeted priorities. In talking with Rachel about the DPP process and the impact of coaching on that process, she revealed that it was

a frightening topic to me. It is a daunting idea to think of changing a [leadership] practice and implementing it school-wide. In our coaching sessions, [my coach] always encouraged me to keep a laser-like focus. She emphasized concentrating on one specific thing and documenting progress, reflecting on that progress and the impact. That seemed too simplistic [a strategy] when, in fact, I had a school that needed a lot of change very quickly. It seemed like a tremendous amount of effort for one small change. I was very wrong. Despite my doubts, I selected a DPP goal that supported our school improvement plan of increasing the rigor of core instruction. I focused my data collection on learning targets and resulting teacher actions when I was conducting my walkthrough observations. I then presented my findings to the faculty. At each data collection point, I talked with my coach. Her support, her questions, and the [related] research she provided always gave me the information I needed to have honest and open discussions with teachers. Each time, the data indicated a positive trend. Each time, student achievement went up [see Figure 6.2]. Not only did student achievement go up, but also, discipline instances decreased, teacher satisfaction increased, and positive results were seen campus-wide. By [zeroing in] on one goal with a laser-like focus and having a coach to guide my thinking, I saw real change. (Rachel Hazel, personal communication, September 24, 2015)

THE COMPONENTS OF IMPACT COACHING

By applying the six functions of change with Rachel during both the construction and the implementation of her DPP (Figure 7.12 presents a sample

FIGURE 6.2 Percentage of Teachers Posting Learning Targets

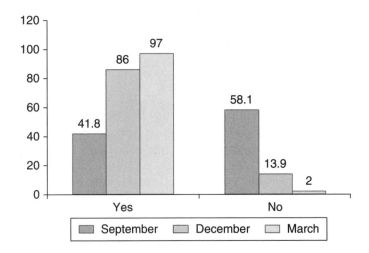

deliberate practice plan), we employed the impact coaching partnership approach strategies we have found to be so critical to coaching done well—the impact coaching cycle. Impact coaching for instructional leadership, as we have defined it previously, has very clear components that enable the impact coach and school leader to respond to the various challenges that present themselves during the change process. The first three components of this process (engage, identify, and teach) are described in the remainder of this chapter. The next five components of the instructional coaching process (model, observe, explore, support, and reflect) are discussed in Chapter 7.

Engagement Strategies for Starting the Leader on the Coaching Journey

What is it that motivates school leaders to want to engage in a coaching relationship? After all, school leaders are very busy people with more things to do than there is time, energy, and resources to do these things effectively. The reality is all school leaders face the same dilemma—more things to do than time permits. Smart principals, like Rachel Hazel, understand that they can't be expected to do everything. So she has to figure out where her time, effort, and influence will count the most. Rachel and her impact coach understand that producing the greatest leadership impact is a sacrificial act. To pull it off, Rachel must steal from other areas of her professional life. In other words, something has to give over here in order for Rachel to make an impact over there. We're talking about significant tradeoffs—serious compromises. What is required is a strong will and a steadfast rationing of personal resources, such as her time, energy, and influence.

Toward that end, principals are constantly engaged in what Everett Rogers (2003) describes in his book *Diffusion of Innovations* as "opportunistic surveillance" (p. 422). What does opportunistic surveillance mean? It means that most principals, as well as organizations, face many problems but possess knowledge of only a few innovations that offer solutions to these problems. So they tend to scan for innovations and then match a promising innovation with one of their school-wide problems of practice. Rachel practiced opportunistic surveillance when she shared with us these feelings:

> *The sheer number of ideas and the amount of research available is overwhelming. It is difficult to process, to know where to start, and, quite frankly, a little frightening.* (Rachel Hazel, personal communication, September 24, 2015)

So Rachel searched the available professional development support that might help her sharply focus on leadership practices that matter most and reached out to an individual she trusted to help her know where to start. Energy management, then, as Rachel and others have discovered, is what motivates principals to look for support and coaching.

Rachel's strategy of finding a coach is one of four that we routinely encounter. What are the processes an impact coach employs to engage leaders in the coaching journey? We are typically confronted with four scenarios: (a) one-to-one interviews, (b) small- or large-group presentations, (c) informal conversations, and (d) senior district leader referral. Each of these approaches will be described subsequently.

One-to-one interviews. You've certainly heard the real estate agents' mantra, "It's location, location, location!" So what does this real estate agent refrain mean? And what possesses real estate agents to repeat it three times? Simply put, it means identical homes can increase or decrease in value due to their locations. It's repeated three times for emphasis so you will remember the important real estate maxim. It's the number-one rule in real estate, and it's often the most overlooked rule.

Similarly, the number-one rule in impact coaching for instructional leadership is relationship, relationship, relationship! Like the real estate mantra, it means similar coaching pairings can either be successful or unsuccessful in their impact based on the strength of relationship between coaches and their coachees. School leaders will not embrace learning with a coach unless they're comfortable working with that coach. It's a matter of trust!

Why should you consider using interviews as a way to engage leaders in the coaching journey? One-to-one interviews help impact coaches achieve, at minimum, four goals. First, they are a way to gather specific information about the leader, school challenges, teacher and student needs, and cultural norms specific to the school. Next, impact coaches can use this information to personalize coaching sessions and other professional learning to the particular needs of the school leader. And interviews enable an impact coach to build the school leader's understanding of the philosophy, methods, and opportunities offered by impact coaching for instructional leadership. Lastly and most importantly, impact coaches establish a relationship between themselves and the school leader.

Small- or large-group presentations. There are times, however, that we have discovered that engaging in one-to-one interviews with busy school leaders is not practical or efficient. For instance, if an impact coach is aware that a group of school leaders are united together in a common enterprise (e.g., school improvement planning, implementing high-yield leadership practices such as effective feedback) that they want to collaborate on, the need to conduct interviews may not be as important. Therefore, an alternative to the former method of engaging leaders in the coaching process is small- or large-group meetings. The learning intentions of these small- or large-group meetings are fourfold: (a) review the instructional leadership professional learning options that exist for school leaders; (b) clarify the partnership perspective foundational to the coaching relationship; (c) explain the practicalities related to impact coaching for instructional leadership; and (d) determine which school leaders want to work with the impact coach and start the coaching journey. Most importantly, impact coaches boost the success of these coaching presentations when they employ impact coaching partnership theories of practice, which use the language of learning and build relational trust by ensuring that school leaders (a) are treated as equals in the process, (b) collaborate by offering choice in learning, (c) seek the voice of leaders in order to activate change, (d) make dialogue rather than monologue the norm, (e) implement assessment on existing practice that leads to action on future practice, (f) embrace the challenge of building relational trust, and (g) acknowledge that learning is hard work.

Informal conversations. Schools are highly social systems, which means that the spread of ideas occurs by people talking with one another (Rogers, 2003). Impact coaches capitalize on this important research finding by weaving together a human network of a few "opinion leaders" (Rogers, 2003, p. 27) that implement high-impact instructional leadership practices that makes a significant impact on learning and student achievement. Simply put, a key part of an impact coach's job is to engineer interconnectivity among and with school leaders. Hence informal conversation is, in many cases, an effective enrollment method.

Senior district leader referral. When an impact coach and senior leaders within a school district work together, there will inevitably be occasions when the senior leadership within the district identifies school leaders who they believe need to work with the impact coach. District leader referral can be a powerful way to accelerate the impact of coaching in a district, but it must be handled with care. If the partnership principles are ignored and struggling school leaders are told they must work with an impact coach (as a condition of employment), the coach can be seen as a reprimand, not a support, and school leaders may come to resent the impact coach's assistance. We recommend a different approach for senior district leader referral, one consistent with the partnership principles. Instead of telling a school leader she must work with an impact coach, we propose that senior district leaders concentrate on the instructional leadership practices that must change and offer the services of the impact coach as one way the school leader can navigate the needed change.

Regardless of whether impact coaches engage school leaders through one-to-one formal and informal conversations, small- or large-format presentations, or district leader referral, what remains is that they communicate their genuine respect for the practice of instructional leadership. Rachel Hazel mused that it was the

reciprocal relationship [with my coach that] has proven to be an invaluable resource to help me find my voice as my school's instructional leader. Having a voice and feeling valued is motivating. (Rachel Hazel, personal communication, September 24, 2015)

Identifying the Most Opportunistic Starting Point

Subsequent to an impact coach's efforts to engage school leaders (through one-to-one interviews, from small- or large-group presentations, via informal conversations, or through administrative referral) in the coaching process, the impact coach will have a list of potential collaborating school leaders with whom to work. The task of identifying with whom the impact coach will be working shifts to the task of clarifying which of the instructional leadership practices (these five big-winner leadership practices were explained thoroughly in Chapter 2) the impact coach has to offer that might be most helpful to the school leader. That is, which of the five research-based instructional leadership practices (Robinson, Lloyd, & Rowe, 2008) or their subcomponents, when implemented at the proficient or higher level, would make the greatest difference to learning for all within the school and produce significant advancements in both student progress and achievement?

Simply put, impact coaches gather data from each of their coachees as to their perceived strengths in the area of instructional leadership, which has shown to make the greatest contribution "to the achievement and well-being" (Robinson, 2011, p. 10) of students. Therefore, based upon the research of Viviane Robinson and her colleagues out of the University of Auckland and on our earlier book (J. Smith & R. Smith, 2015), *Evaluating Instructional Leadership: Recognized Practices for Success*, we devised an "Instructional Leadership Practices Self-Assessment," which is depicted in Figure 6.3.

FIGURE 6.3 Instructional Leadership Practices Self-Assessment

INSTRUCTIONAL LEADERSHIP PRACTICE—DIRECTIONS: Read each statement carefully, and then, check the response (SA–Strongly Agree or A–Agree or SoA–Somewhat Agree or SoD–Somewhat Disagree or D–Disagree or SD–Strongly Disagree) immediately to the right of the statement that is most appropriate for you and your leadership team.

Element 1: Establishing Shared Vision/Mission, Goals, and Expectations—*The leader herself or himself or through her or his designee . . .*	SA	A	SoA	SoD	D	SD
Engages in collaborative problem-solving strategies to reach agreement among teachers about the importance of the current learning and/or performance goals (e.g., by expressing his or her own values and commitments and listening to those of others)						
Eliminates stress that may result from multiple conflicting priorities and work overload by focusing on the two or three of the most important improvement needs						
Creates alignment between overarching school goals and the goals set by content area/grade-level leaders						
Generates ownership among teachers about the learning goals for which they are responsible by engaging teachers in a co-construction of the overarching school goals						
Builds personal commitment among teachers to achieve the goals for which they are responsible						
Ensures that teachers have the knowledge and skills that they need to achieve the goals for which they are responsible						
Sees to it that teachers have the resources needed to achieve the goals for which they are responsible						
Element 2: Strategic Resourcing—*The leader herself or himself or through her or his designee . . .*	SA	A	SoA	SoD	D	SD
Routinely evaluates the degree to which the existing allocation of time, staffing, and money are having the desired impact on the school's priority targets						
Ensures sustained funding for instructional priorities						
Ensures that staff recruitment is based on clear descriptions of teacher effectiveness found within the district's teacher evaluation framework and the students' areas of highest needs						

(Continued)

FIGURE 6.3 (Continued)

Element 2: Strategic Resourcing—*The leader herself or himself or through her or his designee . . .*	SA	A	SoA	SoD	D	SD
Sees to it that the staff recruitment and selection process is subject to an in-depth review and evaluation for continuous improvement purposes						
Knows how time is distributed within her or his school and uses this knowledge to make certain that instructional time is restructured to allocate high-quality instruction to students in the areas of highest need						
Routinely assesses the degree to which relational trust exists among staff in order to successfully navigate the human element of the strategic resources allocation process as she or he works to reorganize the people, time, and money in her or his school to match priorities						
Articulates the relationship between instructional programs being implemented and instructional resources being used and student achievement results being obtained						
Element 3: Ensuring Teacher and Staff Effectiveness—*The leader herself or himself or through her or his designee . . .*	SA	A	SoA	SoD	D	SD
Establishes, with teachers, clarity as to which high-priority Common Core or state standards are orchestrated horizontally within and vertically across all grade levels						
Determines, with teachers, that the teaching of high-priority Common Core or state standards is driven by the use of a common instructional framework						
Confirms, with teachers, a close relationship between the things teachers really value and the teacher-made assessments used						
Achieves a high level of agreement with teachers as to what constitutes effective teaching and learning						
Agrees to use student evaluations of teachers as an index of teaching quality, the results of which drive instructional improvement						
Systematically measures the percentage of teachers whose yearly effect size is ≥ 0.40 ES as a measure of teacher effectiveness						

Element 3: Ensuring Teacher and Staff Effectiveness—*The leader herself or himself or through her or his designee . . .*	SA	A	SoA	SoD	D	SD
Ascertains a high degree of understanding among the staff as to which instructional and leadership strategies and curricular programs are having the greatest impact versus the least impact on student achievement and use the results to inform next steps						
Establishes a high frequency (i.e., monthly) and quality (i.e., making critical sense of teaching and learning) of *LinkingTalks* that occur among teachers and leaders within the school						
Is in classrooms twenty to sixty times a week observing teachers (brief periods of time ten to fifteen minutes each), with subsequent feedback given to teachers						
Systematically and regularly monitors and uses student achievement data to determine program effectiveness						
Element 4: Leading and Participating in Teacher/Leader Learning and Development—*The leader herself or himself or through her or his designee . . .*	SA	A	SoA	SoD	D	SD
Ensures that effective professional learning, as described within the research, drives the design, selection, and implementation of teacher professional learning opportunities						
Routinely participates with teachers as the leader, learner, or both during professional learning opportunities						
Ensures that as a group and as subgroups, teachers examine together how well students are doing, relate this to how they are teaching, and then make the necessary adjustments in pedagogy						
Articulates clear connections between the planned professional development and students' learning needs						
Ensures that teachers' and leaders' deliberate practice plans (i.e., professional growth plans) are linked to student learning needs						
Articulates the system she or he uses to identify teachers with expertise needed to help colleagues address targeted teaching problems						
Routinely measures the degree to which student learning has been impacted as a result of changes in pedagogy coming from professional learning						

(Continued)

FIGURE 6.3 (Continued)

Element 5: Providing an Orderly, Safe, and Supportive Environment—*The leader herself or himself or through her or his designee . . .*	SA	A	SoA	SoD	D	SD
Creates multiple (two to three) opportunities for students to provide feedback about the quality of their classroom and school experience						
Regularly makes use of student surveys as to their sense of safety in a variety of in-school and out-of-school arenas, as well as their perceptions of bullying and intimidation						
Uses the results from student survey information to improve the quality of school life						
Provides multiple (two to three) illustrative examples of actions taken that have redefined procedures and responsibilities designed to continuously reduce the potential risk to students throughout the school						
Makes certain there are minimal interruptions to teaching time and buffers teaching faculty from distractions to their work						
Provides evidence that parent involvement efforts are focused on increasing parental engagement with the educational work of the school						
Systematically evaluates the effectiveness of parent involvement and use the results of the evaluation to improve those efforts						
Identifies and resolves conflict quickly and effectively rather than allowing it to worsen						
Co-establishes, with teachers and students, clear and consistently enforced social expectations and discipline codes						

The five elements of instructional leadership, along with their subelements, interact in an interdependent manner and therefore have "strong reciprocal effects" (Robinson, 2011, p. 10). To illustrate this point, when school leaders, along with their faculty, construct student-learning goals that are clear, school leaders find themselves in a better position to ascertain what teachers need to know and be able to do in order to teach their students and move toward goal attainment. Student-learning goals are more likely to be achieved as a result of providing teachers sustained and intensive professional learning, the type research suggests is related to student achievement gains (Darling-Hammond, Wei, Andree, Richardson, & Orphanos, 2009).

The big idea coming from the research (Robinson, Lloyd, & Rowe, 2008) on how leaders make an educational difference can be condensed as follows:

The more leaders focus their relationships, their work, and their learning on the core business of teaching and learning, the greater will be their influence on student outcomes. (Robinson, 2011, p. 15)

An important distinction to make in this survey is that while school leaders are asked to complete the survey as individuals, you will notice that each school leader is directed to consider each of the subelements of the survey from the perspective of her or his administrative leadership team. Why? Because Viviane Robinson and her colleagues were quick to point out that no one single school leader should or could demonstrate high levels of capability on all five elements. Rather, a more practical interpretation of their findings is that what matters most is the frequency of various instructional leadership practices and not the extent to which they are performed by a particular leadership role (Robinson et al., 2008). Regardless, we use this instrument as a way to begin to prioritize the coaching relationship according to those elements and subelements that will make the most opportunistic starting point: impact! So how might the impact coach use the information obtained from the school leaders' self-assessment?

Teaching the Instructional Leadership Practice to Be Implemented

Once the impact coach and the school leader have identified a high-impact instructional leadership practice to implement, the coach has to teach the leadership practice to the coachee. Alisa Fedigan, principal at DeBary Elementary School, DeBary, Florida, for example, selected a subelement under Element 3 from Figure 6.3: "Ascertains a high degree of understanding among the staff as to which instructional and leadership strategies and curricular programs are having the greatest impact versus the least impact on student achievement and use the results to inform next steps." Specifically, the leadership strategy identified within her deliberate practice plan was to determine "the percentage of staff that proficiently use success criteria and instructional feedback practice ... in their classrooms [monthly]" (Alisa Fedigan, personal communication, January 8, 2017). Translating research into practice is tricky. Jim Knight (2007), in *Instructional Coaching: A Partnership Approach to Improving Instruction*, suggests several tactics that, when used, will enhance a coach's ability to translate research into practice. The specific coaching tactics are as follows:

- Clarify: read, write, talk
- Synthesize, break it down, and see it through [leaders'] eyes
- Simplify

Clarify. Impact coaches need to be thoroughly familiar with and have deep knowledge of the instructional leadership interventions. This means impact coaches need to read, take notes on, and reread the books and research articles that describe the instructional leadership practices that they are sharing with school leaders. That said, impact coaches need to mark up their books and articles, highlight key passages, write in the margins, and tab the contents to make personal connections with the content. Impact coaches then must have a high degree of fluency with these materials such that they can speak about them extemporaneously without actually consulting the books or articles and the notes they have taken.

We have known for some time now that one simple way to cement the research on instructional leadership into our minds is to engage in an active rather than a passive review of the material. That is, if you can recreate the material you've digested then you truly understand it. How do impact coaches recreate the research? Try writing out your understanding of the materials you've read. This activity might take the form of writing blogs; tweeting about essential research concepts to those you are following, as well as to those following you; writing outlines of documents; creating semantic maps or webs; or paraphrasing what has been read into simple language. The critical point is to make the research a part of who you are as an impact coach by writing and talking about what you are reading.

Synthesize, break it down, and see it through leaders' eyes. Once impact coaches have clarified the meaning of research articles and books, they need to synthesize what they have learned and describe the essential features of the instructional leadership practices they have studied. For some, this is accomplished by writing one- to two-sentence statements that capture the critical attributes of the interventions they are sharing with school leaders. The goal here is for impact coaches to be able to identify and summarize what is most important about the instructional leadership practices they are sharing with school leaders.

One of the strongest strategies they could employ would be to work with school leaders to co-create short checklists (see specific examples of these in Chapter 3, Figure 3.9, and in Chapter 7, Figure 7.2) that summarize the critical instructional leadership practices and break them down into the essential components. Good checklists, as Atul Gawande (2009) suggests, "are precise. They are efficient, to the point, and easy to use" (p. 120). Checklists can be powerful implementation tools and can help school leaders remember how to facilitate complex processes. They can clarify for all the priorities and prompt impact coaches, school leaders, and teachers to function better as a team. That is, good checklists help to control for the variability (i.e., individual interpretation of what the leadership practice looks like when proficiently implemented) that inevitably creeps into the implementation practices of well-meaning practitioners. Most importantly, good checklists, just like good teacher-made success criteria, serve to help school leaders know what success looks like and advance their ability to know "Where are you going?" "How you are doing?" and "Where to next?"

Simplify. Impact coaches should use the "Goldilocks principle" when presenting what are oftentimes complex research-based ideas to school leaders. Ideas should not be too simplistic, nor should they be unnecessarily complex. Rather, they should be presented at just the right level. What does that mean? It means impact coaches should not confuse *simplistic* with *simplicity*. Simplistic, according to the MacMillan online dictionary, means treating something in a way that makes it seem much simpler than it really is. The word *simplicity*, however, refers to the quality or condition of being easy to understand or do. Bill Jensen (2000), in his book *Simplicity*, adds further clarification when he writes that simplicity is "the art of making the complex clear" (p. 2).

There are many things that impact coaches can do to make complex research findings clear to school leaders. For some, this is accomplished through storytelling in the form of anecdote, metaphor, simile, and analogy. If coachees perceive stories to be metaphorical in nature, this perception can help them to draw parallels between stories and their own lives, to reframe or see problems in a different light, and to be more receptive to suggested changes in leadership practice.

An example of a story we often talk about in presentations to school and district leaders is the poor use of time in which we as practicing principals engaged, not because we were intentionally trying to waste time but because we simply didn't understand what the research was saying constituted effective use of time and effective feedback. Consequently, we prided ourselves on visiting classrooms frequently (a good leadership practice). We conducted these classroom visits armed with checklists of information to be collected about instructional practices we deemed to be highly desirable (was the objective written on the board, were teachers moving about the classroom interacting with students while they were learning, did teaching practices require students to work in groups rather than individually, were students engaged, etc.). Once our classroom observations were completed, we would leave feedback for each teacher about the presence or absence of these highly desirable instructional qualities. Our feedback to teachers almost always took the form of suggestion or advice, which we have since come to learn is not effective feedback (see Figure 3.8 for a detailed description of the leadership practices associated with effective feedback). Most importantly, as hard as we worked to engage in these leadership practices, they were most likely not helpful to teachers. Thus, our good intentions were a waste of time.

CHAPTER 6: KEY TAKEAWAYS

- Impact coaches recognize that change is a process, not an event. They are better able to meet school leaders' needs when they consider the six functions of change facilitation described by Gene Hall and Shirley Hord (2011): (a) identifying and communicating a shared vision of the change; (b) planning and providing resources; (c) investing in professional learning; (d) checking on progress; (e) providing continuous assistance; and (e) creating a context supportive of change.

- There are several ways in which impact coaches can engage school leaders in the coaching journey. Usually, the greater the likelihood school leaders will be resistant, the smaller the number of school leaders the impact coach meets when introducing coaching. The most effective method is usually one-to-one interviews.

- The Big Five—establishing a shared vision, goals, and expectations; strategic resourcing; ensuring teacher and staff effectiveness; leading and participating in teacher/leader learning and development; and providing an orderly, safe, and supportive environment—can help school leaders and coaches make decisions about where to start with coaching.

- Translating research into practice involves identifying the essence of a body of work created by researchers in a clinical setting and then reconstructing it so that it can be appreciated and proficiently implemented by leaders in their schools.

- Impact coaches can enhance their teaching of high-impact research practices if they use five tactics: (a) clarify, (b) synthesize, (c) break it down, (d) see it through the eyes of leaders and teachers, and (e) simplify.

GOING DEEPER

Further Reading: *Educational Change and High-Impact Instructional Leadership Practices*

The impact coaching process is all about change—changing behaviors, attitudes, views about your role, knowledge, and understanding in order to increase personal and organizational impact. However, much of the actions of leaders around introducing, accomplishing or implementing, and assessing change have occurred in an uneven manner within school districts and within schoolhouses. During a time of abundant research findings and examples of improved instructional and leadership practices leading to a significant, positive influence on learning and achievement, there is a woeful absence of sound implementation practices. Consequently, far too many effective practices are being implemented using superficial, modest, or poor implementation practices. Gene Hall and Shirley Hord have been systematically charting what happens to people and organizations when they are involved in change. They have learned a great deal about the challenges, the problems, and what it takes to be successful. Therefore, we would urge those of you at the front lines who have to implement expected change or those of you who might be leaders of change to read *Implementing Change: Patterns, Principles, and Potholes* by Gene Hall and Shirley Hord (2011).

Also, should you want to know more about what high-impact instructional and leadership practices are, there is no better summary of the research relating to student achievement than John Hattie's (2009) book *Visible Learning: A Synthesis of Over 800 Meta-Analyses Relating to Achievement*. It offers readers brief snippets that contain the essential findings and conclusions from the research on over 138 influences related to improved student achievement.

CHAPTER 7

MODELING, OBSERVING, AND COLLABORATIVELY EXPLORING DATA

> *Coach and student, when they do their jobs well, function not only as practitioners but also as on-line researchers, each inquiring more or less consciously into his own and the other's changing understandings.*
>
> —Donald A. Schön (1987, p. 298)

The focus of the last chapter was on enrolling school leaders into the coaching process, identifying which high-impact instructional leadership practice the school leader will implement, and clearly explaining the selected practice to the school leaders. This chapter is about helping the school leader implement the new instructional leadership practices in a way that is consistent with what the research describes as best practice. Practically speaking, it is about the dialogue between impact coach and school leader and the various tools the coach can use to help shape the coachee's thinking while he is implementing the selected high-impact instructional leadership practice.

IMPACT COACHING PROCESS TOOLS

In the epigraph to this chapter, what does Donald Schön (1987) mean exactly by the notion, if the impact coach and the school leader are doing "their jobs well, [they] function not only as practitioners but also as on-line researchers, each inquiring more or less consciously into his own and the other's changing understandings" (p. 298)? What he means is that in order to be a good impact coach and a good coachee, both the impact coach and school leader must be committed to developing and nurturing a mutually beneficial relationship—clearly an example of the impact coach partnership approach. In other words, both partners must be actively engaged in their profession—one of coaching and the other of instructional leadership. And both partners must inquire not only into how the other's perceptions are changing but also, of equal importance, how their own perceptions are changing as a result of the partnership. You see, that is exactly the definition of a true partnership, an enterprise where both participants have a joint interest and agree to share the associated risks and rewards proportionately. So what are some of the process tools the impact coach will employ to engage both coach and school leader in mutually beneficial dialogue about the data? The remainder of this chapter will explore five impact coaching process tools that cause both coach and school leader to function as practitioners, online researchers, and inquirers into self and other's changing understandings. The five process tools are as follows:

- Modeling the high-impact practices
- Conducting *Linking Walks*
- Engaging in *Linking Talks*
- Designing and implementing deliberate practice plans
- Utilizing success criteria checklists

Modeling the High-Impact Practices

A number of years ago, we took up the sport of fly-fishing. Our coaches are fly-fishing mavens and good friends of ours, Rick and Mary Jane, who own a home on the Madison River just south of Bozeman, Montana—a spectacular setting made famous by the movie *A River Runs Through It*, directed by Robert Redford and starring Brad Pitt, among others. We mention this because the movie trailers often depict Brad Pitt, who is playing the part of Paul MacLean, standing on a rock in the middle of a river, in the Arctic half-light of the Madison Canyon assuming a somewhat angelic nature casting hard upstream and then pivoting gracefully downstream, the fishing line arching several times in an elegant motion called "shadow casting" so that you have some understanding of the complexity but also the artistry of the skill one needs to master to be a good fly-fisherman.

Our fly-fishing training began with Rick and Mary Jane showing us how to hold the rod, the position of the wrist and the metronome motion of the arm; explaining that when you cast a rod, you actually make two casts, a back cast and a forward cast; and telling us that to cast successfully, you need to think and act on the forward and back casts as separate and distinct actions. The back cast is just what it sounds like; it is when the rod tip is moved rearwards, taking the line with it. The forward cast is the opposite. First, Rick and Mary Jane would model for us the cast at the same time that they engaged in self-talk (a highly effective metacognitive strategy).

That is, they talked us through the cast as they were demonstrating the cast. Then they would ask us to do it. When we messed up or when we did it right, they promptly gave us feedback. Time and again, the same pattern repeated itself. Rick and Mary Jane showed us what to do; then they watched us until we got it right. This was the way we learned how to fly-fish—watching our friends, practicing, getting their feedback, and applying that insight to our own practice.

The way we learned to fly-fish from our friends is the way we've learned many—perhaps most—of the skills and behaviors picked up in our life-time: how to ride a bike, drive a car, use eating utensils, change a flat tire, iron a shirt, or use Excel. We seem to learn best when someone shows us how to do it, watches us, and then gives us feedback about our actions. Donald Schön (1987) refers to this process as "imitative reconstruction" (p. 109), a problem-solving process in which the imitator constructs and tests the essential features of the action she has observed—a problem-solving process in which we all have engaged in our lives. Think about it, as children, we learned to play by imitating other children. As adults, we learned to function in an adult world by imitating the adults around us. We learn new physical skills, games, ways of working and interacting with others, practices of everyday life, in part, by imitating others who are already good at these things.

Thus, modeling, observation, and feedback are important—oftentimes essential—strategies for learning. After all, we wouldn't teach someone to swim by giving them a lecture, showing them a video clip of Michael Phelps, giving them a book to read, and then tossing them into the water. And while some leaders swim the great majority of others sink. While we would never consider teaching someone to swim in this manner, when we provide traditional professional development for school leaders, this is pretty much what we do. You will recall in Chapter 1 our assessment of traditional professional development for school leaders as being of dubious quality because it was long on seat time and perhaps inspirational at the time, but it was short on transfer of training. In other words, a great deal of professional development takes place with little to no follow-up, and school leaders often have few, if any, opportunities to see the new instructional leadership practices performed in their schools with their teachers.

Consequently, the impact coaching partnership approach to scaling instructional leadership demands that it be a reflective practice where "the coach's showing and telling are interwoven, as are the [school leaders'] listening and imitating" (Schön, 1987, p. 111). As a result of weaving together these aspects of the coaching partnership, school leaders learn what they could not learn simply through the impact coach's telling or demonstration alone. In brief, the two processes complement one another. The next two subsections address these interdependent aspects of modeling: telling/listening and demonstrating/imitating.

Model: Telling/Listening. Impact coaches spend a fair amount of time in schools with school leaders modeling leadership practices, watching school leaders, and having reflective conversations about what the school leader saw when he watched the impact coach or what the impact coach saw when she watched the school leader. Since many school leaders find the business of observation somewhat intimidating, impact coaches try to keep the experience as informal as possible: "You watch me and reflect or respond; I watch you and reflect or respond."

This "chain of reciprocal actions and reflections" that Donald Schön (1987, p. 114) presents so eloquently in his book *Educating the Reflective Practitioner* begins with a dialogue between coach and coachee to clarify what exactly will be modeled for the coachee. Schön suggests that when coach and coachee coordinate telling and listening, demonstrating and imitating, "each component process fills gaps of meaning inherent in the other" (p. 118) for both thought partners. In other words, the impact coach's descriptions of the research and demonstrations and the school leader's efforts to make meaning and ultimately imitate the practice being modeled provide the necessary information for "reciprocal reflection-in-action" (p. 118). Schön refers to this mutual contemplation as a "ladder of reflection" (Schön, 1987, p. 115), which is made up of four rungs:

1) Designing (identifying the research to be implemented)

2) Description of designing (describing the expected leader actions)

3) Reflection on description of designing (reflection on the meaning the other has constructed for a given description)

4) Reflection on reflection on description of designing (reflecting on the dialogue itself)

In Figure 7.1, we illustrate how a reflective mode of thinking may be introduced into the dialogue between the impact coach and the school leader. The illustration is based on the construction of a ladder of reflection. The idea here is to illustrate how the fact that the impact coach and the school leader define together the high-impact instructional leadership practice to be implemented makes it possible to introduce a reflective mode of thinking.

As can be observed, the school leader improves her understanding of the relationships between the concepts success criteria, feedback, and use of the feedback throughout the dialogue depicted in Figure 7.1. As a result, the school leader feels listened to, supported, and confident as to what her next steps would look like. Conversely, the impact coach's personal reflections acknowledge his attentiveness to the school leader's needs, at the same time stretching the school leader's thinking about the practice of feedback.

Model: Demonstrating/Imitating. In modeling, the first two aspects (telling and listening), give way to the complementary qualities of demonstrating

FIGURE 7.1 A Ladder of Reflection: A Dialogue Between Impact Coach and School Leader

LADDER RUNGS	IMPACT COACH AND SCHOOL LEADER DIALOGUE
Designing [Identifying the research to be implemented]	**School Leader:** I spend a great deal of time conducting classroom walkthroughs and providing teachers feedback, but I am not certain teachers even use the feedback I've given them or find it valuable.
	Impact Coach: You take pride in the time you devote to classroom observations and the feedback you give teachers. You are wondering what you could do to ensure teachers see your feedback as useful and are using the feedback you provide to improve their practice.
	School Leader: Yes, exactly! But how do I do that?
	Impact Coach: The research on feedback indicates that the information you provide teachers must be just in time, just for them, just for where they are in the learning process, and just what they need to move forward. This means that your feedback to them should be around a set of success criteria you have established with them. In some cases I've seen principals use a Feedback Cue Card *[The coach sketches an example of a Feedback Cue Card on a piece of paper for the coachee. See Appendix.]* with teachers to ensure that teachers understand and use the feedback they've been given.
Description of designing [Describing the expected leader actions]	**School Leader:** When you say "success criteria," what is that exactly? And how would that be used with the Feedback Cue Card?
	Impact Coach: For example, I have noticed that there is a school-wide expectation for teachers to improve the quality of questions during their instruction. How do you know if they are implementing the research on teacher questioning in a proficient manner?
	School Leader: Well, I provided our teachers a full day of professional development on *teacher questioning* last month. They all got the same training, so I am assuming that all teachers are implementing the instructional practice based on what they learned.
	Impact Coach: That may be so. However, without clear performance expectations, each teacher will make idiosyncratic decisions about what successful implementation of questioning practices looks like. Establishing success criteria with your teachers for *questioning* ensures more uniform implementation, as they would spell out what the

(Continued)

FIGURE 7.1 (Continued)

Description of designing [Describing the expected leader actions] (continued)	proficient practice (success criteria) looks like. These success criteria are then listed on the Feedback Cue Card, and you provide teachers feedback on the presence or absence of those success criteria. When teachers receive your feedback on the Cue Cards, they identify the specific ways they responded to your feedback, along with how they will use your feedback to improve. Once they complete their responses, they return the Cue Cards to you. This way, you know if they have understood your feedback and how they are using it to improve their practice. The next time you are in their classrooms, you look for they changes they've made.
Reflection on description of designing [Reflection on the meaning the other has constructed for a description she or he has given]	**School Leader:** So you are suggesting that the feedback I provide teachers as a result of classroom walkthroughs be focused on their individual implementation of *teacher questioning*. Interesting. I hadn't thought about identifying the proficient practices that teachers would be engaged in to effectively use teacher questions during instruction, but it makes sense. I also like the idea of knowing whether they have understood my feedback and the adjustments they will make to their instruction, which will inform my next steps.
Reflection on reflection on description of designing [Reflecting on the dialogue itself]	**Impact Coach:** It sounds like the idea of providing "focused" feedback around clearly identified criteria for teacher questioning, which you have developed with and for teachers, resonates with you and supports your earlier concern. **School Leader:** Absolutely. I think that is a good place to start. Hearing myself talk about my feedback to teachers and a strategy to ensure they have understood and are using the feedback has solidified what was in my gut and swirling in my head. I think I know more about some things that I need to pay more attention to, and I know I need to reflect more on what feedback might look like in this school.

and imitating. Before conducting a demonstration, an impact coach must ensure that the school leader is prepared to get the most out of the demonstration—that he has an established set of success criteria, the critical teaching behaviors that will form the basis for the school leader's feedback. We strongly suggest to our coachees that they co-construct these with their teachers rather than develop them individually and then walk them out to teachers. More importantly, the collaborative process of co-constructing the success criteria builds trust within the faculty and, at the same time, creates ownership for the improvement effort. We also urge school leaders to not start the process of co-constructing the success criteria with a blank piece of paper. Rather, they should draw from the excellent work that is normally all around us if we just look for it (for example, see the excellent work out of the Ontario Ministry of Education at http://www.edugains.ca/newsite/aer/aervideo/learninggoals.html).

To continue building on the fictional example presented in Figure 7.1 and teacher questioning, we draw on the very solid thinking in the area of teacher questioning by our friends and colleagues from the Ontario Ministry of Education (2010) titled *Questioning: Assessment for Learning Video Series, Viewing Guide*, which we have adapted to fit our impact coaching for instructional leadership framework (see Figure 7.2).

Assuming that these were the success criteria (Figure 7.2) that the school leader and his staff had co-created, the impact coach and school leader schedule a time to engage in a round of classroom observations where the impact coach observes teachers and provides written feedback while the school leader also takes notes about the observed teacher practices. The observations are followed up with a reflective process during which the impact coach shares her written feedback to teachers, explaining the reasoning behind the feedback to each teacher observed, while the school leader listens, gives operative attention to his comments, and asks clarifying questions of the impact coach. The impact coach's and/or school leader's reflection on his own or the other's practice can yield a description that highlights subtle differences, distinguishes the connections between research and application, and serves to inform the understanding that leads to surface and ultimately deeper understanding. A sample of the reflection-on-practice dialogue between impact coach and school leader is depicted in Figure 7.3.

We have discovered that once an impact coach and school leader go through several rounds of "you watch me" classroom observations, where the impact coach observes teachers and provides written feedback while the coachee takes notes about the observed teacher practices, followed by reflection-on-practice dialogue to get the coachee to a place where she is confident, it is time to flip the roles. That is, the "I watch you" phase of the modeling begins with the school leader conducting classroom observations of teachers and providing the written feedback while the coach takes notes; after practicing these swapped "you watch me" observations, the impact coach and school leader again come together to reflect on the feedback being provided.

As the school leader repeats this process with the impact coach—both the component actions and the reflections on practice—he may, at some point, discover that he has internalized the performance. What began as an imitative reconstruction of the impact coach's demonstrated practice is now something of his own, a new leadership practice to be added to his repertoire of instructional leadership ability.

Conducting *LinkingWalks*

Authors have long enjoyed their ability to coin new words and phrases or spin a new combination of existing words and sayings when describing the topic of their writing. It is considered one of the rewards of the profession. For example, Michael Fullan (2010), in his book *Motion Leadership: The SKINNY on Becoming Change Savvy*, coined the term "simplexity" (p. 16)

FIGURE 7.2 Teacher Questioning Practices Success Criteria Observation Form

| Task: _____ | Grade-Level Dept:_____ |
| Name: _____ | Date: _____ |

TEACHER QUESTIONING SUCCESS CRITERIA: THIS TEACHER . . .	OBSERVED	COMMENTS
Posed and posted for viewing key questions to focus students' thinking at the beginning of a lesson or series of lessons		
Used questions during the lesson to monitor whether students are grasping concepts and to see what they are thinking while the teacher is teaching		
Asked questions to help students think about their thinking (metacognition)		
Posed a question at the end of a lesson to determine if students have achieved the learning goal(s)		
Waited at least three seconds between posing a question and eliciting a response		
Waited at least three seconds after a student's answer before responding		
Used a variety of strategies (i.e., think-pair-share, allowing time for individual reflection and collaboration, no-hands strategy) to engage all students in thinking about a question		
Used closed questions to review, check for understanding, and recall facts		
Used "mediative" questions (i.e., open ended, positive presuppositions about the student, judgment free; using tentative and explorative language; inviting thinking toward knowledge, comprehension, analysis, synthesis, application, evaluation, etc.) to help students become more self-directive		
Used strategies to expose students' thinking (e.g., probing, clarifying, redirecting, synthesizing, summarizing)		
Distributed questions among all students, both those who volunteer and those who don't		
Fostered an emotionally safe learning environment where students felt comfortable saying "I don't know"		

FIGURE 7.3   Reflection-on-Practice Dialogue

LADDER RUNGS	IMPACT COACH AND SCHOOL LEADER DIALOGUE
Designing [Identifying the research to be implemented]	**Impact Coach:** I determined that the most appropriate level of feedback to provide this teacher was at the "self-regulation" level. **School Leader:** How did you come to that determination? And why is that important to providing her with feedback?
Description of designing [Describing the expected leader actions]	**Impact Coach:** It was clear to me from the observation that she fluently used many of the success criteria. The power of feedback involves invoking the right level of feedback relative to whether the teacher is a novice with questioning, somewhat proficient, or possesses a high degree of competency. Therefore, my feedback to her was *"How might you use mediative questions with your students to help them identify and draw on their internal resources to achieve the goals you've set for them?"* How does this feedback compare with the feedback you would have provided this teacher?
Reflection on description of designing [Reflection on the meaning the other has constructed for a description she or he has given]	**School Leader:** Well, I thought her use of questioning was good generally, but I thought she could have done more to engage all students in thinking. So my feedback to her was *"You need to use some strategies such as think-pair-share and talking with table partners to get more kids thinking about your posted question."* **Impact Coach:** So you thought she was fairly adept at using questioning but chose to give her task feedback, which is generally a strategy you would use with novice learners, not with those with some or a high degree of proficiency.
Reflection on reflection on description of designing [Reflecting on the dialogue itself]	**School Leader:** Hmmm, your comment makes me think that I need to do a better job of aligning my assessment of a teacher's proficiency at using questioning with the level of feedback I provide her or him if I want her or him to perceive my feedback as being helpful. **Impact Coach:** How has our time together supported your thinking about feedback and your next steps? **School Leader:** It's made me realize that bringing into play the right level of feedback is key to filling in the gap in learning and helping teachers take the next step toward being assessment-capable learners.

to describe the importance for school leaders to identify the fewest number of "high-leverage, easy-to-understand actions that unleash stunningly powerful consequences" (p. 16).

Next, Viviane Robinson (2011), in her writing about instructional leadership and the relationship between teaching and student learning, used the term "linking talk" (p. 110). In this sense, "linking talk" is used to describe the connection between what has been taught and what students have learned (more on this tool later within this chapter). That is, effective teachers *link* their explanations of their own teaching to their impact on students' learning. We believe that skilled leaders must also be able to *link* their accounts of their leadership and of the collective efforts of teachers (instructional strategies planned and implemented, etc.) to their actual or possible impact on student achievement.

Therefore, in our development of this coaching tool, we have coined the term *LinkingWalks* (LW) to describe our version of a classroom walkthrough protocol. Brief but frequent classroom walkthroughs have become an increasingly popular leadership strategy in recent years for informally observing instructional practices. For example, Robert Marzano (2011), talking about the "instructional rounds" (City, Elmore, Fiarman, & Teitel, 2009) protocol, suggests that it is "one of the most valuable tools that a school or district can use to enhance teachers' pedagogical skills and develop a culture of collaboration" (Marzano, 2011, p. 80).

The *LinkingWalk* process itself is a reflection of several nationally known classroom walkthrough models—*Instructional Rounds* (City, Elmore, Fiarman, & Teitel, 2009), *An Observational Protocol Based on the Art and Science of Teaching* (Marzano, 2010), *Data-in-a-Day (DIAD)* (Ginsberg & Kimball, 2008), and the *McREL Power Walkthrough* (McREL International, 2013). As such, many of the same features contained within the aforementioned walkthrough protocols are also features of our *LinkingWalk* process. Figure 7.4 describes the common walkthrough features contained within both the protocols referenced and the *LinkingWalk* process.

Inasmuch as there are common features between these classroom walkthrough protocols and our *LinkingWalk* process, there are also a number of features that are unique to our process and provide the rationale for why we advocate that schools use this process ahead of others. The features that are distinctive to the *LinkingWalk* process are identified in Figure 7.5.

The purpose of LinkingWalks. *LinkingWalks (LW)* are focused classroom observations conducted by small teams (one to twenty, depending on the size of the school) of school administrators, groups of teachers and/or school/district coaches, instructional leadership coaches, and district leaders. The purpose of the *LW* process is to provide an opportunity to do the following:

- *Collect system-wide data* around high-impact instructional leadership practices aligned with district and school improvement plan and school leader improvement plan priorities.

FIGURE 7.4 Common Features of Walkthrough Protocols Contained Within *LinkingWalks*

CLASSROOM WALKTHROUGHS INCLUDE . . .

- Small teams of educators (one to twenty) engaged in brief (five- to fifteen-minute), informal classroom observations of patterns of teaching and learning instruction across classrooms in order to improve them
- The intent to create a school-wide picture made up of many small snapshots of instruction and learning
- A specific protocol followed, with time spent before each walkthrough to identify and discuss the focus of the observations, followed by a "debriefing" discussion among team members to identify elements that should be shared with teachers
- Discussions based on evidence collected and free of judgment and evaluation
- Tight ties to and an integral component of the comprehensive district and school improvement plan

FIGURE 7.5 Unique Features of the *LinkingWalk* Process

UNIQUE FEATURES OF THE *LINKINGWALK* PROCESS INCLUDE . . .

- A laser-sharp focus on high-impact instructional leadership practices (i.e., those with an effect size ≥ 0.40) in order to take these practices to scale within the school
- The routine and systematic comparison of improvements in high-impact instructional leadership practice with improvements in student progress and achievement developed into "public displays of effection"
- Alignment with school leaders' and teachers' professional growth plans

- *Identify trends and patterns* in classroom environmental issues and/or instructional practice and the impact these practices are having (or not) on student learning.

- *Perpetuate ongoing collegial dialogue* about quality teaching and learning.

- *Learn from other team members* through their observations, inquiry, and perspectives.

- *Deepen collective understanding* about high-impact instructional leadership practices that, when implemented well, can have a significant impact on student progress and achievement.

- *Scale instructional expertise* by dependably identifying and giving recognition to the expertise among teachers, thereby developing collective agency among teachers and leaders whose members acknowledge the variable expertise among their colleagues and work with all in the school to raise the overall level of expertise and teacher and leader effectiveness (Hattie, 2015b).

Prior to conducting the LinkingWalk. Before conducting the *LW* process, the school leader and the impact coach, serving as the *LW* facilitator, assemble members of the *LW* team (i.e., teachers, school administrators, etc.) to review meeting mechanics and team process norms. (*Note:* It is entirely possible for the *LW* process to be conducted with just two individuals—that is, the coach and the school leader being coached—in which case adjustments will need to be made to the descriptions that follow.) Next, the school leader (together with her faculty) identifies the focus question(s) related to the specific high-impact instructional leadership practice to be observed during the *LW*; the school leader explains how this area of focus is connected to the school improvement plan and the practices described in their school's teacher evaluation framework, the classrooms that will be visited, and why those particular classrooms have been chosen for observation. A sample list of high-impact instructional leadership practices, with brief descriptions of those practices and the effect sizes of the practices, is presented in Figure 7.6.

Then the designated leader leads the discussion, during which time team members come to understand the indicators (evidence) that would support the instructional focus (i.e., use of learning intentions and success criteria, teacher questioning, cooperative group work, etc.), agree on data-gathering tools, and develop agreed-upon use of evidence-gathering tools. Lastly, the leader distributes appropriate *LW* templates to each member. Note that we have developed a number of data-gathering tools based on Robert Marzano's (2013) and Charlotte Danielson's (2013) frameworks, as these two teacher evaluation models seem to be the most widely used. Additionally, we have developed evidence-gathering templates with our coachees, some of which are presented in Figures 7.7 and 7.8.

Conducting the LinkingWalk. Each classroom observation takes approximately fifteen to twenty minutes. All team members enter the classroom at the same time. During the observation, *LW* team members do not speak to each other. Team members should unobtrusively locate themselves within the classroom as they orient themselves to the learning space. Once oriented, team members will want to move about the classroom to see the work of a range of students. When appropriate, team members should talk with individual students and/or small groups of students (see examples of questions in Figure 7.7), as student responses to questions posed by team members provide valuable data to share during the full debriefing session. At the end of the agreed-upon time, all team members leave the classroom together and reconvene in the meeting place to debrief for a short time. We have found the following "Tips for Conducting the *LinkingWalk*" to be very helpful:

- Acquaint yourself with the classroom (e.g., grade level and/or subject matter, composition of students).
- Look for posted learning intentions and/or success criteria—what students are being asked to know and to do (the tasks or success criteria).
- Determine what students are actually doing relative to the assigned task.

FIGURE 7.6 Sample of High-Impact Instructional Leadership Practices

HIGH-IMPACT INSTRUCTIONAL LEADERSHIP PRACTICE	DESCRIPTION	EFFECT SIZE
Collective teacher efficacy (expertise)	When we believe that by working together, we can make a difference, it has a positive impact on student learning and outcomes. Effective collaboration happens when structures and relationships enable information and ideas to flow in all directions.	1.57
Assessment-capable, visible learners	Refers to students who can be their own teacher; they can articulate what they are learning and why, describe how they are learning (the strategies they are using to learn), know their next learning steps, use self-regulation strategies, understand the assessment tools being used and what their results mean. These students can also self-assess; they seek, are resilient, and aspire to challenge; they can set mastery goals, ask questions, and see errors as opportunities. Such students are comfortable saying they don't know and/or need help, positively support their peers' learning, know what to do when they don't know what to do, actively seek and use feedback, and have metacognitive skills and can talk about these skills.	1.44
Teacher credibility (in the eyes of the students)	Teacher credibility is vital because students are highly perceptive about knowing which teachers can make a difference to their learning. Instilling confidence through credible teaching will give the students the reassurance and confidence to invest in the lesson's content.	0.90
Providing formative evaluation to teachers	Refers to teachers attending to what is happening for each student in their classrooms as a result of their instruction—when teachers ask "How am I doing?" Highest effects when teachers seek evidence on where students are not doing well.	0.90
Feedback	Among most powerful of influences, especially when it is from the student to the teacher. Feedback is information provided by an agent (i.e., teacher, peer, book, parent, or one's own experience) about aspects of one's performance or understanding.	0.70

- Determine what the teacher is doing and saying relative to the assigned task.

- When appropriate (unless the teacher is directly teaching them), talk with students.

- It is important to remain focused on collecting judgment-free descriptions. This is not the time to analyze or evaluate what you are observing; simply document what you are observing.

FIGURE 7.7 *LinkingWalk (LW)* Student Voice Template

LINKINGWALK (LW) STUDENT VOICE TEMPLATE					
# of students in the class:		Teacher #:	Date:		Grade/Content:
Learning Intentions/Success Criteria:			Time into the lesson:		
			Beginning:	Middle:	End:
Instructional Setting:	Whole Group:	Small Group:	One on one	Centers:	Partners:

Questions *LW* members pose to students include:

1. What are you learning today?
2. What is it that your teacher wants you to know and be able to do as a result of your learning today?
3. What strategies do you use when you get stuck?
4. How will you know if your work is of good quality?

ASSESSMENT CRITERIA	LEVEL 4	LEVEL 3	LEVEL 2	LEVEL 1
Question 1	Learning target paraphrase or success criteria	Directions, activity, task answer	General subject answer	I don't know or unable to answer
Question 2	Learning target paraphrase success criteria	Completion of activity/task. Effort-based answer	General subject answer	I don't know or unable to answer
Question 3	Clear identification of the six school-wide learner dispositions	Identifies several (two to three) of the school-wide learner dispositions	One of the school-wide learner dispositions or teacher-dependent strategy	I don't know or unable to answer
Question 4	Refers to the established success criteria (rubric or checklist)	Seeks answer from a source other than the teacher, peer assessment	Teacher-dependent answer	I don't know or unable to answer

QUESTION	STUDENT 1	STUDENT 2	STUDENT 3	STUDENT 4	STUDENT 5
1					
2					
3					
4					

FIGURE 7.8 Feedback Template

LINKINGWALK (LW) FEEDBACK TEMPLATE					
# of students in the class:		Teacher #:	Date:	Grade/Content:	
Learning Intentions/Success Criteria:			Time into the lesson:		
			Beginning:	Middle:	End:
Instructional Setting:	Whole Group:	Small Group:	One on one:	Centers:	Partners:
Feedback by anyone (record both the frequency of each with tally marks and verbatim examples)					

TYPES AND LEVELS OF FEEDBACK	TALLY MARKS	VERBATIM EXAMPLES
Task		
Process		
Self-regulation		
Self (praise)		
Teacher to student		
Student to teacher		
Student to student		

FIGURE 7.9 Samples of Baseline Evidence Statements

- Out of 28 students, the teacher engaged with 5 students 3 to 7 times, 12 students 1 to 2 times, and 11 students not at all.
- When 8 out of 22 students were asked "What are you learning today?" only 1 student out of the 8 could describe the learning target or success criteria. The other 7 stated the content (i.e., math, science) or described the activity (i.e., cutting, matching, multiplication).
- Student-learning activities were aligned with the stated learning intentions and success criteria in 1 of 5 classrooms.
- Out of 15 minutes of classroom observation, the teacher talked for 12 minutes, compared with the students, who talked for 3 minutes.
- Out of 15 questions asked by the teacher during the observation, 10 were surface or low level and 5 were deep or high level.
- During the 15 minutes of observation, the teacher asked mostly low-level cognitive questions requiring a single response.
- While the success criteria were not posted in classrooms, it was evident when talking with students that they had a clear understanding of what they were expected to do and learn.

Debriefing following the LinkingWalk. Begin by having individuals and/or partners read through their notes and identify recollections, impressions, and supporting factors relevant to the specific classroom instructional practice. Then teams discuss their findings and create baseline statements on chart paper that reflect the qualitative and quantitative evidence collected. Examples of baseline evidence statements would include those depicted in Figure 7.9.

Next, teams or partners create graphical representations (or depictions on chart paper) of the evidence collected in support of the baseline evidence statements. (Graphs and depictions should reflect both a summary of all data collected, as well as data by individual classroom.) Examples of graphs coming from one of our *LinkingWalk* processes are shown in Figure 7.10. Once the data have been graphed, *LW* team members set about recording their personal wonderings and questions.

Then *LW* team members review all displayed evidence. Team members collectively share nonjudgmental observations and wonderings, recollections, and impressions drawn from classrooms visited. Drawing on their own experience and knowledge of research-based instructional practice, as described within their district teacher evaluation model and the research, *LW* team members engage in "challenging talk" (Annan, Lai, & Robinson, 2003, p. 33) focused on deepening their understanding of how the identified instructional practice that was observed compares with the way

FIGURE 7.10 Sample of *LW* Data Graphed

Teacher Formative Assessment

2% Peer Assessment

3% Student Self-Assessment

13% Observation

50% Questions

32% Prompts

Out of 16 K–4 classroom observations (3 repeats), 141 prompts were used to elicit student understanding.

Out of 16 K–4 classroom observations (3 repeats), 221 instances of questions that elicited student understanding were collected.

Out of 16 K–4 classroom observations, (3 repeats), 10 opportunities for students to self-assess against a standard of practice were observed.

Out of 16 K–4 classroom observations (3 repeats), 59 instances of the teacher circulating to monitor student learning and to offer feedback were observed.

Out of 16 K–4 classroom observations (3 repeats), 8 opportunities for students to peer assess against a standard of practice were observed.

Questioning - Overall

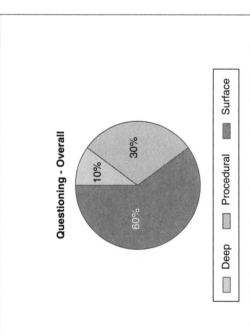

60%

10%

30%

☐ Deep ☐ Procedural ☐ Surface

- Out of 11 classroom observations were a total of 399 questions.
- 121 out of 399 were Procedural Questions – 30%
- 238 out of 399 were Surface Questions – 60%
- 31 out of 399 were Deep Questions – 10%
- 1 out of 11 classrooms observed small-group questioning with a longer wait time.
- 10 out of 11 classrooms observed whole-group questioning with little or no wait time.

119

it is described in the research (process/content). The principal makes notes on the discussion and collects all data, graphics, and baseline evidence statements from *LW* team members. The principal and the coach determine the best way to provide information back to both the teachers whose classrooms were visited as well as the staff as a whole.

Meg Roa, professional development and support specialist, Volusia County Schools, summarized the impact of Learning Walks (Volusia County's description) as

> one of the best professional learning events I've experienced. This job-embedded PD is focused, relevant and provides a powerful collaboration platform for professionals from all levels of experience and expertise to learn together. I truly believe the Learning Walks process has the power to impact instructional practice and transform school culture. (Meg Roa, personal communication March 19, 2017)

Alisa Fedigan, principal at DeBary Elementary School in DeBary, Florida, discovered the power of zeroing in on specific instructional practices they wanted to implement well throughout the faculty by utilizing the *Linking Walk* process. (*Note:* DeBary uses the term Learning Walks.) Specifically, Alisa developed a deliberate practice plan (J. Smith & R. Smith, 2015) or personal leadership growth plan around teachers' proficient use of learning targets and success criteria during their daily classroom instruction. Together, Alisa and her staff co-constructed the success criteria they would accept from these monthly Learning Walks (as she calls them) that would reveal the degree to which a teacher was being clear with students about what she wanted students to learn and what the outcome of this learning would look like. The process involved monthly classroom observations, during which time observers would ask students in those classrooms being observed four questions related to the established learning targets and success criteria. Student responses were then matched to one of four "level" responses (see Figure 7.11).

Student responses to these four questions were then tabulated and summarized each month to enable teachers to collectively analyze and, as a result, make appropriate adjustments to their instructional practice. A summary from three months of observations (October through November) can be seen in Figure 7.12.

"Public displays of effection" (R. Smith & J. Smith, 2016), such as the graph (Figure 7.12) that Alisa created, are a very useful strategy to help her stir the collective thinking of her teachers that lead to collective, as well as individual, instructional next steps! As you compare the October to December results for each question, with rare exception (December, Question 1), you will see a decrease in the number of Level 1 and 2 student responses and a corresponding increase in the Level 3 and 4 student responses. In other words, over time and with increased proficient instruction by teachers, DeBary students were gradually demonstrating greater ownership of their own learning. In brief, Alisa's students were becoming more assessment-capable learners (Hattie, 2012)!

FIGURE 7.11 Learning Target and Success Criteria Rubric

LEARNING TARGET/SUCCESS CRITERIA				
QUESTIONS POSED TO STUDENTS:				
1. What are you learning about today?				
2. What is it your teacher wants you to know and be able to do as a result of your learning today?				
3. What [learning] strategies do you use when you are stuck?				
4. How will you know if your work is of good quality?				
ASSESSMENT CRITERIA RUBRIC	**LEVEL 1 RESPONSE**	**LEVEL 2 RESPONSE**	**LEVEL 3 RESPONSE**	**LEVEL 4 RESPONSE**
Question 1	"I don't know the answer"	General subject matter answer	Directions, activity, task answer	Learning target, "I can" statement
Question 2	"I don't know the answer"	General subject matter answer	Completion of activity/task. Effort-based answer	Learning target, "I can" statement
Question 3	No clear strategy	One strategy or teacher-dependent strategy	More than one strategy, includes resources	Multiple strategies from a variety of sources
Question 4	"I don't know the answer"	Teacher-dependent answer	Seeks answer from source other than the teacher (i.e., peer assessment)	Refers to the learning target, checklist, or rubric

Metacollaboration Through *LinkingTalks*

Forget about being the person in charge, the one at the top of the pyramid, the "my way or the highway" manager. While that stale management paradigm was all about command and control of people and things, the new leadership standard is all about connecting people and resources together. That is, effective instructional leaders are web-masters who weave together a network of human capital! Dr. Russ Quaglia (2016) offers another way of describing this change, suggesting that when principals lead with voice, "principals realize that instructional leadership is the role of everyone within the building and not just the formal leader" (p. 3).

The real sway that instructional leaders have comes from assuming the role of "broker-in-chief" of relationships and scaling collective efficacy within the

FIGURE 7.12   DeBary Elementary School Three-Month Learning Walk Data

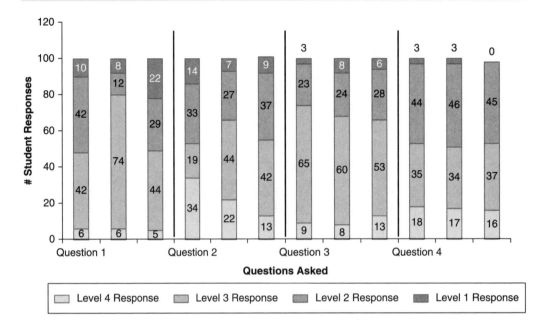

organization. Today's schools are highly complex organizations. Mini cities. Instructional leaders must be able to weave a web of connectivity and collaborative expertise.

To accomplish this, instructional leaders must make certain that everyone has easy access to the school's collective brain. Everyone within the school needs to be sufficiently linked so they know where they are in relation to the schools' goals and what next steps to take for themselves. A highly integrated system such as this operates only when there is a tight web of informed, coordinated effort.

How do you pull this off? You make it easy for everyone to connect with each other, resolve problems at their level, generate ideas, and make and learn from mistakes. Highly skilled instructional leaders hook people up and help them link the accounting of their own teaching/leading to its actual or probable impact on students. To do this, you'll need to circulate. Use strategies that link people up and grow your human capital. This is where the practice of *LinkingTalks* comes into play.

Highly collaborative organizations and groups focus on developing many leaders working in concert, instead of relying on key individuals. Thus, they are like string quartets: members are reciprocally interdependent, using each other's outputs as their own inputs and vice versa. Their interdependence is also complete and immediate. Their work is done only as a unit; they cannot perform a string quartet composition without all of the members working together simultaneously. They are artists who collaborate; they must simultaneously devote their concentration to their own and to each other's playing.

When one listens to good jazz musicians improvise, it is not only the imagination of the improvising soloist that's engaged in the performance but also the imaginations of the other musicians as they support and interact with the soloist. In this sense, jazz musicians participating in improvisation translate their individual musical inventions into a collective performance, playing as one and creating an artifact with its own meaning and coherence. In musical parlance, they call this kind of alignment among musicians "being in the groove" or performing well together.

Highly effective groups of teachers and leaders engaging in dialogue about instructional practice, like the performance of jazz musicians, also get "in the groove" as they translate their individual classroom interventions and the impact of these interventions on student achievement into a collective performance, working as one and creating a collective artifact of instruction and impact with its own meaning and coherence. And just as jazz musicians feel the directions in which the music is developing and make new sense of it, highly collaborative teacher groups intuit the direction conversations are taking and make new meaning out of them. In other words, "conversation is collective verbal improvisation" (Schön, 1987, p. 30), with individual group members continually improvising words in conversations and improvising solutions to problems on the spot—"metacollaboration."

Metacollaboration (a collaboration on collaboration) through "learning talks" (Annan et al., 2003, p. 31) is a process designed to help school leaders guide teachers' collective verbal improvisation about teaching and its impact on student achievement. The aim is to help leaders acquire the knowledge and skills to effectively facilitate this "learning talk" among and with teachers that analyzes the impact of their teaching practices on student learning, evaluates the outcomes of that analysis, and then uses the results to make changes in ineffective practices by creating more effective ones.

Inasmuch as it is critical for school leaders to be able to schedule time for teachers to collaborate and to help facilitate this collective dialogue, there is a "dark side to collaboration . . . call it coblaboration" (Perkins, 2003, p. 149), blab that does not link up the organization's collective brainpower. Too often, collaboration is about sharing resources, instructional units, activities, and war stories and sharing beliefs about why something might or might not work in "my" context. Let us be crystal clear that this is not about increasing the sheer amount of teacher talk within the organization. It is, however, about increasing the kind of talk, "linking talk" (Robinson, 2011, p. 110), that focuses on and is designed to improve teaching and learning. And impact coaches need to help school leaders acquire the knowledge and skills to lead and participate as *learners* in helping teachers figure out how to get classroom and school-wide improvement (Robinson, Lloyd, & Rowe, 2008).

Brian Annan et al. (2003) present a model of teacher talk, which we have modified slightly and renamed *LinkingTalks*, that outlines the types of conversations in which teachers and leaders engage (see Figure 7.13) that proceed from all possible types of teacher and leader talk and conclude with three forms of *LinkingTalk*. Like an onion, these categories of *talk* have many layers—several outside layers once peeled away reveal the heart of all talk—*LinkingTalk*.

FIGURE 7.13 Teacher/Leader *LinkingTalk*

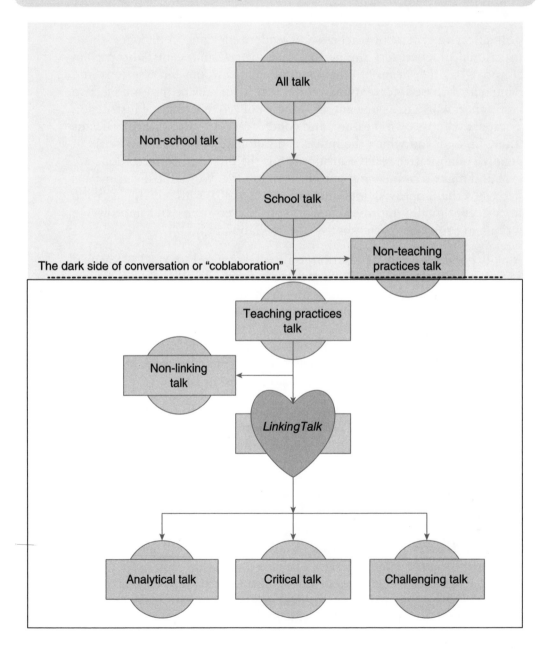

IMPACT COACHING: SCALING INSTRUCTIONAL LEADERSHIP

As you review this model, keep in mind that there are two foundational assumptions that underpin the model. First, the one finding that stands out in time as more powerful than any other is that "the greatest influence on student progression in learning is having highly expert, inspired and passionate teachers" (Hattie, 2015b, p. 2). Second is a collective, ongoing, and synchronized effort on the part of school leaders and teachers to obtain feedback on the impact of teaching on learning (many times from the *LinkingWalk* process), and using that feedback to further shape the instructional process, scale instructional expertise, and improve learning for all is essential. We would propose that there is a third underlying assumption that needs to be added to the good thinking of Annan, Lai, and Robinson. The Annan, Lai, and Robinson (2003) concept of "Learner Talk" (p. 31) doesn't exclude school leaders. Thus, the more skilled school leaders are in creating opportunities for, developing trust among, and providing the resources needed to understand the impact on students of all the teachers, as well as the school leader, and to lead these discussions with and among teachers, the greater the likelihood that the culture of the school will shift to one supportive of improving practice via analysis, critique, and challenge.

Figure 7.13 presents a pictorial storyline in which the category of "all talk" is positioned at the top of the depiction—the outer layer to our earlier onion analogy. All talk includes talk about both schooling as well as non-schooling matters (i.e., weather, sports, family issues, etc.). Beneath these two layers of talk is talk about teaching practices—talk about teaching and learning—or talk that is not about teaching and learning. The first two layers of talk constitute teacher "coblaboration" (Perkins, 2003, p. 149), as we have suggested earlier.

At the heart of all talk is *LinkingTalk*, which is further divided into three types: analytical talk, or talk that analyzes the impact of teaching and leading on student learning; critical talk, or talk that evaluates the outcomes of analytical talk; and challenging talk, or talk about replacing ineffective teaching and leadership practices with more effective ones. Thus, *LinkingTalk* is talk about teaching and leadership, which analyzes, evaluates, and/or challenges the impact of teaching and leadership practices on student learning in order to scale high-impact instructional leadership practices.

The heart of *LinkingTalks*, unlike our own heart, is divided into three chambers (analytical, critical, and challenging). However, similar to our hearts, these three chambers are interrelated. For example, teachers and leaders who challenge each other to change ineffective practices (challenging talk) rely upon judgments of whether these practices were effective or not (critical talk), which is dependent upon how those evaluations were made (analytical talk). One can assume, then, that the weaving together of these three strands of conversation constitutes teaching practices talks. Figures 7.14 through 7.16 depict examples of the three interdependent streams of conversation, one that is teacher based and the other that is leader based.

FIGURE 7.14 Analytical Talk

SAMPLE DIALOGUE . . .	WHY IT IS ANALYTICAL TALK . . .
Example 1 **Mayan:** We should not have attempted to implement both the effective feedback and teacher questioning initiatives. Teachers are complaining that they are feeling overwhelmed, and the two initiatives are taking time away from the teaching of content. **Kristin:** Is one impacting student learning more than the other? **Mayan:** Hmm, I'm not certain. We need to examine pre/post student achievement data as a result of using these instructional practices. It might be that we just need to forge ahead.	Mayan and Kristin are engaging in analytical talk because they a. Have incomplete evidence in order to make an informed decision b. Conclude that they need to examine student achievement data to determine to what degree teacher concerns are impacting student achievement
Example 2 **Jeff:** I am going back to the way I typically give teachers feedback. **Impact Coach:** You have doubts that the way you are attempting to provide teachers feedback now is not working. What are you noticing? **Jeff:** I tried to provide teachers "leveled" feedback, like the research says, but teachers' responses on the self-assessment checklist were mixed. Most teachers responded that the amount of feedback was not manageable. And students' pre/post assessment scores were not very good.	Jeff and his coach are engaging in analytical talk because he a. Has examined evidence (adult practice, as well as student achievement scores) b. Has linked the student achievement scores to his leadership practice

FIGURE 7.15 Critical Talk

SAMPLE DIALOGUE . . .	WHY IT IS CRITICAL TALK . . .
Example 1 **Lindsay:** (looking at a video clip of her attempting to use teacher questioning) Have you noticed that I tend to choose only those students who voluntarily raise their hands to answer my questions?	Lindsay and Julie are engaging in critical talk because a. They have evaluated Lindsay's teaching practice related to teacher questioning based on video evidence

SAMPLE DIALOGUE . . .	WHY IT IS CRITICAL TALK . . .
Julie: Yeah. You're supposed to distribute your questions among all students, both those who volunteer and those who don't. What other strategies are you aware of to engage all students in thinking about your question?	Lindsay and Julie are engaging in critical talk because a. They have evaluated Lindsay's teaching practice related to teacher questioning based on video evidence
Example 2 **Mike:** I didn't facilitate that staff meeting very well. **Impact Coach:** Say more. **Mike:** I provided too much content all at once. The plus/delta feedback from teachers said that they sat for too long a time before they unpacked the content.	Mike and his coach are engaging in critical talk because a. Mike has evaluated the impact of his facilitation (ineffective) based on feedback from teachers b. The coach has asked Mike for evidence for his evaluation

FIGURE 7.16 Challenging Talk

SAMPLE DIALOGUE . . .	WHY IT IS CHALLENGING TALK . . .
Example #1 **Marek:** (discussing next year's budget during a department chair meeting) It appears that we're planning to allocate the same amount of money to this mathematics program. **Silas:** Yeah. I wonder if we should still be using this program? When you look at our state testing data over the past three years, our student scores remain fairly stable. **Marek:** That's true, but I don't believe we are implementing the program with fidelity. When I talk with our colleagues, it seems to me that we are individually selecting which of the components we want to do. If we follow the established success criteria, we should see the kind of impact on student achievement the research suggests.	Marek and Silas are engaging in challenging talk because a. Silas is challenging his colleagues to discontinue a mathematics program based on achievement data that show the program as ineffective b. Marek is challenging her colleagues' practice of not following the mathematics program, which could have influenced the achievement results c. Marek is also suggesting a better practice, strict adherence to the established success criteria, that should positively influence student achievement

(Continued)

FIGURE 7.16 (Continued)

SAMPLE DIALOGUE . . .	WHY IT IS CHALLENGING TALK . . .
Example #2 **Impact Coach:** (looking at Ashlyn's deliberate practice plan, or DPP) You asked me why your ninth-grade writing scores remain at such a low level. Look at your DPP. Your monitoring plan occurred twice last year—once in the middle of the year and the other at the end of the year. **Ashlyn:** What do you think I should do? **Impact Coach:** You are most likely assessing student performance in writing too infrequently in order to have an impact on student writing. Rather than assessing writing performance just two times per year, you should think about assessing it every eight to ten weeks, as it provides more opportunities to make needed adjustments to instructional and leadership practice. **Ashlyn:** Oh, that makes sense! I need to increase the frequency of my assessment of writing. **Impact Coach:** Absolutely!	Ashlyn and her coach are engaging in critical talk because a. Ashlyn's coach is challenging Ashlyn to stop using an ineffective leadership practice (infrequent monitoring) because that is the possible cause of the low writing levels b. Ashlyn's coach is inventing a new practice (more frequent monitoring of student achievement) to replace Ashlyn's ineffective practice c. Ashlyn has invited her coach to critique her leadership practice d. Ashlyn has asked her coach to help her invent a new leadership practice to replace her ineffective one

When impact coaches help school leaders to understand the impact that well-implemented *LinkingTalks* can have on student learning, it reinforces and helps to operationalize several of the "theories of practice" (J. Smith & R. Smith, 2015) we presented previously in Chapter 4. To begin with, teachers and school leaders have to become powerful change activators (TOP 2) of the core business of teaching, leading, and learning by taking ownership for those adult actions that are contributing to the performance of students. Next, teachers and leaders focus on their own learning and debate the impact these practices are having on students and teachers (TOP 1). Lastly, when teachers and school leaders talk to improve practice via analysis, critique, and challenge, together they build a culture of relational trust (TOP 7) by demonstrating a respect for the ideas of others, listening to understand others' points of view, believing in others' capability, and ensuring their words match their deeds.

Designing and Implementing Deliberate Practice Plans

In all fields of human endeavor—from the arts (i.e., music, painting, and writing) to sports (i.e., swimming, running, and golf) to games (i.e., bridge and chess)—great performers of all stripes almost always commit themselves to continually improving their performance, which we call deliberate practice. This unrelenting desire to constantly improve their performance requires them to identify certain "sharply defined elements of [their] performance that need to be improved, and then work intently on [improving] them" (Colvin, 2008, p. 68). Colvin goes on to say that a hallmark of great performers is that they "isolate remarkably specific aspects of what they do and focus on just those things until they are improved; then it's on to the next aspect" (p. 68). Another way of saying this is that learning, regardless of who is doing the learning, is most effective when the individual purposefully engages in deliberate practice that includes active monitoring of one's learning experiences compared with some established goal or standard of practice. More importantly, learning takes place only as a result of monitoring one's progress and using the feedback about one's progress in order to know what next steps to take toward the goal or standard (i.e., the desired state).

As stated previously in Chapter 3, all too often, instructional leadership coaching initiatives are implemented haphazardly, without a clear plan and, more importantly, without an appreciation for the science behind coaching and what it takes to be successful. When coaches work with their coachees to create a plan (see Figure 7.17) that incorporates the essence of Michael Fullan's (2010, p. 16) concept of "simplexity," then the resulting outcome is most likely going to be an example of "coaching done well" (Gawande, 2011, p. 53).

Utilizing success criteria checklists. What is a success criteria checklist? Think in terms of a rubric (or "scoring tool"); it is a way of describing performance criteria based on the expected outcomes and performances of the coachee (or teachers). Typically, rubrics are used in scoring or grading written assignments, performances, or oral presentations; however, they may also be used to inform any type of school leader or teacher practice, which, according to Jonsson and Svingby (2007), enhance the reliable evaluation (the degree to which the teacher's or school leader's practice aligns with the established success criteria) of a performance.

Thus, the success criteria checklists shared with you earlier (see Figures 3.9 and 6.3), along with each of our five "Instructional Leadership Ability Rubrics" (located in the Appendix), consist of a set of scoring criteria (word picture descriptions of leadership behavior) and quality ratings associated with these criteria. In most rubrics, the criteria are grouped into categories so the instructor or supervisor, in our case, and the leader being evaluated can

FIGURE 7.17 Sample Deliberate Practice Plan

DELIBERATE PRACTICE PLAN (DPP)

School Leader's Name and Position: Nick Smith, Principal, Marsh Middle School

Evaluator's Name and Position: Dr. Julie Hellman, Director of School Improvement and Accountability

Target for School Year: 2017–18 SY	Date Target Approved: August 1, 2017

School Leader's Signature: *Nick Smith*

Evaluator's Signature: *Julie R. Hellman*

Prioritized School-Wide Problem of Practice

Our ISTEP+ data reveal significant gaps in student writing achievement between our Hispanic and our white students. In particular, they did not score well on the Writing Process component of the assessment. We may not be providing these students with enough practice with prewriting, drafting, editing, and revising relative to our expectations that they write clear, coherent, and focused expository writing.

SMART+ER Goal (Drawn from your school improvement planning analysis linked to the problem of practice)

Seventy percent of our eighth-grade students (Hispanic) will meet the DOE writing criteria in Grades 6 to 8 and will attain a Level 3.5 or above by June 2017 with monthly reevaluation progress monitoring of student writing.

High-Impact Instructional Leadership Practices (What might be one or two high-impact practices that could leverage goal attainment?)

Focus specifically on the following leadership practices relative to improving expository/narrative student writing . . .

- Planning, coordinating, and evaluating teaching and the curriculum
- Promoting and participating in teacher learning and development

Theory of Action (What is your hypothesis? For example, "If we . . . , then we will . . .")

If we implement differentiated writing instruction, then student writing performance will improve.

LEADERSHIP STRATEGY IN ACTION	STUDENT RESULTS (FORMATIVE ASSESSMENT)	QUALITATIVE BENEFITS	SOURCES OF DATA TO MONITOR
Increase the percentage of faculty implementing differentiated writing instruction at the "proficient"	Increase the percentage of students scoring at the "proficient" and higher levels on a monthly assessment using	• Become keenly aware of the barriers to proficient student writing. • Develop an awareness of the instructional	• Bimonthly rubric results of teachers' self-assessment • Bimonthly rubric results of the school leader's observed assessment

or higher level based on teacher self-assessment bimonthly using a locally developed rubric.	a locally developed rubric.	practices that appear to most help students overcome those barriers, as well as those practices that don't have a positive relationship to improvements in student writing. • Determine whether the selected leadership strategy in action is having the desired impact or not.	• Bimonthly rubric results from student writing performance translated into effect size measures

TASK ANALYSIS *(WHAT ARE SOME KEY THINGS YOU ANTICIPATE YOU WILL NEED TO DO TO ENSURE SUCCESS?)*

1. Schedule and conduct a differentiated writing strategies workshop for faculty.
2. As a result of the professional development on differentiated writing, build a differentiated writing rubric that clearly describes teacher instructional practices in four performance areas (i.e., Exemplary, Proficient, Progressing, and Not Meeting Standards).
3. Construct a student writing rubric.
4. Conduct student writing rubric calibration trainings.
5. Translate student writing rubrics into student-friendly language.

discriminate among the categories by level of performance. In organizational use, the rubric provides an "objective" *external standard* against which leadership and/or teaching performance may be compared.

Most people have difficulty using rubrics reliably at first without some practice. The fact is in order to use an assessment tool effectively, it must be used on a regular basis (more than simply one or two times a year). Rubrics are most effective when school leaders practice using them with their impact coaches and faculty over and over again, making certain to clarify any vague terms or quantify phrases that require further definition. For example, the word implementation is almost always used within principal and teacher evaluation instruments. After all, successfully implementing a variety of initiatives is a critical leadership and instructional role. But the word implementation is vague and requires one to ask such questions as "Implementation to what degree?" Additionally, we often see the phrase "routinely monitoring" being used again within teacher and leadership evaluation documents as if the phrase enjoys some universal understanding. Without providing further clarification, routinely monitoring to one school leader might be interpreted as monitoring three to four times a year, and yet, to another school leader, it might mean six to seven times per year. Consequently, whether school leaders are adopting our success criteria checklists or developing their own checklists, they require clarification and/or revision based on feedback from the coach and/or school faculty. The best rubrics are almost always by-products of an iterative effort. In other words, the effectiveness of a rubric description relies on co-constructing meaning among the impact coach, the school leader, and faculty through feedback, so each can make the appropriate adjustments to their thinking ahead of any formal or informal assessment.

Why develop a success criteria checklist? A success criteria checklist is a means of describing such things as what a proficiently developed deliberate practice plan "looks like" (both at the developmental and implementation levels) when fully implemented (Hall & Hord, 2011). The following "Deliberate Practice Development" and "Deliberate Practice Implementation" rubrics (see Figures 7.18 and 7.19) paint a series of "word pictures" of the school leader behaviors and practices and also describe the behaviors and practices as school leaders move from the "Unsatisfactory" variation toward the "Highly Effective" variation.

Using a success criteria checklist. The deliberate practice implementation and development checklists help impact coaches and those school leaders involved in implementing the deliberate practice plan to develop a common understanding of where the school leader is headed—the learning intention, or having the end in mind. Beginning with the "end in mind" (Covey, 1989, p. 99) or creating the intended action prior to the enacted action helps school leaders focus their efforts on the right work and avoid the problem of the school leader doing things differently based on idiosyncratic interpretations of what the practice looks like. Additionally, the "Deliberate Practice Implementation" and "Deliberate Practice Development" checklists help the impact coach, as well as the school leader, determine where they are and what they need to do to move toward full implementation. For example, the impact coach and school leader can use the checklist to determine progress in developing and implementing the deliberate practice plan and decide where to target specific support that will be most effective in moving the school leader toward the desired state.

Impact coaches should use these two documents to determine what variation (i.e., Highly Effective, Proficient, etc.) within either the development or the implementation of the deliberate practice plan predominates among all of their coachees. School leaders' reflections should be as candid as possible when determining their level of performance; this is not a rating tool but a tool of self-assessment that will help school leaders determine where they are in the development and implementation process and what next steps they need to take.

As a measurement tool, impact coaches may elect to have school leaders self-assess using the "Deliberate Practice Implementation Checklist" monthly. By summarizing the data they collect (i.e., the specific variations that predominate in their coachees), impact coaches can model for their school leaders how to use data to inform leadership behaviors and practice.

FIGURE 7.18 Deliberate Practice (DP) Development Checklist

DELIBERATE PRACTICE (DP) DEVELOPMENT CHECKLIST

Deliberate Practice Priorities: The leader and the evaluator identify one to two specific and measurable priority learning goals related to teaching, learning, or school leadership practices that impact student learning growth. One or two targets are recommended.

HIGHLY EFFECTIVE	EFFECTIVE	NEEDS IMPROVEMENT	UNSATISFACTORY
All criteria for the effective category have been successfully met. In addition: The leader . . . • Assists other leaders in helping them develop a proficient DP • Uses the concepts contained within the DP template to influence other school improvement planning documents • Frequently shares what she or he is learning (both successes and failures) about the effective development of DP plans with other schools, departments, or districts to maximize the impact of the leader's personal learning experience	The leader . . . • Identifies a **Prioritized School-Wide Problem of Practice** that clearly identifies the problem without offering any solutions • Captures a **SMART+ER Goal** for her or his personal growth that aligns with a SMART+ER (i.e., specific, measurable, ambitious, relevant, time-bound, evaluated, and reevaluated) Goal within her or his school improvement plan • Identifies a few (one to two) sharply defined elements of her or his performance that offer the greatest opportunity to leverage her or his knowledge based on research and skills (based on research) in multiple leadership performance areas that are designed to improve student achievement as **High-Impact Instructional Leadership Performance Areas** • Creates a single **Theory of Action** statement that specifically describes implicit or explicit models of how educators must act and what, as a result, she or he hypothesizes will happen to student achievement as a result of being aligned with the SMART+ER Goal	The leader . . . • Identifies a **Prioritized School-Wide Problem of Practice** that clearly identifies the problem but may offer solutions • Establishes a **SMART+ER Goal** that is either unrelated to one of the school's SMART Goals or attempts to focus on more than one SMART Goal within the school improvement plan • Identifies a few (one to two) **High-Impact Instructional Leadership Performance Areas;** however, the indicators selected may not be in areas the research supports as high effect size leadership practices • **Theory of Action** statement is represented in the "if/then" format but lacks clarity or is overly complex and confusing and may not specifically address desired changes in student achievement related to the SMART Goal	The leader . . . • Is unable to produce a completed draft of her or his DP or several elements of the DP template are left blank and/or • Selects a **Prioritized Goal** that is not connected to critical targets identified within the school improvement plan • Identifies more than three areas she or he believes are **High-Impact Leadership Instructional Performance Areas,** and the indicators selected are not in areas the research supports as high effect size leadership practices • Is missing a **Theory of Action** statement or it is not stated in an "if/then" format or fails to specifically identify the hypothesized adult practice and/or its desired impact on student achievement

(Continued)

DELIBERATE PRACTICE (DP) DEVELOPMENT CHECKLIST

HIGHLY EFFECTIVE	EFFECTIVE	NEEDS IMPROVEMENT	UNSATISFACTORY
	The leader . . . (continued)	The leader . . . (continued)	The leader . . . (continued)
	• Constructs one to two observable, subject to frequent public testing, and measurable (i.e., quantifiable; able to be gauged) **Leadership Strategy in Action** statement(s). These strategies are an *obvious* translation (i.e., paraphrase) of the high-impact instructional leadership practices. These strategies are constructed with *formative language* (e.g., "increase the percentage of") and are *time-bound* (i.e., they indicate how often the public testing will occur).	• Does not clearly align the **Leadership Strategy in Action** statement(s) with the theory of action statement. May not be stated in measurable terms or, it may resemble a task analysis	• Makes little or no connection between the theory of action statement and the **Leadership Strategy in Action** statement
	• Converts the results, or "then" statements, from the theory of action into a measurable **Student Results** statement (a formative, teacher-made assessment related to the SMART Goal) that is measured monthly	• Tends to tie the **Student Results** statement to assessments the school may or may not control and are measured less than on a monthly basis	• Tends to tie the **Student Results** statement to large-scale assessments rather than locally developed assessments that can be measured frequently
	• Identifies both the desired leadership and teacher benefits to conducting the research in the **Qualitative Benefits** column	• Focuses the **Qualitative Benefits** section of the plan primarily on how "others" will benefit but not on how the leader herself or himself will benefit from the successful improvement effort	• Uses the **Qualitative Benefits** section of the plan to describe what the leader will do but not the benefits the leader expects as a result of successfully implementing her or his strategy in action
	• Explains in clear terms the **Sources of Data to Monitor** (reflects both the leadership, as well as the student achievement, data)	• Tends to reflect the **Sources of Data to Monitor** against the student achievement data but does not identify the data coming from the measurable leadership strategy in action	• Tends to reflect **Sources of Data to Monitor** against the student achievement data but does not identify the data coming from the measurable leadership strategy in action
	• Provides a detailed **Task Analysis** that makes visible critical next steps	• Provides a **Task Analysis** that contains a list of things to do that looks very similar to the items included within the leadership strategy in action step	• Provides a **Task Analysis**, but it has nonkey, as well as key, next steps—too detailed to be of practical use

FIGURE 7.19 Deliberate Practice (DP) Implementation Checklist

DELIBERATE PRACTICE (DP) IMPLEMENTATION CHECKLIST

HIGHLY EFFECTIVE	EFFECTIVE	NEEDS IMPROVEMENT	UNSATISFACTORY
All criteria for the proficient category have been successfully met. In addition: The leader . . . • Shares the results of her or his action research with faculty, what she or he is learning, and how that learning will influence leadership practices in the future • Publicly reports, including plans and oral presentations, a frank acknowledgment of prior personal and organizational failures and offers clear suggestions for system-wide learning resulting from those lessons • Regularly shares the results of her or his action research, along with some of the things she or he is learning about leadership practices, and the connection to student achievement with other schools, departments, or districts to maximize the impact of the leader's personal learning experience	The leader . . . • Produces clear and consistent evidence that she or he is monitoring and measuring both the leadership strategy or strategies, as well as the impact on student achievement monthly • Documents the changes in leadership practice that are occurring monthly as a result of the monitoring • Publicly displays the graphic depiction of the degree to which the achieved leadership strategies in action compare with the impact on student achievement	The leader . . . • Produces evidence that she or he is monitoring and measuring student effect data but is inconsistent in monitoring and measuring leadership data. Consequently, it is difficult to determine the degree to which the specified leadership practices are impacting student achievement. • Participates in the action research process and provides limited evidence of changes based on data • Might display student results data, but she or he has not yet created a graphic display depicting both the results of the leadership strategies in action compared with the changes in student performance	The leader . . . • Demonstrates no significant effort to work on the targets • Demonstrates an indifference to data and shows no changes in leadership practice compared with the previous year. The data screams "Change!" and the leader's actions say "Everything is fine." • May not even be charting student results monthly, let alone how educators are performing

CHAPTER 7: KEY TAKEAWAYS

- Both partners in the impact coaching relationship must inquire into not only how the other's perceptions are changing but, of equal importance, how their own perceptions are changing as a result of the partnership in order to be seen as doing their jobs well.

- Five coaching process tools that cause both impact coach and school leader to function as practitioners, online researchers, and inquirers into self and other's changing understandings were reviewed. These process tools consisted of modeling the high-impact practices (combining, telling/listening, and demonstrating/imitating); conducting *LinkingWalks* to scale instructional expertise; engaging in and facilitating *LinkingTalks* with and among teachers to analyze, evaluate, and challenge the impact of teaching and leadership practices on student learning in order to scale more effective practices; designing and implementing deliberate practice plans; and utilizing success criteria checklists to gauge the degree of implementation.

GOING DEEPER

Further Reading: *Instructional Leadership and Good Checklists*

For an in-depth discussion of the research on instructional leadership, readers would be well served by reading Viviane Robinson's (2011) *Student-Centered Leadership*, which offers school leaders clear practical descriptions of the "leadership capabilities" (p. 16), the knowledge and skills needed to confidently engage in the elements of instructional leadership.

Use of the checklist by professionals has made it possible for them to skillfully accomplish some of the most difficult things people do—from flying airplanes to building skyscrapers to improving surgical practice. Want to find out more about what makes a good checklist a good checklist? Atul Gawande (2009), acclaimed writer and surgeon, makes a compelling case for the use of "good checklists" (p. 120) in his book *The Checklist Manifesto: How to Get Things Right*. It supports the notion that impact coaches and school leaders need to be clear about the practices they are attempting to implement.

CHAPTER 8

THE END OF IMPACT COACHING: SCALING INSTRUCTIONAL LEADERSHIP

> *The end of THE END is the best place to begin THE END, because if you read THE END from the beginning of the beginning of THE END to the end of the end of THE END, you will arrive at the end.*
>
> —Lemony Snicket (2006)

This short wrap-up chapter has two objectives. First, we provide a brief recapitulation of what we now know about leadership impact coaching, which has been addressed in the book's earlier chapters. Second, we will encourage you—no, challenge you—to move toward a coaching approach that helps you nurture school leaders' voice "in a way that builds relationships, trust, and momentum" (Quaglia, 2016, p. 9) around improvement efforts.

There is always a temptation to add new material in the concluding chapter of a book. We, however, will not do that. We would merely like to say this: In an era abundant with research findings and examples of tested and improved instructional and leadership practices that have led to better processes, we know what to do, so please, let's do it! Lemony Snicket (2006), in the epigraph, suggests, "If you read *The End* from the beginning of the beginning of *The End* to the end of the end of *The End*, you will arrive at the end" (p. back cover). Similarly, if you read *Impact Coaching* from the beginning of the beginning of *Impact Coaching* to the end of the end of *Impact Coaching*, you will arrive at the end of all of this discussion about impact coaching and the need to scale high-impact teaching and leadership practices within our schools and school districts. What, then, do we know about the beginning to the end of *Impact Coaching*?

WHAT DO WE NOW KNOW?

We know that hiring and retaining effective school leaders is critical to teacher effectiveness and, therefore, to student achievement; however, districts are struggling to attract and retain talented, well-trained school leaders in schools largely due to three factors: (a) lack of support, (b) high turnover rates, and (c) the complexities of the job (Hattie, 2015b; Louis, Leithwood, Wahlstrom, & Anderson, 2010; Robinson, 2011). Specifically, research suggests that newly hired principals require two types of support: (1) socialization support to learn about district rules, regulations, the way "things are done around here," and about the targeted reform initiatives, and (2) early career support systems, such as coaches or mentors, for the first two years of the principalship (School Leaders Network, 2014). Think about your system: *In what ways are you providing newly hired principals the type of support they need to stay and thrive within your system?*

We know that when school leaders are coached, the likelihood that new leadership and instructional practices will be sustained and institutionalized is increased to statistically significant levels. Given the fact that resources (time, energy, funding, human, and materials) are limited and the rapid rate of change and learning in today's schools and school systems, we must create systems for supporting school leaders in becoming more focused on the practices that matter the most, making them effective and efficient in learning and applying these practices in order to significantly improve student progress and achievement (Bloom, Castagna, Moir, & Warren, 2005; Bickman, Goldring, De Andrade, Breda, & Goff, 2012; Rowland, 2017). *How are you giving your school leaders the gift of coaching?*

We know that there are a number of well-designed coaching models, and while our impact coaching model contains many of the characteristics identified within other models, our model differs from these other coaching models in two fundamental ways. First, our model, like Jim Knight's (2007) coaching model, reinforces a singular focus on high-impact practices that research concludes have the greatest impact on student learning. Second, the impact coaching model requires that coaches and school leaders evaluate the effect of their coaching and/or leadership practices on learning and achievement. And most importantly, our coaching model expects the coach and school leader to understand the impact on students of all teachers and their own impact as school leaders and to act on that impact. *In what ways are you monitoring, measuring, and using the results of your measuring of school leaders' impact on student achievement to continually improve both personal and organizational performance?*

We know that the issue facing school districts concerned with protecting their upfront investment in highly effective school leaders is less about hiring a coach for this critical position and more about supporting—coaching—the school leaders you hire. In other words, if you evaluate school leaders, then you have an obligation to assist them (i.e., provide coaching, mentoring, professional learning opportunities, etc.) in areas that will make the greatest difference to teachers and students within your schools (School Leaders Network, 2014). Meredith Honig's (2012) research analysis provides support for this idea, suggesting that school districts should consider "shifts in the role of some central offices from mainly management, monitoring, or other hands-off principal support roles to central offices operating as main agents of principal learning" (p. 767). *In what ways are you shifting the role of central-office personnel from managers to leaders of instructional leadership?*

We know that all varieties of school systems (i.e., large, small, urban, suburban, and rural) can engage in impact coaching strategies with and for their school leaders by changing the expectations of those whose primary responsibility it is to evaluate school leaders (i.e., superintendents, assistant superintendents, directors, and school principals) or how they view their role (Honig, 2012). We advocated for ten theories of practice as the lens through which evaluators of school leaders and school leaders themselves must think about the way they interact with school leaders. *What are your theories of practice that underpin school leaders' every action and decision in a school?*

We know that a critical feature of the leadership impact coaching model (one that distinguishes it from other coaching models) is helping school leaders focus on and spend more of their precious time, energy, and influence on those high-impact, big-winner leadership practices that research has shown have a significant impact on student learning (Robinson, Hohepa, & Lloyd, 2009). Achieving a significant leadership impact is a greedy beast. It has a ravenous appetite. And school leaders must ask themselves why they should take food off other plates they are juggling to satisfy this creature's craving. Because this is the beast that effective school leaders are betting on to produce their most significant leadership impact—the advancement of learning for all and increased student progress and achievement.

Besides, we suspect that some of the things that have been eating up school leaders' time and energy deserve to starve. It's all the urgent but unimportant stuff school leaders have allowed to creep into their professional lives that really doesn't contribute much to their impact. It's the insignificant routines school leaders follow out of habit. And it's the urgent but trivial stuff that demands their attention yet contributes little, if anything, to their leadership impact. So what is the answer? Kick these scroungers away from the leadership training table.

Think significant few. Concentrate on the essential leadership practices, such as routinely evaluating your impact, then deliberately activating change based on the results, relentlessly focusing on learning and the impact of teaching;

see assessment as feedback to you as the instructional leader, and engage in dialogue with teachers about the relationship between what they do and the impact their instructional practices are having or not having on student learning. Figure out what to ignore. *How much of your school leaders' time, day in and day out, is spent on the instructional and leadership practices that research suggests have the greatest impact on learning and student achievement?*

We know that the simple but powerful impact coaching cycle we use with clients involves a number of proven successful coaching steps that are embedded within three components: Identify, Learn, and Improve (see Figure 3.1). These three components, along with the embedded steps, create a plan of action for the school leader. The impact coaching cycle, the one modeled by Rachel Hazel, created an ongoing agenda that formed the basis of the coaching interaction. In other words, Rachel's plan of action (deliberate practice plan), like blueprints that guide the day-to-day work of the builder, become the design, the roadmap that directs the actions of teachers and leaders as they work to co-construct a more effective school system that positively impacts student achievement. *What are the "blueprints" that guide your school leaders' day-to-day practices?*

We know that a foundational element to a highly productive coaching alliance is relationships that are mutually respectful and caring, where individuals feel both valued and valuable and help each other, grow mentally, emotionally, and spiritually (Bickman et al., 2012; Garmston & Wellman, 1999; Knight, 2007) and where it is okay for individuals to make and learn from their mistakes. *How are you keeping a pulse on the health of your organizational relationships?*

We know that effective communication between the impact coach and the school leader breathes the first spark of life into the work, and effective communication keeps collaborative effort alive. Nothing else is so crucial to coordination of collective effort. No other factor plays such a precious role in building and preserving trust between the coach and the school leader. Communication following the "open-to-learning conversations" (Robinson, 2011, p. 38) is the make-or-break issue. *In what ways are you helping school leaders acquire and effectively use those conversational lubricants (i.e., pausing, paraphrasing, questioning, etc.) that are the basis for critical, challenging, and accountable talk?*

We know as much now about what happens when people and organizations are engaged in change as we did two decades ago. Thus, the problem educators face is a "doing" problem, not a "knowing" problem (Pfeffer & Sutton, 2000). Given that all coaching partnerships, ours included, are about implementing some sort of change in practice (instructional and/or leadership), we underscored the key change facilitation strategies that school leaders and impact coaches must keep in mind and are most important, according to the research, to make change happen (Hall & Hord, 2011). There are many reasons for school leaders and teachers not to have an impact, and no single reason matches all situations. However, research on implementation identifies a common reason for lack of impact is failure to implement a high-impact practice (Fixsen, Naoom, Blase, Friedman, & Wallace, 2005). *In what ways are you using what we know about change to make certain that the changes you are implementing are being implemented well—not in a mediocre or poor manner?*

Finally, *we know* that there are a number of process tools the impact coach can employ to engage both coach and school leader in mutually beneficial dialogue about the school leader's improvement effort and the resulting data. Specifically, we discussed modeling the high-impact practices, conducting *LinkingWalks*, engaging in metacollaboration through *LinkingTalks*, designing and implementing deliberate practice plans, and utilizing success criteria checklists that promote essential self-regulation practices. *How are you using co-constructed success criteria checklists with your school leaders so that they understand what success looks like along the leadership improvement journey?*

With modeling, the impact coach partnership approach demands that it be a reflective practice where "the coach's showing and telling are woven together with listening and imitating (Schön, 1987, p. 111). As a result of knitting together these aspects of the coaching partnership, school leaders learn what they could not learn simply through the impact coach's telling or demonstration alone. That is, the two processes are interdependent. By observing models in action, school leaders may develop "a conceptual model of the target task prior to attempting to execute it" (p. 2). Think about your school or school system. *How are you amplifying the voice of school leaders (Quaglia, 2016) by modeling for them those high-impact practices they should be expertly using routinely in their schools in order to have a significant impact on teachers and students?*

LinkingWalks, as we noted earlier, are a classroom observation process that contains many features similar to those of other nationally recognized classroom walkthrough protocols (Instructional Rounds, Data-in-a-Day, McREL Power Walkthrough, etc.). However, unlike other similar processes, the practice we have strongly advocated for within this book focuses on high-impact instructional leadership practices (i.e., those with an effect size ≥ 0.40) in order to take these practices to scale within the school, asks the school leader to compare the improvements in high-impact instructional leadership practice with improvements in student progress and achievement and to translate the data into "public displays of effection," and aligns with school leaders' professional growth plan. Thus, the protocol serves to link practice to impact. *How do your classroom walkthroughs help you and your teachers sharply focus on those practices that research indicates produces the greatest impact on student progress and learning?*

Engaging in metacollaboration through *LinkingTalks* is a process designed to help school leaders facilitate teachers' collective verbal improvisation about teaching and the impact teachers' instruction is having on student achievement. The aim of this process tool is to help school leaders acquire the knowledge and skills needed so they are able to effectively facilitate this *LinkingTalk* among and with teachers to analyze the impact of their teaching practices on student learning, evaluate the outcomes of that analysis, and then use the results to make changes in ineffective practices by creating more effective ones. *How do your "Professional Learning Communities" (DuFour, DuFour, & Eaker, 2008), your "Data Teams" (Anderson, 2010), your "Collaborative Cultures" (Garmston & von Frank, 2012), or your "Impact Teams" (Bloomberg & Pitchford, 2017) focus on "the evidence of impact, common understandings of what impact means, the evidence and ways to know about the magnitude of this impact and how the impact is shared across many groups of students" (Hattie, 2015b, p. 24)?*

Designing and implementing deliberate practice plans was discussed as a process tool designed to help impact coaches and school leaders avoid the pitfalls present in many leadership coaching initiatives, which are implemented haphazardly, without a clear plan, and, more importantly, without an appreciation for the science behind coaching and what it takes to be successful. Specifically, we advocated for impact coaches working closely with their school leaders to create a plan (see Figure 7.17) that operationalizes Michael Fullan's (2010, p. 16) concept of "simplexity" in order to reflect a coaching process "done well" (Gawande, 2011, p. 53). *In what ways do your school leaders' improvement plans require them to measure the impact of their leadership practice against the resulting impact on student achievement (Smith & Smith, 2015)?*

The use of success criteria checklists was the final process tool we presented. A good success criteria checklist (Gawande, 2009) is a means of describing only the most critical and important steps in a process. They help to make priorities clearer and prompt school leaders to function better as a team. Much like a pilot who routinely goes over her aviation checklists prior to takeoff, school leaders use checklists to help guide their way through complex processes. Ideally, these checklists paint a series of "word pictures" of the specific school leader behaviors and practices in which they need to be engaged in order to implement any leadership practice well. We expect teachers to make certain that students are clear as to the learning intention and the success criteria that will be used to judge the quality of their performance ahead of instruction. *How do you know if your school leaders are practicing the same set of expectations with teachers? How do you know if your school leaders routinely work with their faculty to co-create the improvement process learning intentions (targets) and then, together with teachers, identify what success looks like along the improvement journey?*

LEARNING ABOUT IMPACT COACHING DURING COACHING

One of the most powerful strategies we have employed that enhances both the effectiveness of impact coaching and the creation of organizational connectivity is to find different ways for impact coaches to learn from those they are coaching while they are coaching. The essential concept of seeking information from your coachees about the quality and effectiveness of your coaching is identical to the vital classroom practice of teachers when they secure feedback from their students about the impact of their teaching. One simple strategy for immediately securing information from the coachee about the impact of the present coaching is to ask. For instance, when the first coaching session is complete, the impact coach might ask the school leader, "How has this conversation helped you think about selecting a high-impact instructional leadership strategy?" Armed with this information, the impact coach can make just-in-time adjustments to his practice to improve effectiveness.

When using the "Success Criteria Checklist" described in Figure 8.1, impact coaches can ask the school leader to respond to the full checklist, or they can have the school leader respond to specific components of the checklist in order to calibrate the effects of coaching behaviors one component at a time. That is, impact coaches can get feedback from the school leader at the end of the coaching cycle or as they progress through the various components—Identify, Learn, and Improve—of the impact coaching cycle.

The point here is we want impact coaches, like the effective teachers about which Dr. Hattie so often refers, that are to "DIE for!" (Hattie, 2015b, p. 18). In other words, similar to our most effective teachers, impact coaches also need to become expert at "Diagnosis, Interventions, and Evaluation." In talking with Dr. Hattie about this clever acronym, he has subsequently added a second "i" to the abbreviation (DIiE). That is, "we want teachers and impact coaches that Diagnose a problem, identify an Intervention, implement the intervention, and then Evaluate the impact of that intervention on learning" (John Hattie, personal communication, July 10, 2017). To be expert at diagnosis requires understanding what each school leader brings to the coaching session—experience, motivations, and willingness to engage and improve. To be expert at coaching interventions requires having multiple interventions (i.e., setting aside unproductive patterns of listening, responding, and inquiring; paraphrasing; asking probing and inquiry questions that either focus or open up the school leader's thinking; pausing to allow for deeper, more elaborated thought; etc.) so that if one intervention does not have the desired effect on the school leader, the impact coach changes to another—learning about implementation during implementation. It also involves knowing the interventions that have a high probability of success, knowing when to switch from one to another, and not using "blame" language to explain why a school leader is not responding appropriately. To be expert at evaluation requires knowing the skills of evaluating and having multiple methods and the ability to calibrate the effects of one's coaching behaviors.

Additionally, we would challenge you to compare your own coaching practices with the statements we developed in three large areas—Identify, Learn, and Improve—in Figure 8.1. Take a few moments now, and do this simple reflective exercise. Be as frank as possible with your self-assessment.

Success Criteria Checklist for the Instructional Leadership Impact Cycle—Consider each of the following statements, and indicate U (Usually), S (Sometimes), or R (Rarely) by checking the appropriate box immediately to the right of each statement.

COMPONENT 1: Identify—The coach and the leader collaborate to set a SMART+ER goal and select a leadership strategy to try to meet the goal.	U	S	R
The impact coach (IC) helped the school leader gather and analyze evidence to identify a prioritized student-learning problem and a related problem of instructional and leadership practice.			
The IC helped the school leader create a clear picture of current reality by collecting, reviewing, and analyzing observation and/or perception data to determine next steps.			
The IC phrased questions to the school leader in such a manner that they invited the school leader into the dialogue and opened up her or his thinking in order to identify a goal.			
The IC helped the school establish a SMART+ER goal.			
The IC assisted the school leader in her or his thinking about the choice of a high-impact instructional leadership strategy that she or he would like to proficiently implement.			
The IC and school leader identified the data the school leader intended to monitor that would help her or him know if she or he is on track as she or he went along, as well as the evidence to know whether she or he has achieved the goal at the end of the specified time period.			
COMPONENT 2: Learn—The coach helped the coachee clearly understand what the research says about the strategy she or he has selected and learn how to proficiently implement the strategy.	U	S	R
The IC interpreted the research and clearly explained the high-impact instructional leadership strategy to the school leader.			
The IC helped the school leader understand what successful implementation of the selected high-impact strategy looks like when implemented well (i.e., co-create the success criteria).			
The IC modeled successful implementation of the selected high-impact instructional leadership strategy.			
The IC planned opportunities for the school leader to practice the leadership strategy, receive feedback, and act on the feedback with the support of the coach.			

COMPONENT 3: Improve—The coachee and the coach monitored how the coachee implemented the chosen high-impact strategy, along with the degree of goal attainment achieved.	U	S	R
The IC helped the school leader assess her or his fidelity of implementation (using the established success criteria).			
The IC assisted the school leader's assessment of the impact the selected leadership practice had on student achievement.			
The IC helped the school leader create graphic displays of the data (measures of the leadership practice along with measures of student achievement) or "public displays of effection."			
The IC helped the school leader know how to use the results of the monitoring to inform next steps in leadership practice.			

Finished with your self-assessment? What are some of the trends and patterns you are noticing in the data? We would imagine that, if you have been candid when determining your level of performance, your self-assessment (like many of the ones we have seen) would contain a number of marks in the "rarely" or "sometimes" columns. Remember, this is not a rating tool but a tool of self-reflection against established success criteria that will help you determine where you might begin your own internal improvement process.

OUR CHALLENGE TO YOU

So impact coaches and school leaders, we leave you with a challenge. It is difficult to put a challenge on paper. We would much prefer to look you straight in the eye and say "We dare you!" In our mind, that's exactly what we are doing. We are on one side of a table. You are on the other. We are looking across at you and saying "We dare you!" We dare you to apply what we know from the research to your existing practices to scale leadership and instructional strategies that the research suggests has the greatest impact on learning and student achievement. We dare you to have the courage to confront performance that may be unsound and potentially harmful to learning for all and student achievement. We dare you to be persistent in your efforts to change your personal leadership performance for the better. You will need to possess determined resolve to say that some things (i.e., feedback practices, implementation strategies, how you approach change, etc.) are simply no longer accepted practice and then stay the course when champions of those unsound, outdated but traditional practices wish to challenge the decision-making process. It won't be easy, but it will be worth it. We wish you a truly memorable impact coaching journey!

Appendices

Impact Coaching Tools You Can Use

The Appendices of *Impact Coaching* contains resources that can be used to apply the content and concepts presented in the preceding chapters. Divided into four major sections, the Appendices provide an example of a feedback cue card and how this tool can be used; detailed rubrics of instructional leadership elements on which school leaders should focus their time, energy, and influence; *LinkingWalk* evidence-gathering templates to focus improvement efforts on five different high-impact instructional leadership practices; and a theories of practice self-assessment tool.

Section 1: Feedback Cue Card

Figure A1.1:   Feedback Cue Card

Figure A1.2:   Teacher Questioning Feedback Cue Card

Section 2: Instructional Leadership Elements Rubrics

Figure A2.1:   Establishing Shared Vision/Mission, Goals, and Expectations

Figure A2.2:   Strategic Resourcing

Figure A2.3:   Ensuring Teacher and Staff Effectiveness

Figure A2.4:   Leading and Participating in Teacher/Leader Learning and Development

Figure A2.5:   Providing an Orderly, Safe, and Supportive Environment

Section 3: *LinkingWalk* Evidence-Gathering Templates

Figure A3.1:   Student Voice (Teacher Clarity) Template

Figure A3.2:   Teacher Questioning/Discussion Template

Figure A3.3:   Learning Intentions (Teacher Clarity) Template

Figure A3.4:   Success Criteria (Teacher Clarity) Template

Figure A3.5:   Feedback Evidence-Gathering Template

SECTION 1: FEEDBACK CUE CARD

Effective feedback is directly connected to what teachers are to learn and to the criteria for successful learning. To ensure that *teachers* have a clear understanding of what they are expected to learn as part of the school improvement process, school leaders state the learning as *learning goals*—brief, concise statements in teacher-friendly language that describe what teachers are to know or be able to do at the end of professional growth cycle.

Similarly, teachers need to share with the school leader a clear understanding of what constitutes successful achievement of the learning goals—success criteria. These *success criteria* also need to be expressed in teacher-friendly language.

When feedback is linked to the learning goals and success criteria, it contains the information that teachers need to progress in their learning. Further, by expressing what teachers are expected to learn and what it looks like when they've learned it in language meaningful to teachers, we empower them with the ability to monitor their own progress and set individual learning goals.

Feedback Cue Card

Feedback is information that is provided by someone or something concerning the qualities of one's practice or actions (Hattie & Timperley, 2007) against a standard of performance. For instance, an evaluator or coach could provide feedback to a principal, a colleague or peer could provide an alternate strategy to the principal, a teacher could provide the principal focused feedback on his leadership impact in the school, a community member could provide parental insights, or a principal could use the Internet or a book or article to check her understanding regarding an instructional practice to help clarify ideas and understandings. Simply put, feedback can come from a variety of sources. However, the information shared becomes helpful feedback if—and only if— learners use the information to try to cause something to happen (improve performance), and the information tells them whether they are on track or need to change course. This is where the "Feedback Cue Card" becomes a handy feedback tool to assist with implementation efforts (see Figure A1.1).

The purpose of feedback is to reduce discrepancies between current understandings, performance, and the learning goal or target (Hattie & Timperley, 2007). To close this learning gap, it is critical that school leaders/teachers first have a clear goal in mind and know the success criteria (what the instructional practice looks like when performed at the proficient and higher levels) and know how well teachers are doing toward that goal. Feedback should answer three questions for the teacher/leader: *Where am I going? How am I going? Where to next?* Feedback that answers the first question, *Where am I going?* affirms the learning goal and what success would look like to accomplish this goal. This type of feedback tells the

FIGURE A1.1 Feedback Cue Card

Learning Intentions/Success Criteria:	Teacher:	Grade/Content:	
# of students in the class:		Time into the lesson:	
	Beginning:	Middle:	End:

LOOK-FORS—SUCCESS CRITERIA This teacher . . .	LEADER FEEDBACK Compare this feedback with the Look-Fors on the left.	TEACHER ACTIONS List specific ways you responded to leader feedback.
Metacognition: Look at the feedback provided and identify two specific steps to improve next time.		

Adapted from Ontario Ministry of Education (2010).

teacher specifically what he needs to improve in order to accomplish the goal. For example, imagine that a school leader and his staff agreed on a school-wide learning goal to increase the percentage of teachers who are using effective questioning strategies during classroom instruction at the proficient or higher levels from 20 percent to 75 percent.

The second question is *How am I going?* Feedback that answers this question tells the teacher what progress he is making toward accomplishing the learning goal by providing feedback on his use of the teacher questioning success criteria. That is, following a professional development session regarding effective teacher questioning strategies, the school leader might conduct a series of classroom walkthroughs during which she looks for teachers' attempts to implement the established teacher questioning success criteria, which would be loaded into the first column of the "Feedback Cue Card" (see Figure A1.2). During the classroom observation, the school leader uses "look-fors" to find the teacher's use of the success criteria and writes her observations in the second column in an effort to engage faculty in meaningful dialogue on key learning intentions achieved. That is, the leader seeks feedback from teachers, in the third column, regarding their understanding of the specific teacher questioning strategies that were used during the lesson, which concepts are clear, which concepts need further explanation, and their plan to implement the strategies in the upcoming week (the bottom row). A copy of the "Feedback Cue Card" is left for the teacher to respond and return to the school leader for follow-up.

This individualized teacher feedback will let the principal know the depth of understanding from the training regarding the strategies taught and the ability of the teachers to apply their learning in the classroom. Additionally, this feedback will give both principals and teachers insights into where their performance is currently in relationship to the goal.

The third question is *Where to next?* Feedback that answers this question helps leaders to know where they are supposed to go next as they work toward goal attainment. Specifically, where should the leader put time, effort, and attention in order to close the gap between the goal and existing faculty performance levels? Using our same example, once the principal had an understanding of the degree to which her teachers had acquired the knowledge and skills to implement teacher-questioning strategies from the original professional development session, the leader could determine next steps in differentiating the learning for her teachers.

SECTION 2: INSTRUCTIONAL LEADERSHIP ELEMENTS RUBRICS

You will recall that an important part of the impact coaching process is helping school leaders focus on and spend more of their precious time, energy, and influence on those high-impact, big-winner leadership practices that research has shown have a significant impact on student learning (Robinson, Hohepa, & Lloyd, 2009). In other words, a distinguishing feature of the impact coaching model is the idea that our coaching partnership is based on the idea that impact coaches must concentrate on high-impact instructional leadership practices. Thus, we have developed five rubrics, one for each of the five instructional leadership elements: 1) establishing a shared vision or mission, goals, and expectations; 2) strategic resourcing; 3) ensuring teacher and staff effectiveness; 4) leading and participating in teacher and leader learning and development; and 5) providing an orderly, safe, and supportive environment.

For each element, a rubric has been created, made up of rich descriptions of leadership practice that are situated along a continuum ranging from exemplary practice on one end to not meeting standards of instructional leadership practice on the other. Additionally, these descriptions of practice are further subdivided into the components of the element or its critical attributes, and several possible authentic examples of what the instructional leadership ability practice looks like according to the degree of proficiency being practiced in order to invite self-assessment and formative feedback. There are four levels of performance: exemplary, proficient, progressing, and not meeting expectations. It is our hope that these rich narrative descriptions (rubrics) of the instructional leadership elements along with clear "word picture descriptions" (Hall & Hord, 2011, p. 48) of each dimension deepen and enrich the reader's understanding of what each is expecting the school leader to know and be able to do—the expectations of instructional leadership ability.

FIGURE A1.2 Teacher Questioning Feedback Cue Card

# of students in the class:		Teacher:	Grade/Content:	
Learning Intentions/Success Criteria:			Time into the lesson:	
		Beginning:	Middle:	End:
LOOK-FORS—SUCCESS CRITERIA This teacher . . .		**LEADER FEEDBACK** Compare this feedback with the Look-Fors on the left.	**TEACHER ACTIONS** List specific ways you responded to leader feedback.	
<ul><li>Posed and posted for viewing key questions to focus students' thinking at the beginning of a lesson or series of lessons</li><li>Used questions during the lesson to monitor whether students are grasping concepts and to see what they are thinking while she or he is teaching</li><li>Asked questions to help students think about their thinking (metacognition)</li><li>Posed a question at the end of a lesson to determine if students have achieved the learning goal(s)</li><li>Waited at least three seconds between posing a question and eliciting a response</li><li>Waited at least three seconds after a student's answer before responding</li><li>Used a variety of strategies to engage all students in thinking about a question (e.g., think-pair-share, allowing time for individual reflection and collaboration, no-hands strategy)</li><li>Used closed questions to review, check for understanding, and recall facts</li><li>Used "mediative" questions (i.e., open ended, positive presuppositions about the student, judgment free; using tentative and explorative language; inviting thinking toward knowledge, comprehension, analysis, synthesis, application, evaluation, etc.) to help students become more self-directive</li><li>Used strategies to expose students' thinking (e.g., probing, clarifying, redirecting, synthesizing, summarizing)</li><li>Distributed her or his questions among all students, both those who volunteer and those who don't</li><li>Fostered an emotionally safe learning environment where students felt comfortable saying "I don't know"</li></ul>				
Metacognition: Look at the feedback provided and identify two specific steps to improve next time.				

Adapted from Ontario Ministry of Education (2010).

Instructional Leadership Element Rubrics

FIGURE A2.1 Establishing Shared Vision/Mission, Goals, and Expectations

	EXEMPLARY	PROFICIENT	PROGRESSING	NOT MEETING EXPECTATIONS
Rubric Description	The impact of leader's actions help others within the district/school apply the nine theories of practice—powerful behaviors, ways of thinking—to their actions, thereby increasing leadership capacity within the district/school.	The impact of leader's actions is both adequate, necessary, and meets the school's needs. Actions relevant to this element are appropriate reflections of quality work with only normal variations.	The impact of leader's actions reflects performance that shows potential but lacks sufficient proficiencies to improve student learning, instructional practice, and/or other responsibilities.	The impact of leader's actions demonstrates that she or he either does not understand what is required for proficiency or, through action or inaction, that she or he chooses not to work toward proficiency.
	In addition to possessing all of the qualities of a "proficient" leader . . . The leader routinely shares with others in the district examples of nonjudgmental dialogue skills she or he has used with staff that check and build commitment to goals, as well as specific problem-resolving strategies that have contributed to a shared understanding of the current situation, which avoids blame and invites a collaborative approach to improvement efforts with colleagues. As a result of sharing these proficient practices with others in the district, there is evidence that by helping others acquire and use the leader's knowledge and skills, the leader also is achieving at proficient or higher performance levels on this element.	**The leader herself or himself or through her or his designees** sets, communicates, and monitors a few (two to three) specific school-wide learning goals, standards, and expectations that have been embedded in school and classroom routines and procedures. She or he develops transparent processes that cause teachers and school leaders to co-create the school-wide learning goals. She or he also inquires, at an early stage, about staff capacity to achieve these prioritized goals. Toward that end, the leader goes to exceptional lengths to listen to staff describe their points of view. Furthermore, she or he guarantees the transparent and shared involvement of staff and others in the process so that there is clarity, consensus, and commitment about the goals.	**The leader herself or himself** sets, communicates, and monitors several (three to four) specific school-wide learning goals, standards, and expectations. However, she or he may not be embedded in school and classroom routines and procedures. Given that she or he sets challenging goals without considering teachers' capacity to achieve them, anxiety exists among some staff. The leader attempts to involve staff in the goal-setting process, with uneven results. Consequently, there may be a lack of clarity, consensus, and commitment to the goals.	**The leader herself or himself** imposes numerous (less than four) poorly worded, vague learning goals, standards, and expectations. Consequently, she or he is not embedded in school and classroom routines and procedures. Because the leader is unaware of teachers' capacity to achieve the goals she or he has raised counterproductive levels of anxiety and resentment among staff. The leader makes no attempt to involve staff in the goal-setting process. Thus, there is a lack of clarity, consensus, and commitment to the goals.

Critical Attributes

EXEMPLARY	PROFICIENT	PROGRESSING	NOT MEETING EXPECTATIONS
The leader herself or himself . . .	The leader herself or himself or through her or his designees . . .	The leader herself or himself or through her or his designees . . .	The leader herself or himself or through her or his designees . . .
• Reflects on and secures feedback about the effectiveness of the collaborative problem-solving (i.e., expressing her or his own values and commitments and listening to those of others) strategies used to reach agreement among teachers about the importance of the current learning and/or performance goals	• Engages in collaborative problem-solving (i.e., expressing her or his own values and commitments and listening to those of others) strategies to reach agreement among teachers about the importance of the current learning and/or performance goals	• Attempts to engage in collaborative problem-solving strategies, but skills in this area are novice, so agreements among teachers as to the importance of the current goals are somewhat mixed, with some agreement and some disagreement	• Attempts to mitigate conflict and/or gain wider staff commitment by setting far too many goals that lack specificity. In doing so, the leader sends mixed messages about what has priority and what does not.
• Reflects on and secures feedback about the process used to help staff understand the need for, commitment to, and belief they have the capacity to achieve priority goals	• Eliminates stress that may result from multiple conflicting priorities and work overload by focusing on the two to three most important improvement needs	• Has begun to prioritize the school's improvement efforts by focusing on three to four school goals	• Establishes goals that are imposed rather than co-created collaboratively through discussion with staff
• Uses and shares with colleagues the information collected through the feedback process to improve others' leadership performance around setting goals, expectations, building commitment, and capacity	• Creates alignment between overarching school goals and the goals set by content area or grade-level leaders	• Understands the importance of having teachers participate in the construction of school goals but has yet to develop an effective process for doing so	• Does not check others' commitments to the goals
	• Generates ownership among teachers about the learning goals for which they are responsible by engaging teachers in a coconstruction of the overarching school goals	• Attempts to create alignment between school goals and personal goals and compromises due to lack of agreement among teachers	• Is unaware of alignment needs between school and personal goals, which creates a competitive climate
	• Builds personal commitment among teachers to achieving the goals for which they are responsible		

153

	EXEMPLARY	PROFICIENT	PROGRESSING	NOT MEETING EXPECTATIONS
Critical Attributes (continued)		• Ensures teachers have the knowledge and skills they need to achieve the goals for which they are responsible • Sees to it that teachers have the resources needed to achieve the goals for which they are responsible	• Is unable to secure broad (i.e., a majority) teacher commitment to goals as they remain uncertain how to reach the goals	• Is unable to secure teacher commitment to the goals as staff don't understand how what they have differs from what they want
Real-World Examples	• *The leader, when asked, identifies at least one colleague at another school within the district she or he has personally coached or mentored regarding the goal-setting process.* • *Other leaders in the district credit this leader as a mentor and reason for their success in this element.* • *When asked, the leader is able to articulately describe the process she or he has used to secure feedback as to the effectiveness of the goal-setting process.* • *The leader is able to provide evidence of how she or he has used the feedback from the goal-setting process to inform next steps*	• *A majority of teachers indicate that the leaders in this building invite them into discussions to build a collective rather than an imposed set of priority goals.* • *A common refrain from teachers in this building is "Leaders in this building listen to my concerns."* • *A majority of teachers strongly agree or agree with the importance of the current learning goals.* • *When asked, most teachers can articulate how what they have now differs from what they truly want—thus, a need to change.* • *When asked, a majority of teachers say they are clear about the learning goals for which they are responsible.* • *A majority of teachers feel personally committed to achieving the goals for which they are responsible.* • *The leader and/or the leader's designees, when asked, can articulate what they have learned from listening to the concerns of others and how that impacted the results of the goal-setting process.*	• *Teachers generally agree that leaders in this building are beginning to involve them in the goal-setting discussions.* • *When asked, teachers express mixed views as to the importance of current learning goals.* • *Many teachers, when asked, are unable to articulate the reason for current learning goals or the need for change.* • *Teachers express mixed views as to how the goals connect to their day-to-day work.* • *Fewer than half of the teachers express commitment to the current learning goals.*	• *When asked, most teachers indicate that the leaders in this building tend to impose goals and expectations without discussion.* • *A majority of teachers strongly disagree or disagree with the importance of the current learning goals.* • *When asked, a majority of teachers express frustration with the multiple conflicting priorities and work overload.* • *Most teachers are unclear about expectations and how the goals connect to them personally.* • *A majority of teachers lack commitment to achieving the goals.*

FIGURE A2.2 Strategic Resourcing

	EXEMPLARY	PROFICIENT	PROGRESSING	NOT MEETING EXPECTATIONS
Rubric Description	The impact of leader's actions help others within the district/school apply the nine theories of practice—powerful behaviors, ways of thinking—to their actions, thereby increasing leadership capacity within the district/school.	The impact of leader's actions is both adequate, necessary, and meets the school needs. Actions relevant to this element are appropriate reflections of quality work with only normal variations.	The impact of leader's actions reflects performance that shows potential but lacks sufficient proficiencies to improve student learning, instructional practice, and/or other responsibilities.	The impact of leader's actions demonstrates that she or he either does not understand what is required for proficiency or, through her or his action or inaction, that she or he chooses not to work toward proficiency.
	In addition to possessing all of the qualities of a "proficient" leader The leader provides clear, convincing, and consistent evidence that she or he ensures school-wide effective use of strategic alignment of resources (human, financial, and material) and individually monitors the impact on student achievement. The leader is skilled in the area of human relations and helps others throughout the district acquire and use these practices so that they too can achieve at the proficient or higher performance levels on this element.	**The leader herself or himself or through her or his designees** uses the strategic alignment of resources (human, financial, and material) to prioritize and justify the allocation of resources. Leaders can determine the type of expertise required to achieve school goals and can legitimately recruit such expertise from within or outside the school. They work to develop relationships with community, higher education institutions, staff developers, and other schools to increase networks of support and resources available to the school. The leader continually evaluates the effectiveness of instructional programs being implemented, instructional resources being used, and the impact on student achievement results. The organization's priority goals drive leaders' use of time and how they organize budgets,	**The leader herself or himself** understands the importance of using strategic alignment of resources (human, financial, and material) to justify the allocation of resources. Because resources have not been prioritized, she or he has diluted efforts to ensure that resources are aligned to school priority needs. The leader inconsistently collects feedback to help determine the effectiveness of instructional programs being implemented, instructional resources being used, and impact on student achievement results. The leader has some understanding of the impact of the strategic	**The leader herself or himself** has little or no understanding of the importance of using strategic alignment of resources to prioritize and justify the allocation of resources. Resources are not used to support school priorities, and the leader has not asked for feedback from staff or students regarding the use of resources in the school. The leader has little to no understanding of the impact of the strategic resourcing decisions she or he is making on staff or

(Continued)

155

	EXEMPLARY	PROFICIENT	PROGRESSING	NOT MEETING EXPECTATIONS
Rubric Description (continued)		schedules, instructional resources, professional development, and staffing. The leader demonstrates the ability to "say no" to funding opportunities that overload teachers and detract from priority goals and abandons programs/practices not aligned with school goals. These leaders are skilled in the area of relational trust and are continually mindful of the impact of the strategic resourcing decisions they are making on their staff.	resourcing decisions she or he is making on staff and has yet to make the needed leadership changes.	students and has not yet or has decided not to make the needed leadership changes.
Critical Attributes	**The leader herself or himself …** • Consistently saves resources of time and money for the organization and proactively redistributes those resources to help the organization achieve its strategic priorities • Continually secures and reflects on feedback from staff and students regarding the allocation of resources to support school priorities and student achievement • Uses and shares with colleagues the feedback collected and modifications made to her	**The leader herself or himself or through her or his designees …** • Routinely evaluates the degree to which the existing allocations of time, staffing, and money are having the desired impact on the school's priority targets • Ensures sustained funding for instructional priorities • Ensures that staff recruitment is based on clear descriptions of teacher effectiveness found within the district's teacher evaluation framework and the students' areas of highest needs • Sees to it that the staff recruitment and selection process is subject to an in-depth review and evaluation for continuous improvement purposes	**The leader herself or himself …** • Irregularly evaluates the degree to which the existing allocation of time, staffing, and money are impacting the school's priority targets. • Is beginning to think about a plan for sustaining funding • Has yet to develop a consistent process for the recruitment/hiring of teachers • Implements the district-wide teacher evaluation framework but does not evaluate the effectiveness of her or his efforts	**The leader herself or himself …** • Has no clear plan for strategically focusing resources on instructional priorities • Has little or no record of monitoring the effectiveness of staff use of instructional time, schedules, teacher evaluation framework, and budgets

Critical Attributes			
EXEMPLARY	**PROFICIENT**	**PROGRESSING**	**NOT MEETING EXPECTATIONS**
or his leadership practices so colleagues' practices become as skilled as the leader's • Has established processes to leverage existing limited funds and increase capacity through grants, donations, and community resourcefulness for the school and district • Is a trusted confidant with district and school leaders and is called upon to share strategic resourcing strategies and systems with other colleagues to improve their overall performance	• Articulates the relationship between instructional programs being implemented and instructional resources being used and student achievement results being obtained • Knows how time is distributed within her or his school and uses this knowledge to make certain that instructional time is restructured to allocate high-quality instruction to students in the areas of highest need • Routinely assesses the degree to which relational trust exists among staff in order to successfully navigate the human element of the strategic resources allocation process while working to reorganize the people, time, and money in her or his schools to match the schools' priorities	• Knows the importance of having a relationship between instructional programs being implemented and instructional resources but has yet to articulate the relationship • Has a limited understanding of how instructional time is used throughout the school • Has not formally assessed the degree to which relational trust exists among staff and is not thoroughly aware of the impact of the strategic resourcing decisions she or he is making on staff	• Has not secured any additional funding for the school • Is unaware of the degree of relational trust among staff in the school

(Continued)

EXEMPLARY	PROFICIENT	PROGRESSING	NOT MEETING EXPECTATIONS
• Results indicate the positive impact of redeployed resources in achieving strategic priorities at the district and school level.	• School financial records reflect alignment of spending with instructional needs.	• Teachers generally agree that leaders involve them in decisions regarding the use of school resources and that the use of these resources is beginning to have a greater alignment with school priorities.	• Teachers self-report that they feel overloaded and are detracted from priority goals due to ineffective use of resources.
• The leader, when asked, identifies at least one colleague at another school within the district she or he has personally coached or mentored regarding the strategic resourcing and has evidence to support that colleague's change in leadership practices.	• Faculty indicate clear protocols for accessing school resources.	• Many teachers, when asked, are unable to articulate a consistent process for the hiring of teachers at their schools.	• Most teachers, when asked, report that they are not aware of the hiring practices used at their schools.
• Other leaders in the district credit this leader as a mentor and the reason for their success in the goal-setting process.	• Teachers self-report that the school recruiting and interview processes are fair and transparent.	• The budget reflects that the leader has made minimal attempts to secure added resources.	• Office budget documents reflect that dollars are not committed or used until late in the year or are carried over to another year due to lack of planning and coordination. There is no focus on resources used on school improvement priorities.
• The leader provides documentation reporting that additional dollars from grants and outside sources have been utilized to support school priorities.	• School improvement plan and budget expenditures are directly aligned.	• The budget reflects inconsistent use in focusing resources on school improvement priorities.	• Schedules and calendars do not reflect attention to instructional priorities.
• When asked, the leader can articulate and provide evidence of the process she or he used to secure feedback from staff and students as to the effective school use of strategic resources.	• Leader's documents reveal recurring involvement in aligning time, facility use, and human resources with priority school needs.	• Less than half of the staff schedules and calendars reflect attention to instructional priorities.	• The budget shows no attempt to secure outside resources.
• Students self-report that they have all of the resources needed at the school to successfully accomplish their learning goals.	• Schedules and calendars reflect attention to instructional priorities.	• Fewer than half of the students asked felt that they had the resources needed to support their learning goals at school.	
	• School-wide teacher questionnaire results reveal satisfaction with resources provided for instructional and faculty development.		
	• Students acknowledge an adequate amount of instructional time is available to them in areas of highest need.		
	• Teachers can describe the process for accessing and spending money in support of instructional priorities.		
	• The leader and or the leader's designee, when asked, can articulate what she or he has learned from securing staff feedback and can share leadership changes she or he has made as a result of the feedback.		

Real-World Examples

	EXEMPLARY	PROFICIENT	PROGRESSING	NOT MEETING EXPECTATIONS
Rubric Description	The impact of leader's actions help others within the district/school apply the nine theories of practice—powerful behaviors, ways of thinking—to their actions, thereby increasing leadership capacity within the district/school.	The impact of leader's actions is both adequate and necessary and meets the school needs. Actions relevant to this element are appropriate reflections of quality work with only normal variations.	The impact of leader's actions reflects performance that shows potential but lacks sufficient proficiencies to improve student learning, instructional practice, and/or other responsibilities.	The impact of leader's actions demonstrate that she or he either does not understand what is required for proficiency or, through action or inaction, that she or he chooses not to work toward proficiency.
	In addition to possessing all of the qualities of a "proficient" leader . . . The leader provides clear, convincing, and consistent evidence that she or he builds the capacity of staff to effectively develop, adapt, and implement rigorous curriculum, implement a variety of rigorous instructional strategies and pedagogical methods, adapt instruction and assessment, and use multiple sources of disaggregated quantitative and qualitative data to address student-learning needs that will close achievement gaps.	**The leader herself or himself or through her or his designees** works directly with and tirelessly for teachers to plan, orchestrate, and evaluate teachers and leaders and leading. She or he engages in four sets of interdependent leadership practices to ensure the quality of teaching: • First, orchestrates a coherent instructional program, a by-product of her or his skill at working with teachers to link their curriculum to stated learning goals. She or he uses common instructional strategies with fidelity and coordinates the curriculum and assessments from grade to grade. She or he ensures that school-sponsored support programs are linked to curriculum, instruction, and assessment within and across	**The leader herself or himself** works directly with teachers to plan, orchestrate, and evaluate teachers. However, her or his engagement in key leadership practices to ensure the quality of teaching is haphazard resulting in • The development of a plan for a coherent instructional program that may not be fully implemented yet. She or he understands the importance of using common instructional strategies but either doesn't know where to start or tries to focus on too many at one time. Coordination of the curriculum and	**The leader herself or himself** does not know and/or chooses not to interact with staff about planning, orchestrating, and evaluating teachers. Consequently, she or he does not know and/or • Is unaware of curriculum needs and has little or no interaction with staff concerning assessment and knowledge and/or skills of assessment literacy and data analysis • Chooses not to interact with staff and teaching with research-based instructional strategies to increase student achievement

(Continued)

	EXEMPLARY	PROFICIENT	PROGRESSING	NOT MEETING EXPECTATIONS
Rubric Description (continued)	Moreover, she or he helps others throughout the district acquire and use these practices so that they too achieve at the proficient or higher performance levels on this particular element.	grades. Leaders strategically accept and reject programs and initiatives that don't support the school's focus. • Second, helps teachers examine together how well students are doing, link this to how well they are teaching (i.e., calculating effect size by cohorts, teachers, and students), and then make improvements based upon those ongoing *Linking Talks*. • Third, has an acute awareness of teaching and learning needs in her or his schools because of a frequent presence within classrooms with subsequent feedback to teachers. • Fourth, she or he has a systematic process for monitoring and then using student performance data to inform continuous program improvement.	assessments from grade to grade is occurring but in a limited number of areas. • Together with teachers, she or he examines how well students are doing; however, she or he may not be linking this to instruction. • She or he understands the importance of frequent classroom observations, but it occurs infrequently and may not always include feedback. • The absence of a systematic process for monitoring and then using student performance data complicates improvement efforts.	to high levels for all students • Focuses primarily on managerial functions of her or his role, which tend to trump classroom observations; thus, the leader's presence in classrooms occurs infrequently, with little to no feedback to teachers • Is indifferent to data and does not use data to change schedules, instruction, curriculum, or leadership practices
Critical Attributes	**The leader herself or himself …** • Builds the capacity of faculty to effectively develop, adapt, and implement rigorous College/Career Standards (CCS) to effectively address all students' learning needs	**The leader herself or himself or through her or his designees …** • Establishes, with teachers, clarity as to which high-priority CCS are orchestrated horizontally within and vertically across all grade levels • Determines, with teachers, that the teaching of high-priority CCS is driven by the use of a common instructional framework	**The leader herself or himself …** • Is aware of the need for high-priority CCS; however, the school is still in the planning stages of developing its priority standards • Has yet to identify and implement a common instructional framework	**The leader herself or himself …** • Does not know and/or is uninterested in knowing of the need to identify high-priority academic standards

Critical Attributes	EXEMPLARY	PROFICIENT	PROGRESSING	NOT MEETING EXPECTATIONS
	• Builds the capacity of staff to effectively implement a variety of rigorous strategies and pedagogical methods (i.e., ≥ 0.40 ES) that help students exceed expectations • Helps faculty adapt instruction and assessments to ensure that all students master content and demonstrate at least a year's growth (i.e., ≥ 0.40 ES) for a year's worth of instruction • Uses multiple sources of quantitative (i.e., percentage of students achieving proficiently or higher on local assessments, percentage of faculty implementing the current professional	• Confirms, with teachers, a close relationship between the things teachers really value and the teacher-made assessments used • Achieves agreement with teachers as to what effective teaching and learning is • Agrees to use student evaluations of teachers as an index of teaching quality, the results of which drive instructional improvement • Systematically measures the percentage of teachers whose yearly effect size is ≥ 0.40 ES—teacher effectiveness • Ascertains a high degree of understanding among the staff as to which instructional and leadership strategies and curricular programs are having the greatest impact versus the least impact on student achievement and use the results to inform next steps • Establishes a high frequency (i.e., monthly) and quality (i.e., making	• Has yet to analyze the degree to which teacher-made assessments align with teacher needs • Is aware of what effective teaching and learning looks like; however, agreement with teachers on these matters is not yet evident • Doesn't understand the research on student evaluations of teachers as an index of teaching quality • Is not certain which instructional and leadership strategies and curricular programs are having the greatest impact on student achievement • Understands the need to have teachers engage in dialogue about the relationship of teaching practices to student	• Leaves the matter of an instructional framework up to individual teachers to determine • Determines what effective teaching and learning looks like, and these views are reflected in teacher evaluations • Is unaware of which instructional and leadership strategies and curricular programs are having the greatest impact on student achievement • Believes that the qualities students bring with them to school are largely unchangeable by their teachers • Is in classrooms less than ten times a month observing teachers' work, with no feedback to teachers

(Continued)

	EXEMPLARY	PROFICIENT	PROGRESSING	NOT MEETING EXPECTATIONS
Critical Attributes (continued)	development training at the proficient or higher levels) and qualitative data (i.e., video diaries, focus groups, interviews) to assess and monitor learning; creates systems for consistent monitoring and frequent (i.e., monthly) collection of data and uses data appropriately to identify student achievement trends and patterns, prioritize needs, and drive improvement efforts	critical sense of teaching and learning) of *LinkingTalks* that occur among teachers and leaders within the school • Is in classrooms twenty to sixty times a week observing teachers' work, with subsequent feedback to teachers • Regularly monitors and uses student achievement data to determine program effectiveness	achievement, but this practice is not school-wide • Is in classrooms ten to twenty times a month observing teachers' work, with feedback to teachers at times • Inconsistently monitors and uses student achievement data to determine program effectiveness	• Rarely monitors and uses student achievement data to determine program effectiveness
Real-World Examples	• *"Our principal ensures that all students get high-quality teachers."* • *The leader, when asked, identifies at least one colleague at another school within the district she or he has personally coached or mentored regarding the his or her knowledge and skills in ensuring teacher effectiveness.*	• *"My school administrator leads formal discussions concerning instruction and student achievement."* • *Understands and uses student data to collaboratively diagnose and resolve teaching problems and to set future goals* • *"My school administrator has a research-based understanding of how students learn."*	• *"My principal promotes discussion of instructional issues."* • *Understands and uses student data to diagnose and resolve teaching problems and to set future goals* • *"My principal's understanding of how students learn is based on her personal experience."*	• *"My principal believes teachers discuss instructional issues when they meet in their content area teams."* • *Uses student data to highlight success in or problems with teaching* • *Student learning is viewed largely as a by-product of students' demographics.*

EXEMPLARY	PROFICIENT	PROGRESSING	NOT MEETING EXPECTATIONS
• *Other leaders in the district credit this leader as a mentor and reason for their success in developing and implementing effective feedback systems* • *"When teachers are struggling, my principal provides support for them."* • *Other leaders in the district credit this leader as a mentor and reason for their success in using multiple sources of quantitative (i.e., percentage of students achieving proficiently or higher on local assessments, percentage of faculty implementing the current professional development training at the proficient or higher levels) and qualitative data (i.e., video diaries, focus groups, interviews) to assess and monitor learning.*	• *"My school administrator uses clearly communicated criteria for judging my performance."* • *"My school administrator makes frequent, at least monthly, classroom observations and provides feedback regarding my instruction."* • *"My school administrator's appraisal of my teaching performance helps me improve my performance."* • *"My school administrator is accessible to discuss matters dealing with instruction."* • *Establishes procedures that ensure faculty will regularly use evidence to review student progress* • *"My school administrator assists faculty in calculating effect size and interpreting test results."* • *"My school administrator clearly defines standards for instructional practices."*	• *"My principal uses the district teacher evaluation criteria for judging my performance."* • *"My principal makes three to four classroom observations per year and provides advice or praise regarding my instruction."* • *"My principal's appraisal of my teaching performance validates for me what I know I do well."* • *"My principal encourages me to discuss matters dealing with instruction with my grade-level leader."* • *Directs faculty to use evidence from the state assessment to determine student progress*	• *"My principal makes one to two classroom observations per year and provides advice or praise regarding my instruction."* • *"My principal's appraisal of my teaching performance is a compliance task."* • *"My principal assumes that if I need to discuss instructional matters, I will do so with my content area teams."* • *Uses student data as a lever to demand better instructional performance*

FIGURE A2.4 Leading and Participating In Teacher/Leader Learning and Development

	EXEMPLARY	PROFICIENT	PROGRESSING	NOT MEETING EXPECTATIONS
Rubric Description	The impact of leader's actions helps others within the district/school apply the nine theories of practice—powerful behaviors, ways of thinking—to their actions, thereby increasing leadership capacity within the district/school.	The impact of leader's actions is both adequate and necessary and meets the school needs. Actions relevant to this element are appropriate reflections of quality work with only normal variations.	The impact of leader's actions reflects performance that shows potential but lacks sufficient proficiencies to improve student learning, instructional practice, and/or other responsibilities.	The impact of leader's actions demonstrate that she or he either does not understand what is required for proficiency or, through action or inaction, that she or he chooses not to work toward proficiency.
	In addition to possessing all of the qualities of a "proficient" leader The leader has clearly demonstrated a record of differentiated job-embedded professional learning focused on implementation of instructional priorities and faculty and student needs. Teachers and leaders routinely share instructional practices, and teachers in the building, as well as school leaders, are asked to share their expertise and experiences within the school, as well as with other schools in the district, to improve the practices of others. Teachers, along with school leaders, see themselves as learners and have established a high degree of relational trust.	**The leader herself or himself or through her or his designees** impacts student achievement by leading and participating in professional learning experiences with staff. She or he applies the professional learning research that shifts teachers' practices and promotes the learning of students. She or he identifies, resources, and implements high-quality collaborative opportunities for teachers, promoting teacher learning in ways that result in changed pedagogical methods and advancements in student learning. Learning includes a specific focus on both student and teacher/leader learning needs, emphasizing the importance of the relationship between instructional/leadership practice and student achievement, offering teachers valuable content that integrates both theory and practice, employing the services of external expertise, and providing time—time for teachers to have multiple opportunities to practice, receive feedback	**The leader herself or himself** attempts to implement and participate in professional learning experiences but has yet to connect the school plan to the research on priority instructional needs and to manage her or his time to be part of the trainings. Time for professional learning is provided but is not a consistent priority and usually takes place during faculty meetings. There is limited evidence of job-embedded professional learning, and teachers have little ownership over the process of advocating for and determining their needs. It is not clear if there is a connection between student	**The leader herself or himself** provides and/or supports large-group unfocused professional learning that reflects little or no evidence of acknowledgment of individual faculty needs or alignment of faculty needs to student achievement needs. Professional learning practices at the school are not monitored and are not necessarily aligned with the school priorities. Staff feel fragmented and unfocused and do not know where to turn to for instructional support.

	EXEMPLARY	PROFICIENT	PROGRESSING	NOT MEETING EXPECTATIONS
Rubric Description	School achievement improvement data reflect the leader and teacher's focus on specific professional learning goals.	(i.e., six months to five years), and have ongoing support as they work to implement new learning. Provides strategic planning whereby leaders and teachers share leadership practices, which strengthens the professional community, resulting in stronger teachers' working relationships and higher student achievement.	achievement and professional development at the school.	
Critical Attributes	**The leader herself or himself …** • Is well versed in the effective professional learning research and has clear, convincing documented evidence showing the degree to which student learning has been impacted as a result of changes in pedagogy coming from professional learning. As a result, she or he has been asked by district and/or school colleagues to be a coach and/or mentor to others. • Is actively involved as a leader and learner during professional learning opportunities at both the school and district levels	**The leader herself or himself or through her or his designees …** • Ensures that effective professional learning, as described within the research, drives the design, selection, and implementation of teacher professional learning opportunities • Routinely participates with teachers as the leader, learner, or both during professional learning opportunities • Ensures that as a group and as subgroups teachers examine together how well students are doing, relate this to how	**The leader herself or himself …** • Attempts to use effective professional learning to drive the design, selection, and implementation of teacher learning but has yet to develop a cohesive plan • Inconsistently participates with teachers as the leader, learner, or both during professional learning opportunities • Has set up planning time for teachers to meet to examine how well students are doing but has not helped teachers see the relationship between student achievement and their teaching to make the necessary adjustments in pedagogy	**The leader herself or himself …** • Is not aware of the effective professional development research; therefore, she or he randomly designs professional learning opportunities for teachers with no attention to monitoring the effectiveness of the professional development • Is absent from professional learning opportunities for teachers or leaders • Leader and teacher deliberate practice plans do not align with high-priority student achievement needs

(Continued)

EXEMPLARY	PROFICIENT	PROGRESSING	NOT MEETING EXPECTATIONS
• Ensures that teachers' and leaders' deliberate practice plans are linked to student learning needs and has helped teachers and other school leaders understand the relationship between student learning and their teaching by helping others track achievement and adult data within their school at monthly planning meetings. The leader has also helped other school leaders in writing, implementing, and monitoring their deliberate practice plans. • Has developed and implemented a comprehensive teacher support plan based on staff needs, strengths, and areas of expertise to distribute leadership throughout the school. This plan has been used as a model within other schools in the district.	they are teaching, and then make the necessary adjustments in pedagogy • Articulates clear connections between the planned professional development and students' learning needs • Ensures that teachers' and leaders' deliberate practice plans (i.e., professional growth plans) are linked to student-learning needs • Articulates the system used to identify teachers with expertise needed to help colleagues address targeted teaching problems • Routinely measures the degree to which student learning has been impacted as a result of changes in pedagogy coming from professional learning	• Has yet to develop clear connections between the planned professional development and students' learning needs • Ensures that leaders' deliberate practice plans are linked to student learning needs but has yet to link teachers' plans to student achievement • Has developed a system to identify teachers with expertise to help colleagues address targeted teaching problems, but teachers are unaware of how to secure support • Has not formally measured the degree to which student learning has been impacted as a result of changes in pedagogy coming from professional learning	• Uses only the assigned building coach or other assistant principals to mentor teachers • Provides minimal opportunities for faculty to engage in collegial professional development processes in the school

Critical Attributes

EXEMPLARY	PROFICIENT	PROGRESSING	NOT MEETING EXPECTATIONS
• *The leader, when asked, identifies at least one colleague at another school within the district she or he has personally coached or mentored regarding the goal-setting process.* • *Other leaders in the district credit this leader as a mentor and reason for their success in the goal-setting process.* • *When asked, the leader is able to articulately describe the process she or he has used to secure feedback as to the effectiveness of the goal-setting process.* • *The leader is able to provide evidence of how she or he has used the feedback from the goal-setting process to inform next steps.*	• *A majority of teachers indicate that the leaders in this building invite them into discussions to build a collective rather than imposed set of priority goals.* • *A common refrain from teachers in this building is "Leaders in this building listen to my concerns."* • *A majority of teachers strongly agree or agree with the importance of the current learning goals.* • *When asked, most teachers can articulate how what they have now differs from what they truly want—thus, a need to change.* • *When asked, a majority of teachers say they are clear about the learning goals for which they are responsible.* • *A majority of teachers feel personally committed to achieving the goals for which they are responsible.* • *The leader, when asked, can articulate what she or he has learned from listening to the concerns of others and how that impacted the results of the goal-setting process.*	• *Teachers generally agree that leaders in this building are beginning to involve them in the goal-setting discussions.* • *When asked, teachers express mixed views as to the importance of current learning goals.* • *Many teachers, when asked, are unable to articulate the reason for current learning goals or the need for change.* • *Teachers express mixed views as to how the goals connect to their day-to-day work.* • *Fewer than half of the teachers express commitment to the current learning goals.*	• *When asked, most teachers indicate that the leaders in this building tend to impose goals and expectations without discussion.* • *A majority of teachers strongly disagree or disagree with the importance of the current learning goals.* • *When asked, a majority of teachers express frustration with the multiple conflicting priorities and work overload.* • *Most teachers are unclear about expectations and how the goals connect to them personally.* • *A majority of teachers lack commitment to achieving the goals.*

FIGURE A2.5 Providing an Orderly, Safe, and Supportive Environment

	EXEMPLARY	PROFICIENT	PROGRESSING	NOT MEETING EXPECTATIONS
Rubric Description	The impact of leader's actions helps others within the district/school apply the nine theories of practice—powerful behaviors, ways of thinking—to her or his actions, thereby increasing leadership capacity within the district/school.	The impact of leader's actions is both adequate and necessary and meets the school needs. Actions relevant to this element are appropriate reflections of quality work with only normal variations.	The impact of leader's actions reflects performance that shows potential but lacks sufficient proficiencies to improve student learning, instructional practice, and/or other responsibilities.	The impact of leader's actions demonstrate that she or he either does not understand what is required for proficiency or, through action or inaction, that she or he chooses not to work toward proficiency.
	In addition to possessing all of the qualities of a "proficient" leader . . . The leader provides clear, convincing, and consistent evidence that she or he ensures the creation and maintenance of a learning environment in which important academic and social goals can be pursued and achieved by focusing her or his time, knowledge and skills on three specific tasks within this element. More importantly, she or he helps others throughout the district acquire and use these practices so that they too achieve at the proficient or higher performance levels on this element. The leader involves the school and community to collect data on curricular and extracurricular student involvement to assure equal opportunity for student participation.	**The leader herself or himself or through her or his designees** creates an orderly, safe, and supportive environment in which important academic as well as social goals can be pursued and achieved by focusing her or his time, knowledge, and skills on three specific tasks within this element: (a) setting and enforcing clear expectations, (b) protecting teaching time and buffering teachers from outside pressures, and (c) addressing staff conflict quickly and effectively. In an orderly environment, teachers, leaders, and students can focus on learning as their highest priority because clear and consistently enforced social expectations and discipline codes have been established.	**The leader herself or himself** understands the importance of creating an environment in which important academic as well as social goals can be pursued and achieved; however, the leader and her or his leadership team may not be sufficiently focused on one or more of the following tasks within this element: (a) setting and enforcing clear expectations, (b) protecting teaching time and buffering teachers from outside pressures, and (c) addressing staff conflict quickly and effectively. As a result, teachers, leaders, and students struggle to adequately focus on learning as their first priority.	**The leader herself or himself** demonstrates little to no understanding of the importance of creating an environment in which important academic as well as social goals can be pursued and achieved. She or he is clearly not focused or is unwilling to focus on critical tasks within this element to guarantee an orderly, safe, and supportive environment. As a result, teachers, leaders, and students are not able to adequately focus their time and energies on learning as the top priority.

	EXEMPLARY	PROFICIENT	PROGRESSING	NOT MEETING EXPECTATIONS
Critical Attributes	The leader herself or himself . . . • Shares with colleagues how the information collected through the feedback processes (i.e., student, faculty, and parent surveys) is used to improve the learning environment. Consequently, the leader can demonstrate how others' leadership performance in this element has also improved. • Regularly reviews the need for changes to expectations, structures, rules, and expectations by engaging staff, students, and parents in a dialogue using	The leader herself or himself or through her or his designees . . . • Creates multiple (two to three) opportunities for students to provide feedback about the quality of their classroom and school experience • Regularly makes use of student surveys as to students' sense of safety in a variety of in-school and out-of-school arenas, as well as their perceptions of bullying and intimidation • Uses the results from student survey information to improve the quality of school life • Provides multiple (two to three) illustrative examples of actions taken that have redefined procedures and responsibilities designed to continuously reduce the potential risk to students throughout the school • Makes certain there are minimal interruptions to teaching time and buffers teaching faculty from distractions to their work • Provides evidence that parent involvement efforts are focused on increasing parental	The leader herself or himself . . . • Tends to rely on large-scale survey data only to understand how students view their school experience • Uses the results from student survey information to improve the school environment. But because the feedback process is infrequent, the improvements to safety may not be very timely. • Struggles to provide multiple illustrative examples of actions taken to reduce the potential risk to students throughout the school • Understands the importance of buffering teaching faculty from distractions to their work, but efforts are inconsistent • Provides some evidence that parent involvement efforts are focused on increasing parental engagement, but the focus	The leader herself or himself . . . • Is unaware or uninterested in securing student perceptions regarding the school environment • Provides some examples of actions taken to reduce the potential risk to students throughout the school, but these tend to be reactionary in nature and not the result of data collection • Does not see the connection between the learning environment and student achievement • Parent involvement efforts are focused on such things as back-to-school nights, parent–teacher conferences, award programs, and so forth, and not necessarily on increasing parental engagement on the educational work of the school. • Demonstrates either no awareness of potential problems and/or areas of conflict within the school or chooses to tolerate, protect,

(Continued)

	EXEMPLARY	PROFICIENT	PROGRESSING	NOT MEETING EXPECTATIONS
Critical Attributes	evaluated data from prior feedback sessions. • Often (at least two times per year) serves as a mentor for peers within the district/school in the area of giving and receiving tough messages to improve their knowledge and skill in this area.	engagement with the educational work of the school • Systematically evaluates the effectiveness of parent involvement and uses the results of the evaluation to improve those efforts • Identifies and resolves conflict quickly and effectively rather than allowing it to worsen • Co-establishes with teachers and students clear and consistently enforced social expectations and discipline codes	may not be on the educational work of the school and does not evaluate the effectiveness of their efforts • Demonstrates awareness of potential problems and/or areas of conflict within the school but may not skillfully or quickly resolve the conflict • Has developed school-wide social expectations and discipline codes; however, they are inconsistently administered	or avoid confrontation, believing they will resolve themselves or go away • Expectations are vague, and discipline codes tend to be established teacher by teacher, which means there is no consistency.
Real-World Examples	• The leader, when asked, identifies at least one colleague at another school within the district she or he has personally coached or mentored regarding the establishment of an orderly, safe, and supportive environment.	• A majority of students surveyed indicate that the leaders in this building invite them into discussions to get a sense of safety in a variety of in-school and out-of-school areas, as well as their perceptions of bullying and intimidation. • A common refrain from students in this building is "Leaders in this building listen to and use my point of view regarding school safety to improve the learning environment."	• Students generally agree that leaders in this building are beginning to involve them in the school safety discussions. • A common refrain from students in this building is "Leaders in this building ask for my opinion regarding school safety; however, I am not certain they are using my thoughts to improve the learning environment."	• When asked, most students indicate that the leaders in this building don't engage them in discussions about school safety. • A common refrain from students in this building is "Leaders in this building don't ask for my input regarding school safety." • A majority of teachers strongly disagree or disagree with the statement "Leaders in this building

	EXEMPLARY	PROFICIENT	PROGRESSING	NOT MEETING EXPECTATIONS
Real-World Examples	• Other leaders in the district credit this leader as a mentor and reason for their success in constructive conflict resolution strategies. • "My principal listens deeply to my views, especially when my views differ from her own." • "My principal expects high standards and constantly checks to see how he is helping others reach them."	• A majority of teachers strongly agree or agree with statement that school leaders work to protect teaching time and buffer teachers from distractions to their work. • "I can rely upon my school leaders to back me up when I face challenging situations with parents." • A majority of parents surveyed strongly agree or agree with statement that parent involvement efforts are focused on increasing parental engagement with the educational work of the school. • The leader and/or the leader's designees, when asked, can articulate how they have used the results of the parent involvement evaluation to improve future efforts in this area. • A majority of teachers strongly agree or agree that school leaders address staff conflict quickly and effectively. • A common refrain from teachers in this building is "I feel free to discuss work problems with my principal without fear of it being used against me later." • "My school leaders communicate and consistently enforce clear expectations, structures, and fair rules and procedures for students and staff."	• When asked, teachers express mixed views whether leaders work to protect instructional time and buffer teachers from outside distractions. • The leader and/or the leader's designees can demonstrate that they collect parent involvement information but may not be able to show how they are using the data. • Teachers express mixed views as to the effectiveness of leaders' efforts to resolve conflict effectively and quickly. • "My principal communicates procedures for students and staff. However, the rules are applied inconsistently."	work to protect instructional time and buffer teachers from outside distractions." • The leader is unable to demonstrate that she or he collects, let alone uses, parent involvement information. • Most teachers, when asked, indicate that school leaders take a hands-off approach to dealing with staff conflict and simply allow the problems to worsen. • "My principal developed and communicates procedures for students and staff."

SECTION 3: *LINKINGWALK* EVIDENCE-GATHERING TEMPLATES

From our work with clients across the nation to implement the process of *LinkingWalks*, we have developed ten to twelve data-gathering tools based on Robert Marzano's (2013) and Charlotte Danielson's (2013) teacher evaluation frameworks, as these two models seem to be the most widely used. What follows are several examples of *LinkingWalk* evidence-gathering templates that allow school leaders and their staff to focus on scaling a single high-impact instructional leadership practice:

- Figure A3.1 focuses on gathering evidence from students (student voice) about teacher clarity (0.75 effect size)

- Figure A3.2 zeros in on teacher questioning (0.48 effect size) and classroom discussion (0.82 effect size)

- Figure A3.3 gathers evidence around teacher clarity (0.75 effect size) regarding learning intentions

- Figure A3.4 gathers evidence around teacher clarity (0.75 effect size) dealing with success criteria

- Figure A3.5 concentrates on gathering evidence about feedback (0.75 effect size)

# of students in the class:		Teacher #:	Grade/Content:	

Learning Intentions/Success Criteria:		Time into the lesson		
		Beginning:	Middle:	End:

Instructional Setting:	Whole Group:	Small Group:	Stations:	Independent:	1:1

What are you learning?	**3**		**2**		**1**	
	Able to describe what they were learning		Described what they were doing		Weren't able to respond	

Student One			**Student Two**			**Student Three**			**Student Four**			**Student Five**		
3	2	1	3	2	1	3	2	1	3	2	1	3	2	1

How will you know when you've learned it?	**4**	**3**	**2**	**1**
	Described how they will know when they've learned what they were focused on	Described when they would have finished the task	Described the teacher in control of telling them what was right or wrong and the teacher who told them they could stop	Couldn't describe how they would know when they have learned what they were focused on

Student One				**Student Two**				**Student Three**				**Student Four**				**Student Five**			
4	3	2	1	4	3	2	1	4	3	2	1	4	3	2	1	4	3	2	1

What do you do when you get stuck?	**4**	**3**	**2**	**1**
	Names and/or describes four to five effective-learner strategies (reviews notes, seeks help from a classmate, rereads material, uses references)	Names and/or describes one to three effective-learner strategies (reviews notes, seeks help from a classmate, rereads material, uses references)	Describes task-oriented behavior answer (sit, raise hand, pay attention, follow directions)	Provides an "I don't know" answer

Student One				**Student Two**				**Student Three**				**Student Four**				**Student Five**			
4	3	2	1	4	3	2	1	4	3	2	1	4	3	2	1	4	3	2	1

Teacher Questioning/Discussion Template

# of students in the class:			Teacher #:	Grade/Content:	
Learning Intentions/Success Criteria:			Time into the lesson		
			Beginning:	Middle:	End:
Instructional Setting:	Whole Group:	Small Group:	Stations:	Independent:	1:1

Questioning?	4	3	2	1
	• Students initiate higher-order questions. • The teacher builds on and uses student responses to questions in order to deepen student understanding.	• The teacher uses open-ended questions, inviting students to think and/or offer multiple possible answers. • The teacher makes effective use of wait time.	• The teacher frames some questions designed to promote student thinking, but many have a single correct answer, and the teacher calls on students quickly.	• Questions are rapid-fire and convergent, with a single correct answer. • Questions do not invite student thinking.

4	3	2	1
Sample questions:			

FIGURE A3.3   Learning Intentions (Teacher Clarity) Template

# of students in the class:			Teacher #:	Grade/Content:	
Learning Intentions/Success Criteria:			Time into the lesson		
			Beginning:	Middle:	End:
Instructional Setting:	Whole Group:	Small Group:	Stations:	Independent:	1:1

What are the learning intentions? (outcomes)	3	2	1
	• The teacher states/writes clearly, at some point during the observation, what the students will be learning. • The teacher's explanation of content is clear and invites student participation and thinking.	• The teacher provides little elaboration or explanation about what the students will be learning • The teacher's explanation of the content consists of a monologue, with minimal participation or intellectual engagement by students.	• At no time during the observation does the teacher convey to students what they will be learning. • Students indicate through body language or questions that they don't understand the content being presented.

What are the learning intentions? (outcomes)	3	2	1
	• The teacher describes specific strategies students might use, inviting students to interpret them in the context of what they are learning. • Students engage with the learning task, indicating that they understand what they are to do. • If appropriate, the teacher models the process to be followed in the task.	• The teacher's explanations of content are purely procedural, with no indication of how students can think strategically. • The teacher must clarify the learning task so students can complete it.	• Students indicate through their questions that they are confused about the learning task.

3	2	1
Sample learning intentions:		

FIGURE A3.4 Success Criteria (Teacher Clarity) Template

# of students in the class:				Teacher #:	Grade/Content:	
Learning Intentions/Success Criteria:				Time into the lesson		
				Beginning:	Middle:	End:
Instructional Setting:	Whole Group:	Small Group:	Stations:	Independent:		1:1

What are the success criteria?	3	2	1
	• The teacher makes the standards of high-quality work clear to students. • The teacher elicits evidence of student understanding. • Students are invited to assess their own work and make improvements; most of them do so.	• There is little evidence that the students understand how their work will be evaluated. • The teacher monitors understanding through a single method or without eliciting evidence of understanding from the students.	• The teacher gives no indication of what high-quality work looks like. • The teacher makes no effort to determine whether students understand the lessons. • The teacher does not ask students to evaluate their own or classmates' work

3	2	1
Sample of success criteria:		

FIGURE A3.5 Feedback Evidence-Gathering Template

# of students in the class:				Teacher #:	Grade/Content:	
Learning Intentions/Success Criteria:				Time into the lesson:		
				Beginning:	Middle:	End:
Instructional Setting:	Whole Group:	Small Group:		Stations:	Independent:	1:1

What feedback are students provided about their learning?	4	3	2	1
	• Students monitor their own understanding, either on their own initiative or as a result of tasks set by the teacher. • High-quality feedback comes from many sources, including students; it is specific and focused on improvement.	• Students are invited to assess their own work and make improvements; most of them do so. • Feedback includes specific and timely guidance, at least for groups of students.	• Feedback to students is vague and not oriented toward future improvement of work. • The teacher makes only minor attempts to engage students in peer or self-assessment.	• Students receive no feedback, or feedback is global or directed to only one student. • The teacher does not ask students to evaluate their own or classmates' work.

4	3	2	1
Samples of feedback include:			

SECTION 4: THEORIES OF PRACTICE SELF-ASSESSMENT TOOL

We have merged Carol Dweck's (2006) thinking on "mindsets" and Viviane Robinson's three capabilities with John Hattie's (2012) ten "mindframes" and enhanced them by adding additional leadership perspectives in order to identify ten common *theories of practice*. These theories of practice buttress our five instructional leadership ability elements (see Section 2) and, together, form the architecture of our instructional leadership ability framework (J. Smith & R. Smith, 2015). Getting leaders to adopt these theories of practice is no easy task. However, changing the hearts and minds of leaders is an essential lever to making and sustaining long-term change (Fullan, 1998).

Consequently, school leaders must understand that behavioral changes almost always precede changes in their beliefs (Fullan, Hill, & Crevola, 2006). So what are these powerful behaviors and ways of thinking that are "likely to have major impacts on student learning?" (Hattie, 2012, p. 160). The ten theories of practice (TOP) represent individual and organizational beliefs requiring changes in how leaders view their roles and practices. The theories begin with a belief that leaders are those who evaluate their impact; activate change; focus on learning over teaching; use assessment as feedback; engage in dialogue; embrace the challenges of teaching, learning, and leadership; develop relational trust; teach the academic vocabulary of learning; reinforce that learning and leading is hard work; and collaborate in order to significantly impact student progress and achievement.

FIGURE A4.1 Theories of Practice Self-Assessment Tool

Directions: Review each of the brief statements describing the ten theories of practice, and plot where you believe you sit presently against each statement on the scale below each statement.

I AM AN EVALUATOR . . .

Leaders believe their fundamental task is to evaluate the effect of their leadership on students' learning and achievement. By seeking evidence to inform their leadership practice, leaders are also asking: (a) How am I doing? (b) Where to next? and (c) How am I going to get there?

Never	Seldom	Sometimes	Often	All of the time

I AM A CHANGE AGENT . . .

This proposition is not making the claim that students are not involved in the learning equation or that all success or failure is indeed the responsibility of the leader; rather, it is claiming that the greatest impact relates to the leader's mindset.

Never	Seldom	Sometimes	Often	All of the time

I TALK ABOUT LEARNING, NOT ABOUT TEACHING . . .

Professional discussions in schools are about learning and not teaching. We debate learning and discuss the impacts we are having on our students and how we know students are learning in our classes. Leaders provide time and support for teachers to be learners and evaluators.

Never	Seldom	Sometimes	Often	All of the time

I SEE ASSESSMENT AS FEEDBACK TO ME . . .

Leaders, like students, need to debate and agree about where they are going, how they are going, and where they are going next.

Never	Seldom	Sometimes	Often	All of the time

(Continued)

I ENGAGE IN DIALOGUE NOT MONOLOGUE . . .				
While there is need for leaders to impart information, and the faculty meeting and/or professional development format is indeed efficient, and while leaders do have specific information to convey, there is a major need for leaders to also listen to teachers' learning.				
Never	**Seldom**	**Sometimes**	**Often**	**All of the time**

I ENJOY THE CHALLENGE . . .				
We need to embrace the challenge and make the challenge what we want it to be. The art of leading is that what is challenging to one teacher may not be to another. We need to pay constant attention to the individual differences and seek commonality so that peers can work with each other and teachers with one another and the leader.				
Never	**Seldom**	**Sometimes**	**Often**	**All of the time**

I DEVELOP POSITIVE RELATIONSHIPS . . .				
So often, we are concerned about the school climate but are forgetful of warm, trustworthy, empathetic climates. The primary purpose is to allow teachers to feel okay about making mistakes and not knowing and to establish a climate that welcomes errors as opportunities.				
Never	**Seldom**	**Sometimes**	**Often**	**All of the time**

I INFORM ALL ABOUT THE LANGUAGE OF LEARNING . . .				
We need to develop a shared language of learning within our school (i.e., learning dispositions), use this language with our staff and students, and share the language with our parent community. Research tells us that when all of our communities understand the importance of deliberate practice of learning, they are more engaged in their children's learning.				
Never	**Seldom**	**Sometimes**	**Often**	**All of the time**

I SEE LEARNING AS HARD WORK . . .				
I teach students and teachers the value of (a) concentration, (b) perseverance, and (c) deliberate practice.				
Never	**Seldom**	**Sometimes**	**Often**	**All of the time**

I COLLABORATE . . .				
When we believe that by working together, we can make a difference, it has a positive impact on student learning and outcomes. Effective collaboration happens when structures and relationships enable information and ideas to flow in all directions.				
Never	**Seldom**	**Sometimes**	**Often**	**All of the time**

Glossary

Effect size	An effect size provides a common expression of the magnitude of study outcomes for many types of outcome variables, such as school achievement. An effect size of $d = 1.0$ indicates that an increase of one standard deviation on the outcome (i.e., improving student achievement).
Fidelity of implementation	Implementation is defined as a specified set of activities designed to put into practice an activity or program of known dimensions. According to this definition, implementation processes are purposeful and are described in sufficient detail such that independent observers can detect the presence and strength of the "specific activities" related to implementation (i.e., fidelity of implementation).
Formative	The goal of formative assessment is to *monitor student and/or adult learning* to provide ongoing feedback that can be used by coaches to improve their coaching and by students and/or adults to improve their learning. More specifically, formative assessments • help students/adults identify their strengths and weaknesses and target areas that need work • help coaches and/or school leaders recognize where the school leader/teachers are struggling and address problems immediately Formative assessments are generally *low stakes*, which means that they have low or no point value.
High-impact instructional leadership practices	All those instructional and/or leadership practices that have an effect size of ≥ 0.40 (which roughly translates into a year of academic growth).
Leadership strategy in action	An *observable* statement, subject to frequent public testing, and measurable (i.e., quantifiable, able to be gauged); an *obvious* translation (i.e., paraphrase) of the high-impact leadership practices; constructed with *formative language* (e.g., "increase the percentage of," "reduce the percentage of," "increase the amount of") as such strategies are intended to be "dipstick" measures used over time rather than goal statements; and *time-bound* (i.e., the strategy should indicate how often the public testing will occur).
LinkingTalks	*LinkingTalks* are a process designed to help school leaders guide teachers' collective verbal improvisation about teaching and its impact on student achievement. The aim is to help leaders acquire the knowledge and skills so they are able to effectively facilitate this *LinkingTalk* among and with teachers to analyze the impact of their

(Continued)

	teaching practices on student learning, evaluate the outcomes of that analysis, and then use the results to make changes in ineffective practices by creating more effective ones.
Linking Walks	*Linking Walks* are classroom walkthrough observations that focus on the fidelity of implementation of high-impact instructional leadership practices (i.e., those with an effect size ≥ 0.40) in order to take these practices to scale within the school. The practice consists of routine and systematic comparison of improvements in high-impact instructional leadership practice related to improvements in student progress and achievement developed into "public displays of effection." The instructional practices being monitored, assessed, and acted on during this highly focused process align with and support the school leaders' professional growth plan.
Pareto principle	Is about the vital few versus the trivial many. That is, 80 percent of the trouble comes from 20 percent of the problems. Or only a few of the problems cause most of the trouble.
Prioritized school-wide problem of practice	A prioritized school-wide problem of practice helps to focus the attention of the leader on a critical aspect of organizational development. That is, of all of the demands on the leader's time and all of the things competing for his attention within the school, what central issue will be the target of his focus? Second, it also ensures that the leadership improvement effort will be an aligned action that benefits both the leader (by helping him improve leadership practices) and the organization (by maintaining a focus on strategic targets, which are a priority for all within the system).
Task analysis	A task analysis is a listing of all of those things leaders must do in order to implement the strategy-in-action. The critical function of a task analysis is to answer the question, "What are all of those important tasks I/we (leaders and school faculty) must complete in order to implement the strategy-in-action and achieve the desired results?"
Theory of action	When school leaders interact with others, they tend to design or plan their behavior and retain theories for doing so. These theories of action comprise the values, strategies, and underlying assumptions that inform leaders' patterns of interpersonal behavior. Theories of action operate at two levels: There are espoused theories that leaders use to explain or justify their behavior. And there are theories in action that are implicit in our patterns of behavior with others. In other words, there are both intended theories and enacted theories. Leaders must construct *explicit* theories of action and assess those theories against the realities of their work.
Rubric	A document that articulates the expectations for an assignment by listing the criteria, or what counts, and describes levels of quality from excellent to poor.
Success criteria	Process success criteria are either reminders of steps (as in a instructional procedure) or ingredients that either must be used (as in implementing change) or could help achieve the learning objective but do not necessarily have to all be used.
Summative	The goal of summative assessment is to *evaluate student/adult learning* at the end of an instructional unit by comparing it against some standard or benchmark. Summative assessments are often *high stakes*, which means that they have a high point value.

References

Allison, E. (2011). *Leadership performance coaching*. Englewood, CO: Leadership and Learning Center.

Anderson, K. (2010). *Data teams: Success stories Volume 1*. Englewood, CO: Lead+Learn Press.

Annan, B., Lai, K. M., & Robinson, V. (2003). Teacher talk to improve teaching practices. *SET Research Information for Teachers, 1*, 31–35.

Beteille, T., Kalogrides, D., & Loeb, S. (2012). Stepping stones: Principal career paths and school outcomes. *Social Science Research, 41*, 904–919.

Bickman, L., Goldring, E., De Andrade, A. R., Breda, C., & Goff, P. (2012). *Improving principal leadership through feedback and coaching*. Evanston, IL: Society for Research on Educational Effectiveness.

Biggs, J. B. (1995). Assessing for learning: Some dimensions underlying new approaches to educational assessment. *Alberta Journal of Educational Research, 41*, 1–18.

Bloom, G., Castagna, C., Moir, E., & Warren, B. (2005). *Blended coaching: Skills and strategies to support principal development*. Thousand Oaks, CA: Corwin.

Bloomberg, P., & Pitchford, B. (2017). *Leading impact teams: Building a culture of efficacy*. Thousand Oaks, CA: Corwin.

Bryk, A. S. (2010). Organizing schools for improvement. *Phi Delta Kappan, 91*(7), 23–30.

Bryk, A. S., & Schneider, B. L. (2002). *Trust in schools: A core resource for improvement*. New York, NY: Russell Sage Foundation.

City, E. A., Elmore, R. F., Fiarman, S. E., & Teitel, L. (2009). *Instructional rounds in education: A network approach to improving teaching and learning*. Cambridge, MA: Harvard Education Press.

Colvin, G. (2008). *Talent is overrated: What really separates world-class performers from everybody else*. New York, NY: Penguin Group.

Commission on Behavioral and Social Sciences and Education. (2000). *How people learn: Brain, mind, experience, and school* (J. D. Bransford, Ed.). Washington, DC: National Academies Press.

Conzemius, A., & O'Neill, J. (2002). *The handbook for SMART school teams*. Bloomington, IN: National Education Service.

Costa, A. L., & Garmston, R. J. (2002). *Cognitive coaching: A foundation for renaissance schools*. Norwood, MA: Christopher-Gordon.

Costa, A., & Kallick, B. (Eds.). (2009). *Habits of mind across the curriculum: Practical and creative strategies for teachers*. Alexandra, VA: Association for Supervision and Curriculum Development.

Covey, J. R. (1989). *The 7 habits of highly effective people: Powerful lessons in personal change*. New York, NY: Fireside.

Danielson, C. (2013). *The framework for teaching: Evaluation instrument 2013 Edition*. Princeton, NJ: Danielson Group.

Darling-Hammond, L., LaPointe, M., Meyerson, D., Orr, M. T., & Cohen, C. (2007). *Preparing school leaders for a changing world: Lessons from exemplary leadership development programs*. Stanford, CA: Stanford Educational Leadership Institute.

Darling-Hammond, L., Wei, R. C., Andree, A., Richardson, N., & Orphanos, S. (2009). *Professional learning in the learning profession: A status report on teacher development in the United States and abroad.* Dallas, TX: National Staff Development Council and The School Redesign Network.

DuFour, R., DuFour, R., & Eaker, R. (2008). *Revisiting professional learning communities: New insights for improving schools.* Bloomington, IN: Solution Tree.

Durlak, J. A., Weissburg, R. P., Taylor, R. D., & Schellinger, K. B. (2011). The impact of enhancing students' social and emotional learning: A meta-analysis of school-based universal interventions. *Child Development, 82,* 405–432.

Dweck, C. S. (2006). *Mindset: The new psychology of success. How we can learn to fulfill our potential.* New York, NY: Ballantine Books.

Eisler, R. (2017, February 1). *rianeeisler.com/partnership-101/.* Retrieved February 1, 2017, from rianeeisler.com

Ellison, J. L., & Hayes, C. (2013). *Effective school leadership: Developing principals through cognitive coaching.* Lanham, MD: Rowman & Littlefield Publishers.

Elmore, R. F. (1996). Getting to scale with good educational practice. *Harvard Educational Review, 66*(1), 1–26.

Fixen, D. L., Naoom, S. F., Blase, K. A., Friedman, R. M., & Wallace, F. (2005). *Implementation research: A synthesis of the literature.* Tampa: University of South Florida.

Fullan, M. (1998). *Change forces: Probing the depths of educational reform.* New York, NY: The Falmer Press.

Fullan, M. (2003). *The moral imperative of school leadership.* Thousand Oaks, CA: Corwin.

Fullan, M. (2009). *The challenge of change: Start school improvement now* (2nd ed.). Thousand Oaks, CA: Corwin.

Fullan, M. (2010). *Motion leadership: The skinny on becoming change savvy.* Thousand Oaks, CA: Corwin.

Fullan, M., Hill, P., & Crevola, C. (2006). *Breakthrough.* Thousand Oaks, CA: Corwin.

Garmston, R. J., & von Frank, V. (2012). *Unlocking group potential to improve schools.* Thousand Oaks, CA: Corwin.

Garmston, R. J., & Wellman, B. M. (1999). *The adaptive school: A sourcebook for developing collaborative groups.* Norwood, MA: Christopher-Gordon Publishers.

Garmston, R. J., & Wellman, B. M. (2009). *The adaptive school: A sourcebook for developing collaborative groups* (2nd ed.). Norwood, MA: Christopher-Gordon Publishers.

Gawande, A. (2009). *The checklist manifesto: How to get things right.* New York: Metropolitan Books.

Gawande, A. (2011, October 3). Personal best: Top athletes and singers have coaches. Should you? *New Yorker,* 44–53.

Ginsberg, M. B., & Kimball, K. (2008, January/February). Data-in-a-day: A new tool for principal preparation. *Principal, 87*(3), 40–43.

Hall, G. E., & Hord, S. M. (2011). *Implementing change: Patterns, principles, and potholes* (3rd ed.). Boston, MA: Pearson.

Hargrove, R. (2003). *Masterful coaching: Inspire an impossible future while producing extraordinary leaders and extraordinary results.* San Francisco, CA: Jossey-Bass/Pheiffer.

Hattie, J. (2009). *Visible learning: A synthesis of over 800 meta-analyses relating to student achievement.* London, UK: Routledge.

Hattie, J. (2012). *Visible learning for teachers: Maximizing impact on learning.* New York, NY: Routledge.

Hattie, J. (2015a). *What doesn't work in education: The politics of distraction.* London, UK: Pearson.

Hattie, J. (2015b). *What works best in education: The politics of collaborative expertise.* London, UK: Pearson.

Hattie, J., & Donoghue, G. M. (2016, August 10). Learning strategies: A synthesis and conceptual model. *npj Science of Learning,* 1–13.

Hattie, J., & Timperley, H. (2007). The power of feedback. *Review of Educational Research, 77,* 81–112.

Heston, B. L. (2013). *Coaching for instructional leadership: A case study of executive coaches and principals* (Doctoral dissertation). University of Connecticut, Storrs.

Honig, M. I. (2012). District central office leadership as teaching: How central office administrators support principals' development as instructional leaders. *Educational Administration Quarterly*, 48(4), 733–774.

Jensen, B. (2000). *Simplicity: The new competitive advantage in a world of more, better, faster*. New York, NY: HarperCollins.

Jonsson, A., & Svingby, G. (2007). The use of scoring rubrics: Reliability, validity and educational consequences. *Educational Research Review*, 2, 130–144.

Joyce, B., & Showers, B. (2002). *Student achievement through staff development* (3rd ed.). Alexandria, VA: Association for Supervision and Curriculum Development.

Knight, J. (2007). *Instructional coaching: A partnership approach to improving instruction*. Thousand Oaks, CA: Corwin.

Knight, J. (2016). *Better conversations: Coach yourself and each other to be more credible, caring, and connected*. Thousand Oaks, CA: Corwin.

Knight, J., Elford, M., Hock, M., Dunekack, D., Bradley, B., Deshler, D., & Knight, D. (2015). 3 steps to great coaching: A simple but powerful instructional coaching cycle nets results. *Learning Forward Journal*, 36(1), 11–18.

Learning Forward. (2017). *Standards for professional learning: Quick reference quide*. Oxford, OH: Author.

Louis, K. S., Leithwood, K., Wahlstrom, K. L., & Anderson, S. E. (2010). *Investigating the links to improved student learning: Final report of research and findings*. Minneapolis and Toronto: University of Minnesota, Center for Applied Research and Educational Improvement, and University of Toronto, Ontario Institute for Studies in Education.

Marzano, R. J. (2010). *An observational protocol based on the art and science of teaching*. Englewood, CO: Marzano Research Laboratory.

Marzano, R. J. (2011). The art and science of teaching: Making the most of instructional rounds. *Educational Leadership*, 68(5), 80–82.

Marzano, R. J. (2013). *The Marzano teacher evaluation model*. Englewood: Marzano Research Laboratory.

Marzano, R. J., Waters, R., & McNulty, B. A. (2005). *School leadership that works: From research to results*. Alexandria, VA: Association for Supervision and Curriculum Development.

McREL International. (2013). *McREL power walkthrough user's guide*. Denver, CO: Author.

New York City Leadership Academy. (2015). *Taking charge of principal support: An in-depth look at NYC leadership academy's approach to coaching principals*. New York: NYC Leadership Academy.

Nottingham, J. (2016). *Challenging learning: Theory, effective practice and lesson ideas to create optimal learning in the classroom*. London, UK: Routledge.

Ontario Ministry of Education. (2010). *Questioning: Assessment for learning video sereies viewing guide*. Toronto, Canada: Ontario Ministry of Education.

Perkins, D. (2003). *King Arthur's roundtable*. New York, NY: Wiley.

Pfeffer, J., & Sutton, R. I. (2000). *The knowing–doing gap: How smart companies turn knowledge into action*. Boston, MA: Harvard School Press.

Prochaska, J. O., Norcross, J. C., & DiClemente, C. C. (1994). *Changing for good*. New York, NY: Avon Books.

Prothero, A. (2015). For principals, continuous learning critical to career success. *Education Week*, 34(18), 10–11.

Quaglia, R. J. (2016). *Principal voice: Listen, learn, lead*. Thousand Oaks, CA: Corwin.

Reiss, K. (2007). *Leadership coaching for educators: Bringing out the best in school administrators*. Thousand Oaks, CA: Corwin.

Robinson, V. (2011). *Student-centered leadership*. San Francisco, CA: Jossey-Bass.

Robinson, V., Hohepa, M., & Lloyd, C. (2009). *School leadership and student outcomes: Identifying what works and why. Best evidence synthesis iteration [BES]*. Wellington, NZ: Ministry of Education.

Robinson, V. M., Lloyd, C. A., & Rowe, K. J. (2008). The impact of leadership on student outcomes: An analysis of the differential effects of leadership types. *Education Administration Quarterly*, 44(5), 635–674.

Rogers, E. M. (2003). *Diffusion of innovations* (5th ed.). New York, NY: Free Press.

Rowe, M. B. (1972). *Wait-time and rewards as instructional variables, their influence in language, logic, and fate control*. Paper presented at the National Association for Research in Science Teaching, Chicago, IL.

Rowland, C. (2017). *Principal professional development: New opportunities for a renewed state focus*. Washington, DC: Education Policy Center at American Institutes for Research.

Saphier, J., & King, M. (1985). Good seeds grow in strong cultures. *Educational Leadership*, 42(6), 67–74.

Scholtes, P. R., Joiner, B. L., & Streibel, B. J. (2001). *The team handbook* (2nd ed.). Madison, WI: Oriel.

Schön, D. A. (1987). *Educating the reflective practitioner*. San Francisco, CA: Jossey-Bass.

School Leaders Network. (2014). *CHURN: The high cost of principal turnover*. Hinsdale, MA: Author.

Seashore-Louis, K., Leithwood, K., Wahlstrom, K. L., & Anderson, S. E. (2010). *Investigating the links to improved student achievement: Final report of research findings*. St. Paul: University of Minnesota. Retrieved September 25, 2010, from http://www.cehd.umn.edu/carei/publications/documents/LearningFromLeadershipFinal.pdf.

Smith, J., & Smith, R. (2015). *Evaluating instructional leadership: Recognized practices for success*. Thousand Oaks, CA: Corwin.

Smith, R., & Smith, J. (2016, August 31). *Instructional leaders—the ultimate web-masters!* Retrieved February 27, 2017, from http://www.corwin-connect.com/2016/08/instructional-leaders-ultimate-web-masters

Smither, J. W. (2011). Can psychotherapy research serve as a guide for research about executive coaching? An agenda for the next decade. *Journal of Business Psychology*, 26, 135–145.

Snicket, L. (2006). *The end: A series of unfortunate events, book the thirteenth*. New York, NY: HarperCollins.

Stahl, R. J. (1994, May). *Using "think time" and "wait time" skillfully in the classroom*. Bloomington, IN: ERIC Clearinghouse for Social Studies/Social Science.

Stober, D. R., & Grant, A. M. (2006). Toward a contextual approach to coaching models. In D. R. Stober, & A. M. Grant (Eds.), *Evidence-based coaching handbook: Putting best practices to work for clients* (pp. 367–388). Hoboken, NJ: John Wiley & Sons.

Talbert, J. E., David, J. L., Chen, P., & Lin, W. (2007). *Evaluation of the New Teacher Center–Ravenswood City School District partnership for system improvement: Year one report*. Stanford, CA: Stanford University, Center for Research on the Context of Teaching.

Talley, G. S. (2011). *Perceptions of the impact of coaching on principal performance*. Statesboro, GA: Georgia Southern University.

Taylor, F. W. (1911). *Principles of scientific management*. New York, NY: Harper.

Volusia County School District. (2012, May 1). *Volusia County Schools*. Retrieved September 15, 2015, from myvolusiaschools.org/Pages/default.aspx: http://myvolusiaschools.org/rtt/Documents/VSEL_Manual.pdf

Wellman, B., & Lipton, L. (2004). *Data-driven dialogue: A facilitator's guide to collaborative inquiry*. Sherman, CT: MiraVia.

Wheatley, M. J., & Frieze, D. (2010). Leadership in the age of complexity: From hero to host. Retrieved December 1, 2010, from Margaret J. Wheatley.

Wiggins, G. (2012). 7 keys to effective feedback. *Educational Leadership*, 70(1), 11–16.

Wiliam, D. (2011). *Embedded formative assessment*. Bloomington, IN: Solution Tree Press.

Yeh, S. S. (2006). *Raising student achievement through rapid assessment and test reform*. New York: Teachers College Press.

Index

Achievement, student, 46, 46 (figure), 47 (figure)
Acknowledge/clarity paraphrasing, 78 (figure)
Adaptive School, The (Garmston & Wellman), 79–80, 80 (figure), 82
Adult practice, school-wide problem of, 33–34
Allison, E., 6, 6 (box)
Analytical talk, 125, 126 (figure)
Annan, B., 124, 125
Approachable voice, 79
Argyris, C., 66, 70
Assessment:
 as feedback, 52 (figure), 55–56, 56 (figure)
 feedback and, 39, 40–41 (figure)
 high-stakes, 180
 learners capable of, 115 (figure)
 low-stakes, 179
 summative, 51, 180
 See also Formative assessment
Assistance, continuous, 87
Assumptions, 74 (figure)

Baseline evidence statements, 118, 118 (figure)
Bennis, W., 70
Better Conversations (Knight), 82
Blase, K., 48
Blended coaching, 7–9, 8 (box), 9 (figure)
Bloom, G., 7
Bradley, B., 29, 30

Carlton, S., 2, 29–30
Castagna, C., 7
Center for Research on the Context
 of Teaching, 13
Challenge, embracing, 52 (figure), 56–57, 57 (figure)
Challenging Learning (Nottingham), 64
Challenging talk, 125, 127–128 (figure)

Change:
 activating, 52 (figure), 53, 54 (figure)
 facilitating, 85–87, 85 (figure)
 first-order, 86
 second-order, 86
 shared vision of, 85
 supportive context for, 87
Change model, 85–87, 85 (figure)
Checklist Manifesto, The (Gawande), 136
Checklists:
 characteristics, 98, 136
 deliberate practice development, 132, 133–134 (figure)
 deliberate practice implementation, 132, 135 (figure)
 feedback, 39, 40–41 (figure)
 impact coaching cycle, 31 (figure)
 See also Success criteria checklists
Choice, 50 (figure)
Clarifying, 98
Classroom visits, 99
Coachees:
 feedback from, 143
 point of view, inviting to share, 73 (figure)
Coaches, impact, xiii–xiv, 12–13, 55
 See also specific topics
Coaching:
 benefits of, 138
 blended, 7–9, 8 (box), 9 (figure), 12
 cognitive, 9–10, 10 (figure)
 collaborative, 8 (box)
 consultative, 8 (box)
 executive, 5, 5 (box)
 facilitative, 8 (box)
 importance of, 139
 instructional, 8 (box)
 leadership, 7, 7 (figure), 13–14

leadership performance, 6, 6 (box)
transformational, 8 (box)
See also Impact coaching; *specific topics*
Coaching conversations, 6 (box)
Coblaboration, 123, 125
Cognitive coaching, 9–10, 10 (figure)
Collaboration, 52 (figure), 61, 62 (figure)
Collaborative coaching, 8 (box)
Collective teacher efficacy, 115 (figure)
Colvin, G., 129
Commission on Behavioral and Social Sciences
    and Education, 75–76
Commitment, 69 (figure), 70
Common ground, establishing, 74 (figure)
Communication:
    about, 65–66
    conversations, performance-related,
        66–68, 67 (figure)
    open-to-learning conversations, 68–72,
        69 (figure), 71 (figure), 73–74 (figure)
    thinking, mediating, 72, 75–81, 77 (figure),
        78 (figure), 79 (figure), 80 (figure)
Comparators, 80 (figure)
Concerns, describing, 73 (figure)
Connecticut Association of Schools, 13–14
Consultative coaching, 8 (box)
Continuous learning, xiii
Conversation maps, 9, 10 (figure)
Conversations:
    coaching, 6 (box)
    informal, 91
    performance-related, 66–68, 67 (figure)
    See also Open-to-learning conversations
Costa, A., 9, 51
Courage, 22
Credibility, teacher, 115 (figure)
Critical talk, 125, 126–127 (figure)

Danielson, C., 114, 172
Data, 118, 119 (figure)
Debriefing, 118, 118 (figure), 119 (figure),
    120–121, 121 (figure)
Deliberate practice plans:
    about, 129, 142
    development checklist, 132, 133–134 (figure)
    implementation checklist, 132, 135 (figure)
    sample, 130–131 (figure)
    use of, 88
Demonstrating/imitating, 106, 108–109,
    110 (figure), 111 (figure)
Description of designing (ladder of reflection),
    106, 107–108 (figure), 111 (figure)

Deshler, D., 29, 30
Designing (ladder of reflection), 106,
    107 (figure), 111 (figure)
Diagnosis, Interventions, implementation, and
    Evaluation (DIiE), 143
Dialogue, 50 (figure), 52 (figure), 56,
    57 (figure), 63–64
Diffusion of Innovations (Rogers), 15, 89–90
DIiE. *See* Diagnosis, Interventions,
    implementation, and Evaluation
Dissonance, 2
District leader referral, 91–92
Dunekack, D., 29, 30
Dweck, C., 176

Educating the Reflective Practitioner (Schön),
    63–64, 106
Effective Feedback Checklist,
    39, 40–41 (figure)
Effectiveness, teacher/leader/staff, 23–24,
    24 (figure), 42 (figure), 159–163 (figure)
Effective School Leadership (Ellison & Hayes),
    4–5, 82
Effect size, 12, 20, 20 (figure), 179
Efficacy, collective teacher, 115 (figure)
80/20 rule, 18–19, 180
Eisler, R., 49
Elford, M., 29, 30
Ellison, J., 4–5, 9, 82
Elmore, R., 15
Engagement strategies, 89–92
Environment, orderly/safe/supportive,
    25–26, 26 (figure), 42 (figure),
    168–171 (figure)
Equality, 50 (figure)
Evaluating Instructional Leadership (Smith &
    Smith), 51, 92
Evidence, graphs of, 118, 119 (figure)
Evidence-gathering templates:
    about, 172
    feedback, 176 (figure)
    learning intentions, 174–175 (figure)
    student voice, 173 (figure)
    success criteria, 175 (figure)
    teacher questioning/discussion, 174 (figure)
Evidence statements, baseline, 118, 118 (figure)
Executive coaching, 5, 5 (box)
Executive Coaching model, 13–14
Expectations, shared, 20–21, 21 (figure),
    42 (figure), 152–154 (figure)
Expertise, teacher, 115 (figure)
Exploratory phrasing, 79, 79 (figure)

Facilitative coaching, 8 (box)
Fedigan, A., 97, 120–121, 121 (figure),
    122 (figure)
Feedback:
    assessment and, 39, 40–41 (figure)
    assessment as, 52 (figure), 55–56, 56 (figure)
    checklist, 39, 40–41 (figure)
    from coachees, 143
    high-impact instructional leadership practices,
        115 (figure)
    professional development and, 39,
        40–41 (figure)
    teachers, gathering from, 39, 40 (figure)
    teachers, providing to, 39, 40 (figure)
Feedback Cue Cards, 107–108 (figure),
    148–150, 149 (figure), 151 (figure)
Feedback evidence-gathering template, 176 (figure)
Feedback template, 117 (figure)
Fidelity of implementation, 44–46, 45 (figure), 179
First-order change, 86
Fixsen, D., 48
Fly-fishing, 104–105
Focus, 11 (figure)
Formative assessment:
    defined, 179
    of impact coaches, 55
    of students, 130–131 (figure)
    of teachers, 115 (figure), 119 (figure)
Friedman, R., 48
Frieze, D., 78–79
Fullan, M., 33, 87, 109, 112, 129, 142

Garmston, R., 51, 70, 79–80, 80 (figure), 82
Gawande, A., xii, 1, 2, 29, 98, 136
Goals:
    shared, 20–21, 21 (figure), 42 (figure),
        152–154 (figure)
    SMART-ER, 34–35, 37, 38 (figure)
Goldilocks principle, 99
Graphs of evidence, 118, 119 (figure)
Gunston, R., 9

Hall, G., 85–87, 85 (figure), 100, 101
Hard-sell approach, 67, 67 (figure), 68
Hard work, learning as, 52 (figure),
    59–60, 60 (figure)
Hargrove, R., 5
Harmony, 2
Hattie, J.:
    DIiE model, 143
    feedback, 55
    impact coaching, 30, 39

mindframes, 51, 176
    Visible Learning, 101
Hayes, C., 4–5, 9, 82
Hazel, R.:
    about, xvi
    assessment as feedback, 55
    challenge, embracing, 57
    change, 53, 88, 89 (figure)
    collaboration, 61
    deliberate practice plan, 140
    dialogue, 56
    engagement strategies, 89, 90, 92
    Identify component, 33, 34 (figure),
        35 (figure), 36 (figure), 37
    Improve component, 45–47, 45 (figure),
        46 (figure), 47 (figure)
    Learn component, 44
    learning, 54, 59, 60
    professional development, traditional, 4
    trust, relational, 58
Heroes, leaders as, 78–79
Heston, B., 13–14
High-impact instructional leaders, 4 (box)
High-impact instructional leadership practices:
    about, 3–4, 19–20, 20 (figure)
    credibility, teacher, 115 (figure)
    defined, 179
    effectiveness, teacher/leader/staff, 23–24,
        24 (figure), 42 (figure), 159–163 (figure)
    efficacy, collective teacher, 115 (figure)
    environment, orderly/safe/supportive, 25–26,
        26 (figure), 42 (figure), 168–171 (figure)
    feedback, 115 (figure)
    formative evaluation of teachers, 115 (figure)
    identifying, 37
    implementation with feedback, 44
    learners, assessment-capable and visible,
        115 (figure)
    Linking Walks, prior to conducting,
        115 (figure)
    Pareto principle and, 18–19
    professional development, 24–25, 25 (figure),
        42 (figure)
    resourcing, strategic, 21–23, 22 (figure),
        42 (figure), 155–158 (figure)
    shared vision, goals, and expectations, 20–21,
        21 (figure), 42 (figure), 152–154 (figure)
    teaching, 97–99
High-stakes assessment, 180
Hock, M., 29, 30
Hohepa, M., 19, 65, 97
Honda, S., 71, 83–84

Honig, M., xiv, 139
Hord, S., 85–87, 85 (figure), 100, 101
Hosts, leaders as, 78–79

Identify (impact coaching cycle component):
  adult practice, school-wide problem of, 33–34
  checklist, 31 (figure)
  goals, SMART-ER, 34–35, 37, 38 (figure)
  high-impact leadership strategy
      to meet goal, 37
  progress monitoring, 37, 38 (figure)
  reality, clear picture of, 34, 35 (figure),
      36 (figure)
  SMART-ER goal, 34–35, 37, 38 (figure)
  student-learning problem, 33, 34 (figure)
Imitating, 106, 108–109, 110 (figure),
    111 (figure)
Imitative reconstruction, 105
Impact, evaluating, 51, 52 (figure), 53 (figure)
Impact coaches, xiii–xiv, 12–13, 55
Impact coaching:
  about, 10–11
  blended coaching compared to, 12
  qualities unique to, 11 (figure), 138
  See also specific topics
Impact coaching cycle:
  about, 30, 31 (figure), 32–33, 32 (figure)
  checklist, 31 (figure)
  Identify component, 31 (figure), 33–35,
      34 (figure), 35 (figure), 36 (figure),
      37, 38 (figure)
  Improve component, 31 (figure), 44–47,
      45 (figure), 46 (figure), 47 (figure)
  Learn component, 31 (figure), 37–39,
      40–41 (figure), 41–44, 42 (figure)
  self-assessment, 143, 144–145 (figure), 145
Impact cycle, instructional leadership,
    ix–x, 144–145
Implementation:
  defined, 179
  fidelity of, 44–46, 45 (figure), 179
  importance of, 140–141
Implementation Research (Fixsen, Naoom,
    Blase, Friedman, & Wallace), 48
Implementing Change (Hall & Hord), 101
Importance, factoring in, 139–140
Improve (impact coaching cycle component):
  checklist, 31 (figure)
  fidelity of implementation, 44–46,
      45 (figure), 179

next steps, determining, 47
  "public displays of effection," 47
  student achievement, assessing impact on,
      46, 46 (figure), 47 (figure)
Improvisation, 123
Informal conversations, 91
Information, valid, 69 (figure), 70
"Innovation Process in Organizations,
    The" (Rogers), 15
Inquiry, 78–79, 79 (figure)
Instructional coaching, 8 (box)
Instructional Coaching (Knight), 49–50,
    50 (figure), 97
Instructional leadership impact cycle,
    ix–x, 144–145
Instructional leadership practices self-assessment,
    92, 93–96 (figure)
Interdependence, 122–123
Interviews, one-to-one, 90–91
Invitational questions, 79, 79 (figure)
Invitations, sincere, 79

Jazz musicians, 123
Jensen, B., 99
Jonsson, A., 129

King, M., 87
Knight, D., 29, 30
Knight, J.:
  Better Conversations, 82
  coaching tactics, 97, 138
  high-impact instructional
      leadership practices, 17
  impact coaching, 29, 30
  Instructional Coaching, 49–50, 50 (figure), 97
  partnership principles, 49–51, 50 (figure), 62

Ladder of reflection, 106, 107–108 (figure),
    111 (figure)
Lai, K. M., 124, 125
Language, vague, 80–81, 80 (figure)
Language of learning, 52 (figure), 59, 59 (figure)
Leaders as heroes, 78–79
Leaders as hosts, 78–79
Leadership coaching, 7, 7 (figure), 13–14
"Leadership in the Age of Complexity"
    (Wheatley & Frieze), 78–79
Leadership performance coaching, 6, 6 (box)
Leadership strategy in action, 130–131 (figure),
    134 (figure), 179